ACROSS THE FENCE

The Secret War in Vietnam

MAC SOG

By John Stryker Meyer

Published by SOG Publishing
349 Marazul Street
Oceanside, California 92057-7343
www.sogchronicles.com

Publisher: John Stryker Meyer

E-mail:idahoonezero@sbcglobal.net

Cover photo: Spike Team Idaho prior to launching into target Echo Four on 6 October 1968. Photo provided by John Stryker Meyer

Cover design by Bob Jones and Jacquie Cook

Back cover photo: Members of ST Idaho gather in front of the CCN Mess Hall shortly after returning from training in early 1969. From left: Nguyen Cong Hiep, team interpreter; Chau; Tuan, grenadier; John S. Meyer, One-Zero; Nguyen Van Sau, Zero-One; Cau; Son; Douglas L. LeTourneau, One-Two; Hung and Lynne M. Black Jr., One-One.

BISAC Subject Headings:
BIO008000 BIOGRAPHY & AUTOBIOGRAPHY / Military
HIS027180 HISTORY / Military / Special Forces
HIS027070 HISTORY / Military / Vietnam War

Library of Congress Control Number: 2011900173

ISBN-13: 978-0-9832567-0-0
ISBN-10: 0-9832567-0-5 (previously ISBN 0-9743618-1-X)

Edition: 10 9 8 7 6 5 4 3 2SAN: 860-1062

DEDICATION

This book is dedicated to all SOG reconnaissance team members, both U.S. Special Forces and indigenous troops, as well as to every man in every air support unit, especially the Kingbee pilots of the 219th South Vietnamese Air Force's Special Operations Squadron, who worked daily with SOG teams on the ground, across the fence, in America's secret war. This book is also for every man in SOG and their support units who made the ultimate sacrifice.

With My Deepest Appreciation…

After my loving wife of 16 years, Anna Marie Avery Meyer, the mother of our five children, I would like to thank the following people for their role in getting the *new edition* of Across The Fence printed in 2011, eight years after the first edition, printed by Real War Stories, hit the streets of America.

M. Lisa Allen
Stephen Bayliss
Lynne M. Black, Jr.
Mark Byrd
Charles Borg
Jacquie Cook
Dennis J. Cummings
Louis DeSeta
Robert S. Jones
Mike Keele
Douglas L. LeTourneau
Faith Kristin Meyer
John McGovern
George Miller
Robert J. Parks
Joe Parnar
John E. Peters
Alan Wise
Don Wolken
Ron Zaiss

And, Anna and I would like to salute our parents, Henry and Dorothy Meyer, and William Dennis Avery and Renee Hamel—who have moved on to the big LZ in the sky.

TABLE OF CONTENTS

ACKNOWLEDGMENTS

In 1973, I wrote my first SOG-related piece in my student newspaper The Signal, at Trenton State College in Trenton, New Jersey. Dr. Robert Cole, the college's first full-time journalism professor and Dr. Nadine Shanler Schwartz, the newspaper's advisor, both suggested that I write a book. At that time, I had been out of Special Forces for more than three years. The thought had never occurred to me to write about my time in South Vietnam and across the fence, especially since I had signed a government document in 1968 pledging to never write or talk publicly about SOG for 20 years. Additionally, the anti-Vietnam/anti-Vietnam veteran sentiment in the country at the time made it difficult to find a publisher who would buy the concept of a Vietnam book that dealt with real people striving against unbelievable odds in a politically handicapped war.

The first person to actually pay me for writing about SOG was Soldier of Fortune editor and publisher Robert K. Brown, a former Green Beret who had fought along side the indigenous people of South Vietnam as well. More important, many years ago Brown had suggested that I write a book, too. Not only is he a fellow former Green Beret and a generous publisher, but a man who backs friendship with action and deeds, not hollow words.

Over the years several members of the Special Operations Association, all former SOG personnel, suggested that I write a book on SOG. Among them were men I had run missions with on Spike Team Idaho and men from CCC and CCS. Since the early days of our marriage, my wife Anna, and her mother Renee Hamel and her father, William Avery, a WW II Marine, had quietly urged me to set pen to pad to write about SOG. Three years ago, one of the great unsung heroes of SOG, Pat "Mandolin" Watkins told me, "You have to write a book. I don't care how, but write something. Get the first book published. Our people are dying off. We have to capture their stories. After the first book, you'll be able to do more stories and the men in SOA will trust you because you've been on the ground across the fence and survived Laos, Cambodia and North Vietnam." My first One-Zero, Robert J. "Spider" Parks echoed those sentiments that year during the ceremony at Ft. Bragg, North Carolina, where SOG veterans received the Presidential Unit Citation 28 years after SOG was shut down in 1972. Nowhere on God's earth, are there two men I respect more than Watkins and Parks. They had put their lives on the line time and again when I was on the ground with ST Idaho and for other SOG teams and platoons. And to me, they were the Green Beret big brothers who never lost patience with me, always helped me when they could and never cast judgment while happy to offer sage advice and counsel.

That same year, Special Operation Association member and former SF medic Joseph F. Parnar approached me at the annual SOA reunion in Las Vegas and repeated what Watkins had said, adding, "I've read your stuff. You can write. You've got to do a series of books on SOG before we all die off." SOA member and former CCC One-Zero and fellow Trenton, New Jersey native Tom Waskovich has been nudging me for years to get something down on paper. Also my friend Bill Deacy, who ran reconnaissance missions from CCS and CCN, encouraged me to write a book after we appeared together in a one-hour History Channel feature on SOG.

Then I ran into old friend, SOA member and ST/RT Louisiana One-Zero David Maurer, who wrote one of the best SOG books, The Dying Place, and he urged me to write something. The Dying Place knocked me out when I first read it and later when I reread it. Maurer is a SOG warrior who also survived the Ia Drang Valley during his first tour of duty with the First Cav. He told me that a small publishing company called Real War Stories was going to re-release The Dying Place, which had gone out of print many years ago. He suggested that I call Dennis J. Cummings, of Real War Stories. At that time, I had written a Memorial Day story in May 2002 for my newspaper and had penned a piece about meeting ST Idaho interpreter extraordinaire Nguyen Cong Hiep for the first time in 30 years, after assuming that Hiep was dead. Both pieces generated a lot of positive reaction from within the newspaper and from the communities that the newspaper covers in north San Diego County. And, my wife Anna again told me that she'd completely support any writing efforts for a book, which meant spending extra time with our five-year-old daughter, and she told me that if her mother were alive, she'd urge me to write it in no uncertain terms.

Finally, I asked Maurer for Cummings's phone number and before long we agreed that Across the Fence would be the first in a series of SOG books told from the perspective of the men who were actually on the ground, across the fence in "Indian Territory." As this book goes to press, the interviewing has begun for the second in this series of SOG books.

Others who have offered suggestions and assistance before, during and after the writing of this book were: Major General Eldon Bargewell; John MacIntyre, who told me I should write a book about Phu Bai and C&C, but said he feared that no one would believe the stories that emanated from America's secret war across the fence; Roy Bahr, former CO for FOB 1, 2 and 3; Clyde Sincere, former XO at Phu Bai and CO at the Mai Loc launch site and one of the original SF men who served with 'The Father of Special Forces' Colonel Aaron Bank, with the first SF unit in 1952; Bill Shelton, former CO at Phu Bai and Mobile Launch Site 3; Lynne M. Black, Jr., ST Idaho team member and fellow One-Zero; Doug Le Tourneau, former ST Idaho and ST Virginia member; Rick Howard and Rick Estes, former recon men from FOB 1; Nguyen Cong Hiep, ST Idaho interpreter; SF/SOG Sergeant Jeffrey L. Junkins; Walt Herring, former managing editor, Trenton Times; Kent Davy, Editor, North County Times; Adrian Silva, SF troop and longtime friend; J.W. August, managing editor KGTV; Tom Morrow, North County Times columnist; Ron Ferguson, ASA Vietnam vet from Phu Bai; Ernie Acre, CCS recon man and author; Bill Donnelly, USMC Force Recon Vietnam vet; Tom Cunningham, ST Louisiana member; Ron Zaiss, ST New Jersey member; George Sternberg, ST Oregon team member; Don McKinney, legislative aide to D. Issa; Tom Missett, former North County Times publisher; Don Davis, author and former UPI reporter in Vietnam; Stephen Cavanaugh, the former Chief SOG; Michael Byard, CCN operator; Jim Hetrick, member of the original ST Idaho and SOA president; Colonel Thinh Dinh, pilot, 219th South Vietnamese Air Force Special Operations Squadron and his son James Q. Dinh; Major Nguyen Van Tuong, pilot, 219th South Vietnamese Air Force Special Operations Squadron; Major Nguyen Quy An, pilot, 219th South Vietnamese Air Force Special Operations Squadron; Tony Herrell, ST Louisiana member and FOB 3 veteran; Bob Garcia, FOB 2/CCC recon man; "Rock" Myers, SOG veteran; Cliff Newman, CCN veteran; Colonel Jack "Iceman" Isler, former CCN CO; and Brad Ryti, USMC "Scarface" crew chief, aviation historian and friend. Also, Joe Perone and Ian Shearn, of the Newark Star Ledger, and my brother and sister David and Linda Meyer. To all these people, I am deeply grateful.

Of course, behind every publisher and writer, there has to be a talented, patient and thorough editor, and I've been privileged to work with M. Lisa Allen. Not only is she a fine editor, but she showed me how to refine the writing style of first-person voice.

I am especially gratefully to my wonderful wife, Anna, for her support and encouragement over the years. I am also thankful for my children, Faith, Meredith, Alaina, Ryan and Evan, and my parents Dorothy and Henry Meyer. I love you all very much.

I want to thank each person named here for helping me at one level or another during the creative process, which led to this, my first book.

INTRODUCTION

To a great extent history relies on first-person accounts provided by eyewitnesses. When what you see and hear is classified top secret as was the case at MACV-SOG during the Vietnam War, history for those outside its need-to-know range is nonexistent. For those within the inner circle it becomes oral history that's only spoken of when among one another and then only in whispers.

John Stryker "Tilt" Meyer's tour of duty with SOG was at FOB 1 in Phu Bai and Command and Control North, which unquestionably ran the "hottest" targets of any of the C&C camps. His job was running reconnaissance missions across the border of South Vietnam into the North Vietnamese Army's sanctuaries in Laos, Cambodia and North Vietnam. There was no job during the war more dangerous or more hidden in secrecy. Time and again, Meyer and the other members of the small recon team he was a member of risked all to gather intelligence and disrupt the NVA's supply chain that snaked its way down the now infamous Ho Chi Minh Trail.

As a U.S. Army Special Forces soldier Meyer was well trained to observe what was truly there and discount what wasn't. He had a ringside seat on a history that nobody at the time ever expected would be revealed to outsiders. In addition to experiencing this vicious secret war firsthand, as a respected recon man he was taken into the confidence of some of SOG's most legendary figures. In the camp club and hootches he heard stories of harrowing close calls and brutally fierce firefights that at times became epic.

History might be compared to rain driving down on a roof. Given enough time it will leak through, as was the case with the ultra-secret MACV-SOG. It took the better part of three decades before the U.S. government officially admitted that these missions into Laos, Cambodia and North Vietnam ever happened. Still, admitting something occurred is a lot different than telling the stories that make up its history. And history at its best is not the dry recitation of facts and dates. History comes alive when the eyewitnesses to it reveal the day-to-day dramas that played out during its making, and the minute details that give it verve and color.

Writing history with life takes more than just being an eyewitness to it. It also takes a gifted writer. The stories that follow are sterling examples of what occurs when these two elements unite.

David A. Maurer
Recon team leader, MACV-SOG
Command and Control North 1968-70.

ACROSS THE FENCE

The Secret War in Vietnam

Chapter One

WELCOME TO C&C

The old Army deuce-and-a-half pulled up in front of House 22, the CIA/Special Forces operated safe house in Da Nang, and someone inside the truck called out, "Everyone with orders to C and C, let's go." My fellow green-as-grass Special Forces soldiers and I casually picked up the M-16s we had been issued in Nha Trang and headed toward the transport truck. More than a dozen of us climbed into the back. It was May 1968. We were triple volunteers: we had volunteered and graduated from the Army's parachute jump school in Ft. Benning, Georgia, made it through the Qualification Course at the Special Forces Training Group in Ft. Bragg, North Carolina and after attending the 5th Special Forces Group (Airborne) in-country training program, we had volunteered to serve in MACV-SOG's Command and Control.

During Special Forces training at Ft. Bragg, several of the Green Berets teaching various courses told us to avoid C&C because the duty was rough and the Special Forces casualties were high in the top secret unit. During communications training, where we learned how to send and receive messages in Morse code, Sergeants Wagner and Russo and Sergeant First Class Paul Villarosa also advised that we avoid C&C. Villarosa was a living legend. He had served three

This three quarter-ton truck was often used for transporting SF soldiers. Here, troops are getting ready to leave the firing range in Phu Bai. From left: John "Bubba" Shore, Charles Borg, John S. Meyer, Bill Barclay—with cigarette, Lynne M. Black Jr.—with beret, and Phouc, of ST Idaho, standing.

tours in Vietnam with the Special Forces. His advice to us was to go to an A Camp for our first tour of duty in Vietnam. Check out C&C from afar before volunteering for the secret, but deadly, operation. Despite all the warnings, Rick Howard, John MacIntyre, Rick Estes, Tony Herrell, Mark Gentry, Bob Garcia, Bobby D. Leathers, myself, and a few others volunteered to serve in C&C. I had been in training or in between training cycles since entering the Army on 1 December 1966. In May 1968, we were finally shifting gears from being in a training mode to an operational mode. None of the rumors prepared us for what followed.

We were about to quietly enter America's secret war in Vietnam. The deuce-and-a-half drove to the northern end of Da Nang, near the Da Nang Air Base, and deposited us in front of a nondescript building where C&C Headquarters was located. After standing around in the Army tradition of "hurry-up-and-wait," a Sergeant Major told us to enter the building. As we settled into our chairs, some of us began to pull out pads or small notebooks, as we had done for more than a year in classroom situations.

"You won't need those," the sergeant major said. "Put away all pens, pencils and notebooks. This is a top secret briefing. All of you have either obtained a top secret clearance or will do so in the near future or you wouldn't be here." The business-like sergeant major went on to explain that we were not allowed to discuss with anyone what was discussed inside that classroom. He asked Mike Byard from Trenton, New Jersey to hand out forms while he spoke. Byard seemed like an old pro to us. He had been in-country three months and had run several joint missions with Navy SEALs as a communications specialist. Now that he was officially entering C&C, Byard was getting the same treatment as the rest of us. The sergeant major looked at the open door to the briefing room and ordered someone to shut it.

"Welcome to the Command and Control Detachment of the 5th Special Forces Group, Airborne, 1st Special Forces, United States Army Special Operations Augmentation, Studies and Observations Group, or simply C and C," the sergeant major said. "Gentlemen,

After these Special Forces soldiers graduated from the Special Forces Qualification Course in December 1967, they were sent to the U.S. Army Southeastern Signal School, Ft. Gordon, Georgia for radio teletype training before being assigned to SOG in S. Vietnam. Among the Special Forces who ran recon missions from FOB 1, 3 or 4 were: Rick Estes, far right in first row; Mark Gentry, far right in second row, John MacIntyre to his right and John S. Meyer, to his right; Richard Jennings, far right third row and Floyd Iron, second from left, third row. Missing from the photo are Rick Howard, who ran missions with ST New Jersey and Robert Garcia, who ran recon mission at FOB 2 in Kontum. (John S. Meyer photo)

before you is a confidentiality agreement." This was a binding contract where all of us acknowledged that we would not discuss C&C with anyone outside of the special augmentation group. "You can't tell your girlfriend, your mother, no one." If anyone asked about our assignments, we were to simply say that we were with the 5th Special Forces Group in Vietnam. The agreement was binding for 20 years. If anyone violated this agreement, that individual could face federal prosecution, resulting in stiff fines and incarceration, and ruin any future government or security employment opportunities. We were prohibited from writing anything about the operation, forbidden from keeping diaries, taking photos, making drawings or tape recording notes of any sort. The sergeant major advised us that anyone who didn't want to sign the agreement could leave. No questions would be asked. Anyone who wanted out would be returned to the conventional Special Forces headquarters in Nha Trang. No one left the room.

The sergeant major told everyone that C&C staff would read all mail, including all letters we wrote and received. When he said that our mailing address would be Drawer 22, with an APO in San Francisco, Rick Howard knew it wasn't a regular Army mailing address. This was something very different.

"Gentlemen," the sergeant major turned toward a generic map on the wall, "the North Vietnamese Army controls these 'neutral' countries," and pointed to Cambodia and Laos, located to the west of the Republic of South Vietnam, and of course, North Vietnam. For several years, the North Vietnamese Army had moved soldiers, supplies, rockets, guns and propagandists south into the eastern provinces of "neutral" Laos and Cambodia through an ever-increasing network of trails and roads called the Ho Chi Minh Trail Complex. The NVA had a division called the 559th, so named because the North Vietnamese government formed it in May 1959, for the sole purpose of expanding the Ho Chi Minh Trail and moving supplies south. The NVA had 30,000 to 40,000 troops, conscripted laborers and enslaved indigenous personnel in Laos alone.

Once the supplies were cached, the NVA units would strike into

South Vietnam from their sanctuaries when and where they wanted. When the units wished to withdraw from the battlefield, they did so, often retreating into Cambodia and Laos to regroup and resupply in preparation for the next attack while conventional U.S. and South Vietnamese armed forces were forbidden to pursue them across the border. Green Beret A Camps were built along the border to act as an early warning system, as well as to provide the local people with basic military training and to improve their living conditions. The efforts of the Green Berets and their indigenous troops in those A Camps weren't enough. This was where C&C entered the picture. Platoon-sized elements called Hatchet Forces, or the smaller 4 to 12-man reconnaissance teams, code-named spike teams, went "across the fence," as the border between the countries was known. Both penetrated deep into Laos and Cambodia to monitor, interdict and report on the NVA forces along the Ho Chi Minh Trail.

"Now listen up real close," the sergeant major said. "When you go across the fence, you will carry no identification of any manner, shape or form." That meant no identification papers, no dog tags, no diaries, no photos, no love letters and certainly no green berets. Everyone would wear sterile fatigues, with no company insignia, no nametags, no unit designators, no jump wings or Combat Infantryman Badges. Why? Without giving anyone a chance to respond, he said that because Laos and Cambodia were "neutral," the United States government could publicly proclaim that the U.S. respected that "neutrality." Thus, if we were killed in Laos, Cambodia or North Vietnam, the U.S. government would deny having anything to do with us. The United States government would explain that no Americans were stationed in Laos or Cambodia, which was technically accurate. The U.S. government had "plausible deniability" if we were captured or killed. And if captured, we were to speak a foreign language.

"Don't tell them who you are," he ordered. "Remember, technically, under the terms and conditions of the Geneva Accords, your status is different than the Air Force and Navy pilots shot down over North Vietnam. They're in uniform. They're identifiable as U.S.

servicemen. C and C men don't fall into the category of prisoners of war." We were in effect, spies, although the sergeant major never used that word. It sounded like we were James Bond without the Astin Martin, the women or the made-for-movies escapes. He also didn't tell us that spies had no protection under the Geneva Convention and that we could be summarily executed if captured.

To further aid the deception, C&C personnel would have a choice of weaponry to carry to the field that was second to no other unit in the Vietnam War. C&C purchasing agents had the latest in weapons for us, from Colt's CAR-15, which was a shortened version of the M-16, and experimental Stoner weapons systems to the older automatic submachine guns, such as those used in World War II, like the British Sten gun, the M-3 "grease gun" and the .45 caliber Thompson. We also had access to the Israeli 9mm Uzi. Handgun options ranged from the reliable Colt .45 and Smith & Wesson .38 Special, to the Browning Hi Power 9mm, German Luger and Beretta. Weapons would be issued from S-4 personnel at one of six C&C Forward Operation Bases: FOB 6 at Ho Ngoc Tao; FOB 5, Ban Me Thuot; FOB 4, Da Nang; FOB 3, Khe Sanh; FOB 2, Kontum; and FOB 1 at Phu Bai.

"Make no mistake about it," the sergeant major told us, "the NVA know where Special Forces soldiers are." In the previous 30 months, the NVA had overrun the original FOB 1 at Kham Duc; the Special Forces A Camp at Lang Vei, a short distance west of Khe Sanh; A Loui in the A Shau Valley; and they had hammered the A Camp at Bu Dop, which had an air strip FOB 6 recon teams and Hatchet Forces used as a launch site.

Then the sergeant major repeated a line that many of us had heard several times during the last year of training. "Don't underestimate the soldiers in the NVA because many of them now carry the new AK-47, which holds 36 rounds." Our CAR-15s held only 18 rounds. What he said next shocked the commo men in the room: Paul Villarosa had been killed in early 1968 on a C&C mission during his fourth tour of duty in South Vietnam. What went unsaid was, if the NVA could get to a professional soldier like Villarosa, you rookies better learn fast about how this sort of war is fought. The sergeant major reiterated how the NVA defeated France in 1954, wrapping up nine years of guerrilla warfare with a stunning victory at the battle of Dien Bien Phu in North Vietnam. And then he gave us one more chilling fact—missions across the fence had no conventional military units for support. No artillery, no resupply and no conventional U.S. or South Vietnamese ground troops.

"You're out there by yourselves, beyond the range of friendly artillery. And because you're so far west of South Vietnam, when you make enemy contact, especially in Laos, it'll take friendly helicopter units more than an hour to get to you."

At some point, he called for a break. Outside, the mood was much more somber than when we had entered the classroom. MacIntyre pulled me aside.

"Jesus, Tilt, you've done it now! You've got us into a secret war and I can't tell my parents about it. My dad fought at the Battle of the Bulge and I can't write and tell him about what we're doing. But if I'm killed in Laos or North Vietnam, you gotta promise me you'll tell my dad the truth. Can you believe they got Villarosa?" The Villarosa announcement had rocked all of the communications specialists. Those of us who had been trained by Villarosa at Ft. Bragg stood silently, wondering what had happened to the veteran Green Beret. He was a short, wiry, intense bantam rooster of a man who could send or receive two separate transmissions of Morse Code simultaneously—a receiver in each ear, and a pencil in each hand. He was a tough teacher, yet always gave the recruits who wanted to learn Morse code extra classes at night and on weekends, if needed. In spite of all his training, he had bought the farm. The gravity of what we were undertaking was beginning to sink in and no one was laughing or kidding around anymore.

Personally, I felt an odd mix of excitement, nervousness and fear. I was excited to be a part of a top secret operation. It was so top secret that Robin Moore didn't mention it by name in his groundbreaking book on Special Forces, The Green Berets. I was nervous because I was a rookie in a war where Villarosa had been killed by the NVA. I was afraid of being a part of what some had described as the most dangerous operation in the Vietnam War. The prospect of operating deep behind enemy lines, similar to what the Office of Strategic Services, the forerunner of the CIA, did during World War II was daunting, especially when there were no friendlies across the fence. Everyone, from farmers and woodcutters to NVA troops, would be out to get us.

When the briefing resumed, the sergeant major retraced several key points from the first part of the top-secret background briefing before mentioning the rules of engagement. He explained that because most C&C missions across the fence would be deep into Laos, Cambodia or North Vietnam, there would be no traditional support from Army and Marine Corps units. Once engaged with the North Vietnamese Army, the Pathet Lao or Khmer Rouge in Cambodia, conventional forces would be prohibited from coming to our aid. There would be no tank support, no armored personnel carriers. Only C&C assets would be allowed to cross the border. Again, the reconnaissance teams would be so deep into enemy territory that the only way help could arrive would be via aircraft, mostly helicopters. In 1968, most of the choppers had no night-flight capabilities. And the weather in Southeast Asia often severely limited helicopter flights. Thus, we were not to engage the enemy unless they fired first. If the mission called for the spike team or Hatchet Force to initiate contact—that was a different matter. C&C assets would be on hand to give us support.

Then the sergeant major turned to code names. Every person in C&C had a code name that was issued by C&C and was to be used for security purposes during any radio transmission. Rick Howard got saddled with "trustee." Trustee wasn't nearly as cool as Don Loomis's "trooper." In other C&C briefings, SF troops got to choose or invent their own names. Doug Le Tourneau asked for and got "Frenchman." Lynne M. Black, Jr. had always wanted to change his first name to Jack, so he chose "Blackjack." If we didn't use our C&C code names we were to use our team-designated positions. On reconnaissance teams, the team leader's designation was One-Zero, the assistant team leader was One-One and the radio operator was One-Two.

I said I'd probably use my nickname "Tilt," as my fellow troops knew me. The sergeant major's assistant told me to pass it on to the S-3 (operations center) personnel. If I was on a mission and got separated from my team, the code name could play a critical role in search and rescue personnel attempting to verify my exact identity and to insure that I wasn't held captive by enemy forces.

There was one more detail: we were given a password comprised of three questions and answers. These were written down and would be used to positively identify us if we were captured. Black's questions and answers were:

Question 1: Who's your father?
Answer 1: That old alcoholic?

Question 2: And your mother?
Answer 2: Still sending me lemon cookies.

Question 3: Is your brother still sick?
Answer 3: He died from his wounds.

As the briefing wound down, the sergeant major told us that we'd be shipping out to the different FOBs ASAP. Once we landed at the FOBs, we would find each operational base highly compartmentalized and that we would be given briefings and operational reports on a "need-to-know" basis. He explained that within the individual spike team or Hatchet Force, it was wise to ask as many questions as possible from the senior members. However, he advised us not to ask a lot of questions about other operations and missions that were classified.

"If you have a need to know, someone will tell you," he said. "Otherwise, don't ask. If a person is captured by enemy forces, it's better that the captured individual not know about other operations that he is not directly involved with." Again, the logic and reasoning was chillingly simple.

The ride back to House 22 was quiet. The days of joking and

fooling around in Training Group were behind us. When we pulled up in front of House 22, MacIntyre and I noticed the tough-looking, no-nonsense Chinese Nung personnel on security duty. We walked across the grassless front yard, past a guardhouse, up the steps and into the building. Straight ahead was the bar. To the left of the bar were a hallway and a sitting area complete with a television, radio, board games, the latest edition of Stars and Stripes and several empty Coca-Cola and beer cans. Down the hall were the living quarters of the non-commissioned Special Forces sergeant who ran the building, Sergeant Losey, and the kitchen area. Off the hallway to the right was a staircase that wound upward to the second story.

MacIntyre stopped at the bar to purchase two Cokes while I went upstairs to grab a shower. Even though it was only May, the temperature and humidity were far worse than Georgia, North Carolina or New Jersey, combined. In addition, MacIntyre and I had been told repeatedly that "anyone could be the enemy" in guerrilla warfare. Being on guard mentally and physically at all times was draining. Add all of that extra caution to the heat and humidity, and Da Nang was a very uncomfortable place.

At the top of the stairs, I found myself in a large room filled with double bunk beds and several cots. On top of one double bunk, sweaty and naked, was a couple heavily involved in the rapture of the moment. They never even noticed me scurry past. When I got to the open shower area, I found an SF trooper showering, while a naked Vietnamese woman squatted in the water, washing herself. Sergeant Losey had explained earlier that the prostitutes were given weekly checkups for venereal disease and what the regular prices were. MacIntyre and I were still adjusting to having prostitutes so readily available and so open about their business. I hesitated to walk into the open shower area. The older SF sergeant could tell I was still new in-country.

"Don't stand on protocol around here. I ain't queer and she won't hurt you, now," he said, pointing to the young prostitute, who was still washing herself.

After a quick shower, I returned to MacIntyre, who was sipping his Coke in the sitting room downstairs. There were several SF soldiers dressed in older jungle fatigues lounging around as well. MacIntyre quickly filled me in on the latest: several of our guys had already shipped out to FOBs 2, 3 and 4. One of the old sergeants drinking a beer had heard another veteran SF troop say that the North Vietnamese Army was really getting its act together across the fence. And the only good news MacIntyre had to report was that the cooks were grilling steaks for dinner, there would be ice cream for dessert and we had missed the last ride to FOB 1. For a few minutes we hunkered down in our seats, waiting for someone to yell at us for not shipping out ASAP. Before long, we got into an intense game of Scrabble and soon went searching for a dictionary, as our dalliance brought no repercussions.

While we tried hard to land our Scrabble pieces on the bonus squares, an attractive young lady came to work behind the bar for the late shift. Her name was Hahn. She was barely over five feet tall, had dark, intelligent eyes, a short haircut and was dressed conservatively, unlike the prostitutes floating around House 22 that night. The steaks came. MacIntyre and I went to the bar, ordered Cokes and started eating, while beginning a tentative dialogue with Hahn. When a couple of intoxicated CIA employees rudely suggested that she go upstairs with them, she politely, but firmly, told them to bug off, and one of the SF sergeants informed them that Hahn was Losey's girlfriend. Once MacIntyre and I assured her that we had girlfriends back in the U.S., she relaxed a bit when talking to us. She told us she was Catholic, she worked in House 22 to help her mother, she spoke three languages, including French, and was thinking about getting a job as an interpreter. As the evening wore on, her sense of humor surfaced more frequently. Just talking to her seemed to take the edge off an otherwise unnerving day.

Shortly before midnight, a few shots were fired down the street from House 22 and MacIntyre and I jumped off of our seats and squatted on the floor. The veteran SF soldiers in the room looked at us and tried to keep their laughter to themselves.

Sometime after midnight, we retired to the bunk beds upstairs.

We both slept on the lower bunks, believing that if House 22 were mortared, the upper bunk would give us added protection. MacIntyre and I both remembered our first night in the 5th Special Forces Group compound in Nha Trang when the Viet Cong mortared the base. At least two rounds slammed into the barracks next to ours. The explosions were unbelievably loud and terrifying. One second we were asleep, the next second incoming 82mm rounds exploded on the indigenous troops' barracks, showering our roof with debris. There were horrifying screams from the wounded. Everyone ran out of the barracks to the weapons room, only to find that transient troops couldn't retrieve weapons unless the duty officer was nearby with a key. We ran to a nearby bunker that faced the perimeter, expecting a full charge of Viet Cong. Instead, illumination rounds popped overhead and slowly descended to earth on their parachutes, eerily lighting up the night and revealing nothing but some water buffalo outside the perimeter.

MacIntyre and I overslept the next morning and missed another ride to Phu Bai. A surprised Hahn greeted us at the bar. After a few minutes of polite chatting, we ordered steak and eggs, as they had several steaks left over from the previous night. As we waited for the steaks, MacIntyre grinned and asked if I remembered that night in D.C. The night in question was during the weekend when the Lang Vei A Camp was overrun by the NVA and we had been sitting in a bar, watching it on television. That night, during the winter of '68, we looked at each other and said several times that we were certain to die during our tours of duty in Vietnam. We went home, withdrew all of our money from our savings accounts and drove back to Ft. Gordon, where we were going though radio-teletype training. For several weeks, MacIntyre and I drove to a restaurant at the Augusta, Georgia airport and had steak dinners, with baked potatoes and drinks, as often as we could get off base. We vowed that we weren't going to leave our money behind for our relatives to fight over. Sitting in Da Nang, we reminisced about that night in D.C., which seemed light years past, when in fact it had only been a few months.

That short time at House 22 was educational for another reason.

Staff Sgt. John Allen standing in company formation with the Hatchet Force element at FOB 1. Allen was the ST Alabama One-Zero and sole survivor when ST Alabama was hit by several NVA elements in early 1968. Allen had to escape and evade through enemy lines before he was rescued from the target area. Note red scarf worn by Hatchet Force members in the KKK, all Cambodian troops. (Photo courtesy of Ron Zaiss)

As MacIntyre and I missed our flights to Phu Bai, a few men from the Special Forces Mike Force came in to relax. They talked about several missions they had recently run, including one where they went out to rescue a C&C recon team that had run into a world of trouble. During the discussion they talked about how happy they were that they weren't assigned to C&C. They mentioned that in March, an entire reconnaissance team from FOB 4 had disappeared while running a mission in Laos. They talked about Spike Team Alabama from FOB 1 losing all of the Americans on the team except one, Sergeant John Allen, who miraculously survived the ordeal. MacIntyre and I looked grim.

Finally, the next day we got up early, rode a truck to the Da Nang Airport and boarded a camouflage-painted Sikorsky H-34 helicopter piloted by Vietnamese from the 219th Vietnamese Air Force. The old H-34s were powered by a nine-cylinder Wright Aeronautical Corporation "Cyclone" R-1820 engine which had powered the legendary B-17s of WWII fame. Special Forces soldier John Hutchens joined us for the flight from Da Nang to Phu Bai. As we boarded the chopper through the door—it had only one door, which was on the starboard side—the Vietnamese crew chief pointed us toward the canvas seats on the port side of the aircraft. The crew chief took a look at us and then went outside for a second and started gesturing to the pilot. We sat down, facing the open door.

When it was time to go, the old nine-cylinder engine sounded like it wasn't going to start. After some urging and cussing, it finally sputtered to life. Once the engine warmed up, the sputtering changed into a powerful-sounding purr. The entire aircraft took on a new rhythm. I assumed the Vietnamese pilot would simply lift off and head north. Instead, he rolled the aircraft outside the hangar area and down a cement road toward one of the main runways. As we rolled toward the runway, a sortie of Air Force F-4 Phantom jets roared

A Kingbee helicopter takes off from FOB 1, Phu Bai, heading north up Highway 1 toward Hue and Quang Tri. (Photo courtesy of Doug LeTourneau)

past, screaming into the sky, heading north. Finally, the H-34 rolled out onto the main runway. The pilot lifted the tail of the aircraft and we rolled down the runway, gaining speed until we had enough transitional lift. Our takeoff was far less dramatic than the Air Force jets.

The radial engine purred as we slowly climbed over the mountains and over the Hai Van Pass. Once we leveled off, the H-34, code-named "Kingbee," flew parallel to Highway 1, the only north-south road from Hanoi in North Vietnam, to Saigon in South Vietnam. As we glided up the coastal road, I was struck by the beauty of the land below, as well as by the bomb craters from the present war. After awhile, we passed the Phu Bai Airport, which sat to the east of Highway 1 and handled both commercial and military aircraft. While passing the airport, the crew chief spoke briefly into his headset and cast a quick glance at the three of us. The Kingbee moved from the east side of Highway 1 to the west. As the aircraft gently shifted across the road, the 2nd Army of the Republic of Vietnam (ARVN) Training Center appeared on the east side. It was a huge complex with a high wall that faced Highway 1.

Without warning, the engine suddenly revved up, increasing its RPMs as the aircraft dipped down a brief moment before beginning an abrupt ascent. MacIntyre looked at Hutchens, who obviously didn't know what was happening. Before a word could be spoken, the helicopter made a hard turn to the right while still in the climb. The H-34 rotated 90 degrees, turning the aircraft onto its side. The quiet, peaceful ride up Highway 1 became terrifying, as we saw nothing but the ground beneath us. MacIntyre grabbed the seat and yelled, "Oh, shit!"

I glanced at the crew chief, who had a broad grin on his face as he described the reactions of MacIntyre and Hutchens to the pilot. The centrifugal force of the radical maneuver held us in the aircraft, although that scientific fact hadn't done anything for our nerves. Before it registered that we weren't going to fall out, the H-34 completed a 180-degree turn and plummeted toward FOB 1.

At the last possible moment, the skillful Vietnamese pilot leveled

E
N
S
W

(LEFT)
This is one of the best aerial photographs of FOB 1, with the helicopter launch pad and Highway 1 at the bottom on the western edge of the facility. On the far right (south) is the 2nd ARVN Training Battalion. On the far left (north) is the old French minefield that continued east, eventually wrapping around the eastern perimeter.
Inside the compound, beginning at the lower left are five buildings of various size for the Hatchet Force troops. The next central building is the shower, with the water towers on the right (south) side. Moving east, the next two buildings that run north and south are the old French barracks built during the French-Indochina War that ended in 1954. The first building is the officers club. The next building is NCO housing. The next four small buildings are additional housing for enlisted personnel. The fifth building was built in July 1968 to house helicopter pilots assigned to FOB 1, including the Musket gunship crews of the 176th Assault Helicopter Company from the Americal Division. Only a few feet further east is the Green Beret Lounge. The Dispensary is the next building followed by the motor pool, which has the last large building on the left (north side) of the camp. At the top of the photo is the rappelling tower.
To the right are the ammo dumps, followed by the Mess Halls. The indig facility is on the far right while the U.S. eating area is on the north side. The northwest corner of the U.S. Mess Hall is the beginning of the football field, which has a Jeep driving through it. The next set of buildings that run north and south are S-4 on the east side and the S-1, S-2, S-3 shops and mailroom on the west side. The next trio of buildings with three buildings each, are the indig troops billets. The one exception is the northeast corner that was the Commanding Officer's office. Housed in that first set were recon troops and the remaining two buildings were mostly Hatchet Force billets. (Photo courtesy of Ron Zaiss)

off for a few seconds, heading south, before rolling the chopper onto its right side again and turning west. He leveled off again as he eased around to the west side of Highway 1 and brought the chopper down. The wheels had barely touched the ground when the crew chief jumped out and told us to exit posthaste. The rotor wash covered us with dust, sand and grit. As we walked away from the aircraft, a three-quarter ton pickup truck pulled up with a C&C reconnaissance team in the back. Six members of Spike Team Idaho, led by Sergeant First Class Glen Oliver Lane, the One-Zero, boarded the aircraft. As we loaded our gear into the truck, the Kingbee rained more dirt and sand upon us as it lifted off and headed west toward Laos.

Chapter Two

LIAR'S DICE

The three-quarter ton truck drove across Highway 1 and through the gates into the FOB. A three-foot wall of old sandbags and a tall wall that was the northern end of the 2nd ARVN Training compound bordered the road on the south. The north side of the road had its own three-foot wall of sandbags that formed a series of bunkers built behind the team buildings. These buildings were a series of three bunkhouses, built side by side. The road went more than 100 yards before the first turn, between the housing for indigenous personnel assigned to the Hatchet Force. Farther down, there was another set of team houses for all of the indigenous personnel assigned to spike teams. Each team had its own room. Turning left into the next roadway led directly to the CO's and XO's office on the left, and the mailroom, S-3, communications, S-2 (intelligence) and S-1 (personnel) shops on the right, again in a series of buildings with three roofs constructed side by side. On the east side of those buildings was S-4, where we picked up all supplies. Immediately east from S-4 was the officers' barracks. The enlisted housing consisted of five smaller buildings east of the officers' quarters, and east of those buildings was the Green Beret Lounge and the dispensary.

As we unloaded our gear from the truck, the driver told us to

Two security guards stand outside the front gate to FOB 1, Phu Bai. To the right of the gate is the 2nd ARVN Training Center. The long fence separates the training center from the top secret FOB 1 compound. On a few occasions, snoopy reporters tried to gain entrance to the camp, but were summarily dismissed. On one occasion, a magazine reporter was told: "Leave or die here, now." (Photo courtesy of Stephen Bayliss)

stack our stuff by S-3 and that someone would eventually explain FOB 1 to us. He noted that the helicopter was en route to put ST Idaho into a target area and that at least one other team was already on the ground, with the possibility of a Hatchet Force gearing up for an A Shau Valley operation. In a few minutes the Executive Officer of FOB 1, Major Clyde Sincere, approached us, quickly introduced himself and asked us if we were all SF-trained communications specialists. We all nodded our heads in the affirmative. Sincere said that was good news because commo personnel were needed both at FOB 1 and FOB 3 at Khe Sanh. I cringed inside. MacIntyre looked at me askance. Two months earlier, MacIntyre and I had watched the Khe Sanh siege live on television. At that time, we, like most of America, didn't realize that a top secret SF camp was located next door to the besieged Marine encampment. Sincere further explained that since this was our first tour of duty in Vietnam with SF, we'd all probably get slots inside the various commo sheds in the beginning. At that moment there was a need for commo personnel, and after we learned the ropes of camp life, we could apply for slots with the Hatchet Force or spike teams. He directed us to report to the mailroom for obvious reasons, go to S-1 to hand over our personnel papers and then to S-4 to get some basic supplies, weapons and ammo. Sincere told us that FOB 1 was an old French barracks that hadn't been hit by Viet Cong guerrilla forces or elements from the North Vietnamese Army since the Tet Offensive earlier in the year. He said the original French minefield around FOB 1 to the north and east had a second minefield beyond it, dug by SF personnel. Additionally, different elements had conducted night patrols and area ambushes since Tet, in a fashion similar to the SF A Camps throughout South Vietnam. Before setting up the ambushes, someone in FOB 1 would tell the local residents at Phu Luong, the small village north of the base, to stay indoors after 2200. After that hour, anyone who walked into an ambush kill zone was considered to be the enemy and dealt with accordingly. Sincere wasn't one to mince words. The major excused himself.

Sincere was too modest to tell us that he was in the original

Facing the camera is Maj. Clyde J. Sincere Jr., standing with other officers in front of the S-2 shop at FOB 1, including Maj. Bill Shelton, the second officer to Sincere's left. (Photo courtesy of Doug LeTourneau)

SF unit formed at Ft. Bragg in 1952 and he had served under the "Father of Special Forces" Colonel Aaron Bank. Sixteen years later, he remained a shadow warrior, an SF troop who cared about the welfare of the men serving under him, as well as doing all within his power to get the mission accomplished.

As MacIntyre, Hutchens and I exited the S-1 shop, I heard a familiar voice shout, "Is that Private Meyer? Is that my catcher? What are you doing hanging out with that traitorous dog from B Company?" Because we were emerging from the relative darkness of the S-1 shop, our eyes were still adjusting to the intense brightness outside. The voice belonged to Staff Sergeant Robert J. "Spider" Parks. I was the A Company catcher, MacIntyre, the traitorous B Company dog. We were happy to see a familiar face, MacIntyre included, even if it was the pitcher from A Company. "Let me show you boys around, even you, you B Company puke."

Spider had graduated from Training Group a training cycle ahead of us. He was a member of ST Idaho, the same team that had taken off right after we landed. He walked us inside the S-3 (operations) shop. Once again, the visual contrast was startling after standing outside in the glaring sunlight, and then stepping into a poorly lit room. On the right and left were desks we half-stumbled past. Spider explained that the back room to the right was the commo center. We entered the back room to the left, which was the briefing room, where pilots and team leaders met with S-3 and S-2 prior to launching a mission.

Spider pulled aside a black cloth hanging over a huge map of Southeast Asia. He pointed to Phu Bai and went straight across the map to the A Shau Valley. He told us that Sergeant Lane and ST Idaho were going into a target designated W-5, or Whiskey Five. The map had a series of grid overlays designating each target area. There were a series of A targets which were near the A Shau Valley, and AS targets, for targets in and around the valley itself. North, in Laos, were G, or Golf targets, and west of the DMZ, in Laos, were MA targets. He told us the A Shau targets, the Whiskey targets and Oscar Eight were notoriously deadly. He mentioned the A Shau

SF A Camps getting overrun, and how the FOB 1 teams had been hammered recently in targets around the valley. Only a few months earlier, NVA soldiers attacked ST Alabama near the valley. The NVA relentlessly pursued and fought the team for days. Enemy firepower on the ground prevented any helicopters from extracting the team. Only the One-Zero lived through the ordeal, escaping by going through the enemy ranks at night, leaving behind the team members who had been killed in the horrific combat. This was the same story we had heard from the Mike Force guys at House 22.

Spider told us that ST Idaho had been inserted without a hitch and that the radioman had given a "team okay" after being on the ground for ten minutes. He explained that all of the air assets used during the insertion of the team, the Vietnamese-piloted H-34s, the helicopter gunships, the propeller-driven A-1E Skyraiders and any fast movers (jets) remained on station until the team on the ground gave a team okay. Nonetheless, Spider was anxious. Looking at the map, there were symbols for anti-aircraft positions that pilots had encountered in recent weeks. As I looked at the symbols, I remembered watching World War II movies where U.S. pilots were briefed on German anti-aircraft positions and how the German ack-ack wreaked havoc on American aviators. I thought about the B-17s flying high at more than 200 miles per hour and still getting hammered. I realized we might encounter anti-aircraft weapons in helicopters flying slightly over 100 mph and a lot closer to the ground. Another twist to the war I hadn't anticipated.

Spider stuck his head back into the S-3 shop and asked if there was any word from ST Idaho. Someone answered no, and told him that the Vietnamese Kingbee pilots had landed and were coming in for a drink and some chow. Our impromptu briefing ended as Spider headed us back outside into the harsh glare and ever-present humidity. As we went outside, the three-quarter ton truck pulled up with the Kingbee pilots and aircrew members. They were a unique group. Most wore tailored gray or black flight suits with a holster and gun slung low on their hip, giving them the appearance of modern day cowboys with baseball caps. When they jumped out of the truck, most walked with varying degrees of swagger. They were cocky, and as Spider quickly pointed out, most of the Kingbee pilots were as good as any American pilot. Spider asked one of them how the insertion went and the answer was "No sweat. No VC." The pilots continued walking to the bar. Regardless of the bad press some Vietnamese military units had received during the last year, the indigenous forces and the men of the 219th Vietnamese Air Force were fearless. As we spoke, someone from S-1 came out and told the three of us that we could stay in the temporary bunking area a few doors down from the CO's office. MacIntyre and Hutchens picked up their duffle bags and moved out. Spider intervened and told the S-1 desk jockey that I'd stay with him in his room until it was determined what my duty assignment would be at FOB 1. He looked at MacIntyre and told him that there was no room for a B Company puke.

Spider and I headed north on the sandy road in front of S-3, crossed the main street and angled slightly to the right to the enlisted quarters for Americans in the old French barracks. We walked down a concrete sidewalk in front of barracks rooms with their front doors open. As we passed the rooms, we heard a broad selection of music: one room had Jefferson Airplane's Surrealistic Pillow booming from a reel-to-reel stereo, the next room had Johnny Cash's "I walk the Line" blaring. Next was Glen Campbell singing "Wichita Lineman" and the Byrds ended the musical tour. Spider pointed out that most of the country and western music was played by the older SF troops who had been in the Army for several years, while the cutting edge rock 'n roll was played by the younger SF troops. I walked into his room and placed my gear in a wall locker before we moved out to the club. In the Green Beret Lounge, it was no different; the jukebox had many selections from both sides of the music aisle. I hoped country and western didn't dominate the jukebox or this was going to be an unduly long war.

Spider moved toward the bar. I missed a step down and stumbled after him. At the bar, Spider ordered a cold drink. I asked for a Coke and the bartender apologized, saying that the only soda he had was Dr. Pepper. He had been out of Coke for weeks, but he had pallets full

From left, with back to camera standing in front of the ST Idaho Vietnamese team room at FOB 1, Phu Bai, is former ST Idaho One-Zero, Robert J. "Spider" Parks, ST Idaho interpreter Nguyen Cong Hiep and Khanh "Cowboy" Doan, who fought along side Black on Oct. 5, 1968. (Photo courtesy of Ron Zaiss)

of Dr. Pepper. Damn! I hated the taste of Dr. Pepper. I asked Spider what kind of war we were fighting if a man couldn't get a Coca-Cola. He shrugged his shoulders and headed for a table near the jukebox. I followed. I was amazed at the different languages I heard; one group was speaking Russian; at another table some SF troops were speaking Hungarian; at another, the men sounded as though they were speaking either Chinese or Japanese. Spider pointed to a table where they were speaking German and commented that it was an East German dialect. The career SF men practiced their language skills as much as possible, regardless of where they were stationed. Among the men at the tables were Special Forces soldiers assigned to South Vietnam on temporary duty status from the 1st Special Forces Group based in Okinawa. The 1st had been sending teams to C&C for several years on a six-month assignment. Some were on their second or third tour of duty in Vietnam, all in the secret war. On the wall of the club were yellow signs with the names of the men from the various 1st SF detachments.

After a while, Spider said it was time for lunch, but he wanted to stop by S-3 to see if there was any word from ST Idaho. He walked back to the commo shack and asked if there was any word from the Whiskey Five target. The commo guy said Covey had flown nearby for a commo check at noon, but couldn't raise anyone from ST Idaho. The news brought a frown to Spider's face as we headed out toward the mess hall. He said that no commo from a team on the ground meant one of three things: the team couldn't talk because they were fighting the enemy, or they couldn't talk because the enemy was too close, or the simplest reason, the team was experiencing radio trouble.

As we neared the mess hall, Spider told me I was in for a surprise. "We have one of the best cooks in all of Vietnam. The head cook here used to be a chef in a big hotel in Hanoi, but moved south to get away from the Communists. The brass in Saigon believes that because we have the roughest assignment in Nam, we should eat right." For breakfast, the chef usually cooked eggs to order and had pancakes or waffles, hot cereal, and sides of sausage, ham or bacon.

Lunch always consisted of at least two main dishes. Dinner had the best of the leftovers from lunch and a new entree. The milk was cold. There was ice for drinks. In this mess hall no one complained about the food.

After lunch, two members from ST Oregon, Mike Tucker, tall and handsome, and George "The Troll" Sternberg, a no-nonsense fireplug of a man, approached Spider, asking about Lane. They had heard ST Idaho had missed the noon commo check and they were worried. Spider voiced his concerns as well, while noting that Lane was a veteran SF troop who had several reconnaissance missions under his belt.

Spider took me over to S-4 for some basic supplies: ammo for my M-16, a Colt .45 and ammo for it, and a carton of hand grenades. I met MacIntyre and we headed back to S-1 for more personnel matters. While there, we heard that the other spike team had declared a Prairie Fire Emergency, code for having made enemy contact and that the team needed to be extracted from the target as soon as possible. FOB 1 jumped to life as the Kingbees revved up for action. UH-1 gunships from the HML 367 squadron joined them; these Marine aviators were known by their unique radio call sign of "Scarface." A few hours later, word circulated through camp that the team in trouble had been successfully extracted from Laos without casualties or loss of aircraft. While the aircraft were returning to Phu Bai, the camp erupted with a few rounds of gunfire and a flurry of activity from the indigenous barracks where personnel from the Hatchet Force lived. There had been a card game and the loser had returned and thrown a hand grenade into the room, killing a few people and wounding several more. Since the indigenous troops were heavily armed, the compound had more than a hundred men of different ethnic groups ready for a firefight…right there! The mix of hate, blood and weapons created a tense atmosphere as the SF medics rushed to the team room to save whomever they could. After several volatile minutes, the SF troops and their veteran indigenous leaders brought calm back to the camp. We were shocked by the sudden brutality among the local troops, but kept our best poker faces in place. As the dust cleared, MacIntyre and I headed to the club to write letters home to our parents and girlfriends. We had our first permanent address in Vietnam after being in-country nearly a month.

By nightfall, all attention was on ST Idaho. Spider and several other spike team members were very concerned because there had been no commo from the team. Covey hadn't been able to raise anyone all day. Spider explained that a Green Beret, usually an experienced C&C member who ran missions into Laos, North Vietnam or Cambodia, could be a Covey rider, whose job it was to talk to the men on the ground and to assist the Air Force pilot in any manner possible. Covey and his SF Covey rider flew an extra mission that night, but to no avail. The airborne command aircraft that flew over Southeast Asia 24 hours a day were unable to raise ST Idaho during the night, either.

By early morning, the mood in camp was grave. Spider said ST Oregon had been selected to run a Bright Light mission into the Whiskey Five target to investigate what had happened to ST Idaho. Mike Tucker and George Sternberg were the veteran recon members of ST Oregon. Tucker was a no-nonsense One-Zero who had many missions under his belt. Sternberg had run several missions from FOB 3 at Khe Sanh during the highly publicized siege of the Marine base in early 1968. Together on ST Oregon, both men respected each other's prowess in the field so much that they rotated One-Zero duty with strong results. They were among the first to photograph NVA bulldozers cutting swaths through the triple canopy jungle to expand the Ho Chi Minh Trail Complex. They photographed NVA tanks, including one shot where the NVA star was visible, prior to the NVA hitting and overrunning the Lang Vei A Camp west of Khe Sanh. They had captured an NVA POW and were flying back to FOB 1 in a Kingbee when one of the team members discovered that the POW was a woman. Sternberg and the team member holding the POW were so startled that they loosened their grip momentarily. The woman bolted from the H-34 and jumped to her death.

Former Idaho team member and medic Stephen Perry was added to their team. Tucker opted to take one Vietnamese team member

George "The Troll" Sternberg, of ST Oregon at the firing range in Phu Bai a short while before ST Oregon ran the Bright Light Mission in May 1968. ST Oregon's mission was to locate, and if possible, bring back any members of ST Idaho. The enemy's response was instant and violent wounding every member on the team, including one S. Vietnamese team member who was KIA (Killed In Action). Sternberg had one of his jungle boots shredded by grenade shrapnel. (Photo courtesy of Ron Zaiss)

from ST Idaho, Ha, on the mission. Ha was highly respected by the veteran SF men. He was fearless in the field, but more important, he could provide insight into ST Idaho tactics. S-3 forced Tucker and Sternberg to accept a Vietnamese lieutenant on the team as part of the joint-training program where Vietnamese officers were sent to C&C to learn about special operations, a decision which didn't sit well with either of them.

Spider explained that a Bright Light team went in armed to the teeth, carrying only weapons, ammunition, hand grenades, bandages and maybe one canteen of water. No food. Bright Lights were the most dangerous of all missions, designed to go in after downed pilots, lost or injured SF team members or to bring back the bodies of SF troops or fliers killed in action. On most Bright Lights, there were plenty of NVA waiting. Tucker and Sternberg rounded out their Bright Light team with the best indigenous team members from ST Oregon. Spider was designated to fly in the "chase" Kingbee, which was a chopper that had a medic or extra SF personnel on board. If the lead Kingbee went down, the chase ship was designated to rescue them.

As the Kingbees lifted off from FOB 1 with ST Oregon, there was only one unspoken thought between MacIntyre and me: if ST Idaho vanished in Laos, what would happen to ST Oregon? Regardless of the odds, Tucker, Sternberg and Perry knew and respected Glen Lane and they would not rest until they found ST Idaho or at least attempted to find out what had happened to the team.

After the long flight across South Vietnam, the Kingbees inserted ST Oregon on the same LZ where ST Idaho had been inserted, a small hill near a bomb crater. From the LZ, ST Oregon's point man found Idaho's trail through grass only a foot or two tall. The trail led down the hill. Within minutes, team members heard NVA in several locations hitting sticks together in an effort to force the team to move in a certain direction. At first, Sternberg hoped the NVA were beating the sticks in an effort to get Oregon and Idaho to move in a certain direction. They followed ST Idaho's tracks indirectly through the grass and down the hill. Ha, Sternberg and Tucker knew that Lane

ST Oregon One-Zero Mike Tucker on the Phu Bai range with his team. (Photo courtesy of Ron Zaiss)

often planted little anti-personnel mines called "toe poppers" to hurt NVA trackers and to give his team warning of enemy activity on their trail. Because the vegetation was thin, the team increased the distance between team members. Tucker soon saw an NVA flag on a post in the ground. Sternberg observed a large road at the bottom of the hill and an empty guard booth. Perry saw the guard booth and realized this was a road heavily traveled by NVA and Pathet Lao troops. Across the road, Tucker saw more than a dozen armed NVA soldiers heading toward them, but unaware of ST Oregon's exact location. Team members heard several trucks in the distance moving in their direction. Tucker wasted no time. He ordered the team back to the bomb crater while signaling Sternberg to radio Covey to report the enemy activity and the need for TAC Air ASAP. Tucker wanted to keep the high ground advantage as long as possible. There was no question about it; the NVA knew another spike team was in the area and it was only a matter of minutes before Oregon would be fighting for its life.

Sternberg pulled out his URC-10 emergency radio and immediately made contact with air assets in the area. As ST Oregon moved into the bomb crater, several NVA soldiers opened fire on the team. Sternberg felt like he was in the middle of an old TV western, as the NVA rounds kicked up the dirt around him. The NVA fusillade increased in ferocity and the entire team suddenly realized that among the weapons being fired at them were Colt CAR-15s, weapons only carried by C&C spike teams. The NVA soldiers were now close enough to throw hand grenades into the large bomb crater. The team was spread around the lip of the crater, fending off attacks. Suddenly three or four NVA soldiers ran down the incline straight toward ST Oregon, firing on full automatic. Sternberg thought several of the NVA were high on some sort of drug because even after he shot one of them twice, the momentum of the soldier's body continued to carry him toward the team before collapsing. Another NVA charged toward Sternberg, carrying grenades. As the enemy soldier started to throw a grenade the Ohio native opened fire with his CAR-15. The rounds slammed into the NVA soldier's body, tearing out huge

USMC UH-1E pilot George Miller receiving his captain bars during a promotion ceremony in a secure area. During 1968, Miller flew many missions with HML-367 (Scarface) including the May 1968 Bright Light mission by ST Oregon searching for ST Idaho when it disappeared. Among the many SOG missions that Miller flew were several sorties on Oct. 5 in support of ST Alabama. Miller also had the distinction of being one of the few American airmen to see a uniformed Russian in the DMZ during late 1968. Miller was awarded the Distinguished Flying Cross stemming from a SOG mission where his UH-1E was heavily damaged by enemy gunfire while supporting an FOB 1 recon team. HML-367 (Scarface) is based at Camp Pendleton today where it continues to engage America's enemies in Iraq and Afghanistan.

chunks of flesh and shredding his uniform. But somehow the enemy soldier continued his forward movement. More important, he threw the grenade. It was an American M-26 frag.

Sternberg grabbed the grenade and threw it toward several charging NVA. Several more Chicom (Chinese Communist) grenades were hurled into the crater, but most of them failed to detonate. The ones that did explode caused minimal damage to team members. Meanwhile, Sternberg directed several air strikes by Air Force F-4 Phantom jets between the bomb crater and the road. Then the single prop A-1E Skyraider strafed above the crater where more NVA soldiers were firing down on ST Oregon. The Skyraider's first gun runs were so close, Sternberg could count the rivets in the warplane. When the Skyraider's wingman followed with a second gun run, Tucker and Sternberg watched in awe as the 20mm cannons instantly shredded the wood line and all the NVA in it. The gun runs left Sternberg covered with dirt, wood chips and leaves. He handed his sawed-off M-79 grenade launcher to one of his Chinese Nung team members, nicknamed "Monkey." The Nung fired his M-79 into the air, using the 40mm high explosive rounds as small mortar fire, while using Sternberg's M-79 to fire directly into charging NVA soldiers.

Another NVA charged the bomb crater and threw an M-26 hand grenade toward the team. To Steve Perry's horror, he saw the M-26 sail into the bomb crater and land a short distance from his feet. The SF medic was applying a bandage to one of ST Oregon's Nungs who had been shot in the calf by an AK-47 round. As he moved to protect the Nung, the M-26 exploded, killing the young Vietnamese lieutenant who was on the other side of the bomb crater. It blew the jungle boots off Steve Perry and peppered him and several team members with hot shrapnel. Sternberg got hit in the leg, hip, elbow and head. Shrapnel shredded one of his jungle boots. The power of the M-26 explosion left Perry with no feeling from the shoulders down. He feared the shrapnel had caused a spinal column injury. Through the din, Tucker quickly inspected Perry's back for wounds or bleeding and found none. The impact of the explosion had temporarily stunned Perry. Still, he was amazed to be alive.

By now, several team members were wounded from hand grenade shrapnel or AK-47 gunfire. The fact that the shrapnel was from U.S. grenades led to the general assumption that the NVA had killed ST Idaho. Tucker directed a few more close air strikes. Sternberg's URC-10 emergency radio stopped working. He stuffed the dead battery in his chest pocket and slammed a new one into the radio. Then the NVA lobbed mortar rounds toward the bomb crater. Sternberg was pissed because he knew he couldn't catch a mortar shell and throw it back. Shortly, the NVA mortarmen began to bracket the bomb crater with incoming rounds. As the mortar rounds marched toward the crater, Tucker directed Scarface to execute strafing runs. Right behind the gunships, the first Kingbee landed to pick up the most seriously wounded members of ST Oregon. Sternberg, Perry, Ha and the most seriously wounded Nung boarded the first Kingbee, which quickly lifted off from the LZ. The second Kingbee landed to pick up the remainder of the battered team.

As the remainder of ST Oregon boarded the second Kingbee, Sternberg's chopper circled the LZ to observe when the second aircraft cleared the LZ. The first Kingbee circled close enough that Sternberg and other team members fired their CAR-15s and M-79s down at the NVA. An enemy bullet ripped through the Kingbee's thin metal wall, lifted Sternberg from the window and drove him across the floor of the H-34. The impact of the AK-47 bullet broke two of his ribs and slammed him into the wall at the front of the passenger's compartment. Sternberg sat on the floor amid the hydraulic fluids that were leaking from the Kingbee. He was too stunned to move as several more enemy rounds ripped through the chopper. Ordinarily, as the commo man on the ST, Sternberg would have radioed Covey on the PRC-25 or used the URC-10 frequency to give a team okay upon extraction from the target. Tucker, in the second H-34, assumed Sternberg was his usual efficient self; however, Sternberg was staring at the life-saving URC-10 battery he pulled from his chest pocket.

Because no one had radioed Covey to indicate the team was

clear from the target, Spider directed the chase ship to land on the LZ to insure that all of ST Oregon was extracted successfully. It was also a last act of desperation. He had hoped against all odds to see Lane, Robert Duval Owen or one of the Vietnamese team members of ST Idaho. He saw no one. Spider jumped aboard the H-34 as a mortar round exploded in the bomb crater and dozens of weapons fired upon the Kingbee. After the chopper lifted off, Covey directed more air strikes into the target area.

Of the three Americans on that Bright Light, Perry was the most seriously injured. Of the Vietnamese, Ha had 94 shrapnel wounds in his body. The rest of the team had varying degrees of shrapnel wounds. Tucker, Perry and Sternberg were flown to Da Nang for preliminary emergency medical treatment before they were flown to Japan and Hawaii.

Back at Phu Bai, there was a collective sigh of relief that ST Oregon had survived the short-lived, but ferocious Bright Light mission. The loss of ST Idaho, however, hung over the camp like an invisible fog. Spider was the first person I spoke to after that Bright Light. He went straight to the bar, unable to believe that ST Idaho had vanished. The complete lack of clues added to the mystery. Were they killed? Were they wounded, captured and now prisoners of the NVA? MacIntyre voiced everyone's next thought. Before he'd be captured by the NVA, he said, he'd kill himself with a round from his CAR-15 or pretend to be dead and blow up as many NVA as possible with one final hand grenade. There was no doubt in my mind; I'd never be taken alive. From that day forward, I always carried an M-26 frag grenade on the upper hook of my web gear. It was the last one I'd use.

While MacIntyre and I wallowed deeper into the morose topic of suicide, Sincere came in and asked Spider to go outside for a moment. Against the day's backdrop, MacIntyre was nervously rejoicing in the fact that he was assigned to a spike team, rather than getting stuck in the commo shack. When we had landed at FOB 1 a few days earlier, the S1 staff sergeant told us that there were about 30 spike teams in camp. Those teams were either operational, training to become operational, shut down for illness, or in the case of ST Alabama, completely rebuilding because the NVA had killed almost everyone on the team. The math was disturbing; 30 had shrunk to 28. With all of the Americans on ST Oregon en route to stateside hospitals, the number shrank by one again. Within three days, two of the most veteran spike teams at FOB 1 had been knocked out of action by the NVA.

"Welcome to C&C," MacIntyre muttered.

We had heard about ST Asp from FOB 4 vanishing in Laos, presumed KIA on 28 March 1968, but there were others: Sergeant First Class Robert L. Taylor, killed 4 April; ST Bear from FOB 3, KIA, Laos; Major George Quamo, U 17 crash, died 14 April; FOB 5 based spike team members Sergeant First Class Leroy N. Wright and Staff Sergeant Lloyd F. Mousseau, KIA, Fishhook area of Cambodia, 2 May; FOB 2 based Lieutenant Joseph C. Shreve, KIA, Hatchet Force operation, 1 May; FOB 1 based ST Alabama team members Specialist Fifth Class Kenneth M. Cryan and Private First Class Paul Chester King, KIA A Shau target, 4 May; FOB 1 Hatchet Force Sergeant First Class Ronald J. Miller, KIA, 12 May; and FOB 1 based Master Sergeant Robert D. Plato and Sergeant First Class John Hartley Robertson, KIA, Kingbee helicopter crash, Laos, 20 May. Additionally, five SF troops were killed at FOB 3 from mortar and artillery shrapnel between 15 and 21 April 1968: Specialist Fifth Class Charles M. Corry, Specialist Fifth Class Daniel F. Sandoval, Sergeant Dennis Thorpe, Sergeant First Class Stefan Mazak and Specialist Fifth Class Samuel R. Hughes. MacIntyre and I didn't personally know any of the KIAs, but the sheer number in that short period of time was sobering. Most of them were veteran Special Forces soldiers. Being as green as we were made us all the more nervous, but not scared enough to quit C&C. As we sat at a table in the Green Beret Lounge, someone at the bar told a really bad joke and was roundly chastised for the poor attempt at humor.

"Sometimes you have to laugh to keep from crying," was the response. MacIntyre excused himself to meet with the team to plan the next day's training, which would include an early morning physical training session, and a run outside FOB 1. He said he liked the "little people," a term of affection among SF personnel for the indigenous troops, on his spike team. Most of the Americans towered above their Southeast Asian counterparts. I was going to tag along, but the comfort of the air-conditioned club was far more preferable to the oppressive heat outside. I pulled out some stationery to write another note home. No way could I mention any of the KIAs or where they died. Even though I had been in-country nearly a month, not one piece of mail from home had arrived, not even from Grandmom Stryker, who always faithfully wrote to me whether I was away at summer camp or basic training or jump school. The lack of mail made me wonder if the C&C censors had found something in one of the letters that had put a hold on the rest.

In a little while, Spider returned to the club. With a drink in his hand, he moved over to my table and broke out the large leather cup used to play liars' dice. He shook the five dice in the cup and slammed it down on the table. After peeking under the cup, he told me what he had. It could be two pairs, three of a kind, four of a kind, or on very rare instances, five of a kind. If I believed him, I had to roll the dice and exceed the combo he had called. If I called his bluff, and he actually had the hand he called, or a hand greater than he had called, I lost and I bought the next round of drinks. After a few rounds of liars' dice, Spider asked me if I'd rather go to the commo shack after learning about the C&C carnage of the last two months, or join ST Idaho as a radio operator.

The gauntlet had been dropped.

Chapter Three

THE LITTLE THINGS

A few days before, the decision would have been easy. Now, however, the thought of sitting in a commo shack after going through 17 months of training to join a secret operation seemed anticlimactic. Spider was the new One-Zero of ST Idaho and Don Wolken, of Kansas City, Missouri, would be the team's new One-One. Spider asked me if I had ever directed TAC Air in close air support strikes or worked with a Forward Air Controller (FAC) using helicopter gunships. I nodded my head yes. I hesitated to tell him that I had only called in air strikes far away from my position during training in Nha Trang.

Spider, sensing my hesitation, explained that there were three golden rules to directing close air support from TAC Air assets while on the ground. First, make absolutely sure the Covey knows exactly where the spike team is. Second, never, ever, call in an air strike that goes across the team. Never! Third, always work the assets around the team's perimeter, as though it were a large box. If I wanted to direct an air strike to the north of the team, I'd request the air strike to be delivered with the aircraft flying from east to west, or vice versa, depending on terrain, weather and enemy weapons. Exactly how close to the perimeter was determined by a combination of ordnance the aircraft was carrying, vegetation, wind and how close the enemy forces were to the team. Then he told me not to talk to Covey the way I talked when I played centerfield, as I tended to chatter a lot while playing defense. The more activity that was going on while the team was engaging the enemy, the more slowly and calmly I had to speak into the radio. If the Covey rider couldn't understand me, I was not only wasting his time and mine, but I was putting the team at risk.

As I mulled that thought over, he asked me if I wanted to meet the Vietnamese members of the latest rendition of ST Idaho. Without waiting for an answer, Spider was up and heading toward the clubhouse door. We walked west, past the S-4 building on the south side, past the S-1, and past the CO's office to a row of rooms occupied by the indigenous team members of spike teams in FOB 1. The first Vietnamese team member he introduced me to was Nguyen Cong Hiep, the team's veteran interpreter, who spoke three languages and understood the North Vietnamese dialect. Hiep was wearing sunglasses, even though we were inside the team room. He had been in special operations for more than two years. Next was a Vietnamese airborne noncommissioned officer (NCO) recently assigned to the team. He was the only Vietnamese on the team with a uniform and rank displayed on the uniform. Then he introduced me to Nguyen Van Sau, the Vietnamese team leader of ST Idaho. Sau had been working in special operations for more than three years. A farmer prior to joining C&C, Spider told me Sau could smell the enemy before any shots were fired. He appeared to weigh no more than 100 pounds soaking wet. Before I could shake his hand, he rattled off a few quick comments to Hiep while turning slightly sideways. I asked Hiep what he said. Hiep was reluctant to interpret. Spider urged Hiep to interpret Sau's remarks, as Sau politely, but reluctantly, shook my hand while shaking his head back and forth.

I was trying to be cool and not appear as green as I was. This was a big moment. How I got along with the indig, or little people, could make or break my SF career. After further urging, Hiep told me that Sau had said I appeared to be a young soldier, similar to some of the young 15-year-old Vietnamese men he had hired for the team in recent days. Additionally, my feet were too big and I was too tall. He said I would make too much noise in the jungle. I tried my best to hide the sting Sau's candor had on my pride, however, I had to acknowledge that he had survived more than three years of combat in C&C operations and I was the rookie. I bit my tongue. Next, Hiep introduced me to Phuoc. Sau was training Phuoc to be the next point man on ST Idaho. Tuan was the team's M-79 man. Hiep said Tuan could hit a fly with a high-explosive round from 500 meters. They were the veterans of ST Idaho. The new hires were Son, 16, Chau and Cau, both 15. Last was Minh, a quiet man who reminded me of a Vietnamese version of "Bashful" from Disney's Snow White and the Seven Dwarfs.

As dinnertime was near, Spider and I left the team room and headed to the U.S. mess hall while the Vietnamese walked east to the indigenous mess. Both were under the same roof, but were separate entities, with separate menus. We found Wolken, joined him for dinner and marveled at the chow, noting that this was by far the best food any of us had eaten during our time in the armed services. After dinner, Spider took Wolken and me over to S-4 to get our weapons and gear up to speed. Spider introduced me to the slovenly-looking S-4 staff sergeant, who promptly announced that he had no more CAR-15s because so many spike team members had lost them in the field. Spider politely reminded him that when a spike team is wiped out, the last thing on the Americans' minds is getting their CAR-15s back to S-4 to help the supply sergeant balance his weapons inventory. Spider asked him if he had any BAR (Browning Automatic Rifle) web gear. He told me the 20-round 5.56mm magazines fit snugly into the old pouches on the World War II-era web gear and the harness was comfortable, as compared to the regular Army issue web gear. Spider also made sure that Wolken and I had signed out two Colt .45 semi-automatic pistols with the warning that we should never go anywhere in Vietnam without some sort of weapon on our person.

After Wolken and I returned to our room with all of our new

supplies, weapons, rounds and weapon-cleaning equipment, MacIntyre stopped by our room and noted that he already had a CAR-15, which was lighter, shorter and generally viewed as more reliable in the field than the old M-16 I was toting around. He asked me if I had received a Browning Hi Power 9mm pistol. I said no. He had one and wanted to show it to me. I went with MacIntyre to his room, which was a few doors away from the CO's office. We had only been in there a few minutes when automatic weapons fire erupted at the western end of the compound. MacIntyre and I cautiously stepped outside of his room and onto the sandy road. Several of the indigenous troops came running around the corner, all heavily armed, carrying CAR-15s, M-16s or M-79s. MacIntyre looked at me. I shrugged my shoulders as Spider's words echoed in my mind. Never go anywhere in Vietnam, even in the compound, without a weapon. I was weaponless. And suddenly, I was real nervous.

Several more indigenous troops and senior Green Berets came running around the corner, heading toward the western end of camp where the shots had been fired a few seconds earlier. I suddenly found a young Vietnamese running toward me with his M-16 pointed at my face! In a matter of seconds the young 15-year-old was right in front of me, speaking in agitated Vietnamese with his M-16 still pointed at my face. I couldn't tell what the heck he was saying, but I recognized him as Cau, one of the new hires on ST Idaho. His M-16 had a magazine in it. His finger was on the trigger. I told him I was on Spike Team Idaho with him and I moved the barrel away from my face as images of coconuts exploding during M-16 weapons training roared through my head. And then he was gone, running around the corner to the main road. MacIntyre and I just stood there dumbfounded, before retreating to his room and grabbing whatever weapons were lying on his bed.

"Jesus, Tilt! He could have killed you, just like that! And he's on your team?" I didn't say a word. Never had an M-16 barrel looked so large.

Another indigenous poker game had gotten out of control and one unhappy player took out his frustration with a M-16, which created more work for the talented SF medics we had at FOB 1. Within a matter of minutes, the senior SF personnel and key indig personnel calmed the camp down. MacIntyre and I found Spider, explained what happened, and asked if this camp violence was a regular occurrence in FOB 1. He said that there were several separate and distinct ethnic groups in FOB 1, all of which had one thing in common: they hated each other. The Cambodes hated the Vietnamese, who hated the Montagnard tribesmen, all of whom hated the Chinese Nungs. Spider jokingly said that most of the members of the different ethnic groups would just as soon kill members of the other groups as kill the Viet Cong or North Vietnamese Army troops. The inbred hatred stemmed from hundreds of years of history in Southeast Asia, none of which we had time to study. The best rule of thumb for the SF personnel was to make sure that the groups didn't mix in camp and to encourage them to save their killing urge for the enemy. Spider assured me that he and Sau would have a chat with Cau and me in the morning.

The next day started with the 0700 formation in the dirt road between the enlisted barracks and the S-4 building. As we stood in formation, I could hear the now familiar roar of the Kingbees heading toward FOB 1. Within seconds, the sortie of Kingbees roared up Highway 1, pulled the hard banking right turn toward the east, and swooped down upon the formation. Buzz, buzz, buzz, the old Sikorsky H-34s flew low to the ground. The lead chopper's front wheels almost touched the trees standing next to the enlisted personnel barracks. We enjoyed watching the Kingbee pilots disrupt morning formation. Formations were dreadful affairs. The person giving the morning briefing usually cursed the interruption, which won an extra note of appreciation from those of us standing there.

Formations were the bureaucratic side of military life that most of us hated. It was at formation that it would be announced that the entire company area needed to be policed—cleaned of any trash, shell casings or beer and soda cans. It was there that it was announced which spike team was responsible for making the morning and afternoon water runs, for making the trash runs, for

From left, squatting, Lynne M. Black Jr., holding his CAR-15, with an XM-148, grenade launcher attached to it. The XM-148 fired the same 40 mm round that the M-79 grenade launcher fired. John S. Meyer holds a sawed-off M-79. The M-79 stock was trimmed and the barrel was cut back severely to make it lighter and less cumbersome in the field. (John S. Meyer photo)

making supply runs to FOB 3 at Khe Sanh, for filling sandbags, and it was at formation where it was announced when memorial services would be held for the SF troops killed in action or listed as missing in action. During the first few weeks in FOB 1, I attended at least three memorial services for fallen SF comrades. Services were held in the mess hall. The last one I attended was for Lane and Owens. During the service, the chaplain hesitated on Lane's name. This was the last official function honoring Spike Team Idaho members, and the chaplain couldn't remember Lane's name. I didn't care if he had attended a dozen memorial services for other branches of the military at Phu Bai that day. I was so angry I never attended another memorial service at FOB 1. The services soon stopped anyway, because there were so many casualties. No official announcement. They just stopped.

It was bad enough that ST Idaho was officially listed as MIA, but it was worse that we couldn't tell their families the truth. This was the price an individual paid for participating in a secret war. If I died, no one would tell my mother the truth, either.

Agonizing over such issues ended as Spider packed up ST Idaho for a trip to the range for weapons familiarization. We fired, stripped and cleaned every weapon in the S-4 arsenal, from the .50 caliber machine gun to a wide variety of submachine guns. Spider told us that our primary weapon of choice, the CAR-15, was the most important object to any spike team member. Go nowhere without it. Although I was still carrying the old M-16, it became inseparable from me, except when I went to the mess hall and to the club. Once on the range, we set up small targets with scraps of wood and metal left from other military groups. Spider made sure that Wolken and I, and any new members on the team, fired thousands of rounds from the hip, and the hip only. In a firefight you wouldn't have time to lift your weapon to your shoulder. The old M-16 felt awkward, but it never misfired. And after a while, firing from the hip became more comfortable. As the day wore on, we brought out the M-79 rounds. Over and over we fired at set targets. The three Americans also carried the sawed-off M-79s. The stock was cut off, leaving enough wood to firmly grip the weapon. The barrels were chopped back several inches, removing the flip-up range sight near the end of the grenade launcher.

At first, the training was slow. Day after day, Spider drilled us relentlessly. In the morning, after formation and cleanup details, the entire team suited up and marched out of camp to practice immediate action drills, how to react to ambushes from the front, from the rear and from the flanks. Spider took us through basic patrol tactics and techniques, drilling into us lessons he had learned from Lane. Occasionally, we set up night ambushes outside FOB 1, as intelligence reports said there was still NVA and Viet Cong movement outside the village of Phu Luong. The nights we ran our ambushes were without incident. Apparently, the local folks and the Viet Cong listened to our psy-ops propaganda and stayed off area trails at night. During those night ambushes, Spider used some of the first night-vision equipment. It was heavy and primitive, but it was the first night-vision equipment that didn't use infrared. The Starlight scope dramatically amplified any light in the area, enhancing our ability to see into the night. But it gave off a greenish light from the rear lens, thus anyone using it had to be careful not to let the light endanger team security.

It was during one of our night ambushes that we heard something odd on the radio. ST Idaho and another spike team set up ambushes in different sectors outside FOB 1. Sometime after midnight, we could hear the sound of mortars firing from FOB 1 into the grid where the other team was set up. As ST Idaho hunkered down, I switched the PRC-25 dial to main operational frequency and to the base camp alternative frequency in an effort to see what was generating the mortar support. At one point, I heard an American shouting, "We're being overrun! They're coming through the lines…give me more fire!" From our position, however, we could hear the rounds exploding and some CAR-15 gunfire, but no AK-47 gunfire from enemy troops. Then, just as suddenly as the mortar fire had started, it stopped. I radioed a friend at the Comm Center and he told me not to worry, there was no enemy activity. When we returned to base in the morning, no one was talking about the mortar fire. Finally, Spider told me that the radio transmission I heard was from a radio operator who had taken too many "green bombers," or "uppers," to stay awake. What I hadn't heard on the radio was his report that the team was being overrun by pink elephants—strictly a feat of his imagination. Welcome to the world of drugs in combat. During training, I had heard stories of Filipino rebels getting drugged up and charging into U.S. lines. The Colt .45 was developed solely for the purpose of stopping those warriors. Some suggested that Hitler's storm troopers used variants of methamphetamine to keep an aggressive edge in combat. No one, however, had warned us of the side effects of the green bombers. The pink elephant story stuck with me a long time. I never carried uppers, fearing their impact on me physically. Hell, I scared myself without being under the influence of drugs.

By the end of June, our team was becoming a cohesive unit. It was clear that Spider had the utmost respect for Sau, the senior, most experienced recon man on our team. He was quiet. He had deep-set eyes that could become very intense. During rappelling training, both from the tower in FOB 1 and from Kingbees, Sau assisted Spider in putting the team through training. When the Vietnamese members of the team erred, Sau dealt with them. Sometimes his message was nothing more than a harsh, burning glare. Sau was Spider's counterpart on the team, the Vietnamese team leader, or Zero-One. Hiep was number two, or Zero-Two, again because of experience. Phuoc had emerged as a strong point man for the team with Sau working closely with him, spending hours talking about everything from the obvious to the subtle nuances of remaining alive in the jungle in Laos, Cambodia or North Vietnam.

Spider worked with Wolken and me. Wolken was a career Army man who seemed to enjoy SF and being on ST Idaho. He spoke softly and emitted a quiet, deadly seriousness. I felt good being the radio operator on the team. I knew that if the shit hit the fan, I'd be on the radio, working the close air support. By the end of June, ST

MACV-SOG men pioneered extracting Special Forces soldiers from the jungle via ropes attached to helicopters. At the end of the rope, in the early configurations of that extraction method, was a McGuire Rig. Such an extraction was dangerous, even when simply practicing due to many factors, such as wind and spinning. During extractions from targets, the teams were always under heavy enemy fire, which increased the dangers and the odds of getting out of a target alive. On occasion, the NVA would wait until the men started to lift off from the LZ before they would open fire on them. (Photo courtesy of Stephen Bayliss)

Idaho was ready for practice missions.

Meanwhile, my best friend MacIntyre told me that his team was ready to pull a mission into an Alpha target. The Alpha targets were located near the A Shau Valley and were considered to be just as deadly for spike teams as the valley itself. MacIntyre was excited and scared. He swung wildly between the two emotions. On one hand, he had a chance to prove to his father that he had the right stuff, that he could serve his country with pride. On the other hand, after watching all of the casualties of war, the anguish of participating in a secret war was especially painful. Several times he asked the obvious question: What happens if I buy the farm out there? We vowed that if either of us "met our maker" across the fence, the survivor would make sure the other's parents knew the truth. Six months earlier, we used to joke about our parents, what a pain in the ass they were. His mother thought I was a bad influence on him and my mother seemed to hold MacIntyre in low esteem for the same reason—a familial juxtaposition that he and I laughed about often. Now, however, as MacIntyre stood on the threshold of being the first member of our group to enter the Prairie Fire Area of Operation, we suddenly cared about what our parents and friends thought about us, especially if we were killed in action.

As MacIntyre's team geared up for the Alpha target, there was only one thing that bothered him: the One-Zero was a lieutenant with no experience on the ground, no combat experience and little time on his spike team. Yet because he was an officer, he was the One-Zero. That really irked MacIntyre. Not that John MacIntyre wanted to be the One-Zero; we simply hated most young lieutenants. Earlier in the year while going through the radio teletype training at Ft. Gordon, Georgia, MacIntyre and I had several run-ins with the young lieutenants running the company, which ended with both of us getting busted in rank and pay for insubordination. They had a total of eight Article 15s for me and nine Article 15s for MacIntyre, after we violated orders about being in the barracks by 2230. We often left base immediately after formation at 1700 and just ignored orders. We'd return to base around 2225, when the sergeant would

This is a close-up view of men lifting off from the FOB 1 launch pad, which was across Highway 1, from the compound. Such extractions were easier in practice because the helicopters and the men at the end of their ropes didn't have to contend with trees and jungle growth that exceeded 100 feet. (Photo courtesy of Stephen Bayliss)

inspect the barracks. Then, around midnight, we'd drive back to Augusta, Georgia. Needless to say, some of the utter hatred we had for those lieutenants spilled over onto MacIntyre's young One-Zero. Regardless, MacIntyre pushed on.

Finally, it was his team's turn to go across the fence. I drove the truck that took MacIntyre's team out to the helicopter pad. The mission was a simple area reconnaissance. They were ordered to get on the ground, stay in for at least five days, report any enemy activity and if the opportunity presented itself, capture an enemy POW. MacIntyre was scared. I told him that was a good thing and not to let the lieutenant do anything stupid. MacIntyre believed his lieutenant was a good man who would not do anything to hurt the team. A gifted football player who had turned down a scholarship to Notre Dame, he understood team play, both as an athlete and a Green Beret. MacIntyre said the insertion plan was simple: he would sit in the door while the young lieutenant squatted behind him. MacIntyre would be searching the LZ for enemy activity and the lieutenant would be scanning the tree line for bad guys. As the Sikorsky H 34s roared to life, I told MacIntyre to be careful with the elephant grass—thick-bladed grass that grew from a few feet to as high as 12 feet. Spider and Staff Sergeant Pat "Mandolin" Watkins had told us repeatedly, when landing on an LZ with elephant grass, don't jump out of the chopper until the H-34's wheel touches the ground or you can actually see terra firma. If you can't see the ground, don't jump. Completely disregard whatever the door gunner says because all the door gunner wants to do is get the hell out of there. He isn't jumping from the chopper into the Prairie Fire AO.

I told MacIntyre I'd buy him his first cold soda upon returning to FOB 1. As the Kingbees headed west toward Laos, I stood there, watching the choppers until they disappeared. When I went back to camp, Spider assured me that Watkins and the young lieutenant had picked a good LZ. It was covered with elephant grass, but it was flat. The plan called for the Kingbees to drop the team on the edge of the grass near the tree line. That way, once the team was on the ground, it could bolt for the jungle and move out posthaste, after giving a team okay to the Covey. Spider also told me that because the Alpha target was near the A Shau Valley, Watkins had plenty of air assets ready to respond to a Prairie Fire Emergency.

MacIntyre and I had become real close buddies during Training Group. He was a damned good softball player and always taunted Spider, Tony Herrell and me during the games between Company A and MacIntyre's Company B team. Now, after a year of camaraderie, he was going into the biggest contest of his life and I was standing on the helicopter pad. We had covered each other's flanks in bar fights, during football games with the legs (non-airborne troops) at Ft. Gordon, and in our dealings with those damned lieutenants. We had agreed that at some point, we had to get on a spike team together.

Knowing that the flight would take more than an hour before the team touched down on the LZ in Laos, I returned to my room for awhile, before heading to the Comm Center, after getting Spider's okay. One of our crew was monitoring the radios. He told me the Kingbees were over the LZ and spiraling in. In any mission, this was the hairiest part. Insertion. Going into "Indian country."

Something was wrong. The second Kingbee was called off from inserting the team. From our end, we could only hear the radio transmissions of Watkins, the Covey rider flying in the Cessna O-2. The lead Kingbee returned to the LZ to pick up the team. MacIntyre's team was receiving some fire from NVA troops. Then the radio grew eerily silent. I was standing on pins and needles, dying to know what happened. Was MacIntyre's team okay? Were there any casualties? It seemed as though an eternity passed before Watkins radioed that MacIntyre's team was extracted from the LZ under light to moderate enemy small arms fire. The team had one casualty; one American had a broken ankle.

An hour later, the Kingbees returned to the helicopter pad. Several in our group were waiting for MacIntyre, along with the SF medics who had their ambulance on site. Again, I was showered with the prop wash, but I had to see my pal. MacIntyre was dirty. He looked pissed and scared. As the medics handled the lieutenant, MacIntyre and I headed to the truck for the short ride back into camp.

"What happened? What was it like, Mac?"

After looking around to make sure nobody could hear him, MacIntyre said, "The poor son of a bitch jumped out of the helicopter too soon." He explained that the Kingbee had settled into the middle of the LZ, in high elephant grass. "The damned door gunner tried to get me to jump out before I could see the ground." He was tempted to jump early, he said, but waited until the right wheel touched the ground before exiting the helicopter. The H-34 rose a few feet off of the ground. MacIntyre said the elephant grass was so tall that it completely covered him when the prop wash hit it. He saw the lieutenant jump from the chopper when it was still several feet off the ground, instead of waiting a few more seconds. The Vietnamese team member exited without a problem. MacIntyre couldn't see the lieutenant, but he could hear him cursing in pain and he radioed Covey to hold the second Kingbee.

As MacIntyre and the Vietnamese team member moved toward the hurt lieutenant, enemy forces fired several rounds into the air. "Jesus H. Christ! It was scary as hell out there and we only had light contact," MacIntyre said. The three of them were on the ground and the NVA opened fire, although from a distance. MacIntyre threw an M-26 frag in the direction of the enemy's gunfire. The Vietnamese team member fired sporadic rounds toward the AK-47s. When the Kingbee returned to pick up the three spike team members, the NVA gunfire increased, but it didn't generate enough firepower to deter the H-34 from landing in the elephant grass. When the Kingbee lifted off from the LZ, every team member opened fire with his CAR-15 on full automatic.

Although MacIntyre had been on the ground for only a few, scary minutes, I could see the sweat stains on his jungle fatigues and headband. As we drove into FOB 1, MacIntyre turned to the Vietnamese team member who had been on the ground with him.

"You number fucking one!" he said, which was the supreme compliment; being "number ten" was the ultimate insult between recon men. The team member smiled and nodded his head, acknowledging the compliment. MacIntyre turned to me and

PFC John MacIntyre sits on a wall shortly before launching into his first mission with ST Louisiana in June 1968 at FOB 1 Phu Bai. (Photo courtesy of Rick Howard)

explained that the Vietnamese team member was cool on the ground. Real cool. The indigenous team member's demeanor on the ground had helped him keep his composure. MacIntyre drove the Vietnamese team member to the indigenous troop barracks and dropped him off, promising to return with cold drinks and chow for the entire team. He dropped me off at the club to get a case of soda, while he rustled up some sandwiches at the Mess Hall. After a quick visit with the lieutenant, MacIntyre reported to S-3, then to S-2 for a quick report on the short-lived mission. A few minutes later he walked into the club, his rucksack still on his back, his CAR-15 still in his hand. I pulled him aside and suggested that he shower, because he reeked from sweat. I told him I would have to make a water run so he'd have enough water for a shower.

At that time, we had to transport water to FOB 1 from a compound south of FOB 1, off of Highway 1. I drove the old truck down the highway with my trusty M-16 by my side, and a Colt .45 strapped to my hip to get a load of water. On the way back, a vehicle passed me and narrowly missed the front left bumper as he pulled sharply in front of me. I hit the brakes hard to avoid a collision. Some of the water in the tanker splashed forward, forcing open one of the two lids on the tank portion of the truck. Water cascaded through the holes in the old, torn canvas roof and onto the hood. Aside from being soaked, I returned to camp intact.

After our showers, MacIntyre and I returned to the club for sodas. Now MacIntyre was a little more confident. Although he had been on the ground for only a few minutes, MacIntyre found the experience both stimulating and terrifying. He said that when the Kingbee began to spiral downward toward the LZ, he was nervous, but ready. When the chopper went into a hover, he got pissed at the door gunner who tried to get him to exit the ship too soon. After reviewing every detail several times, MacIntyre told me that he and I had to get on a spike team together after we had crossed the fence a few times to get experience. Then we had an instant argument about who would be the One-Zero and who would be the One-One. MacIntyre's position was that because he was the first man on the ground, he would have the most missions and I would be his junior. I reminded him that during our football games at Ft. Gordon, I was the better quarterback and that he was a great receiver who usually followed my directions, emphasis on me telling him what to do. Our argument carried on into the night.

The Fourth of July arrived within a few days. At the morning formation, Sergeant Major Harris told us that all U.S. personnel would be on full alert and stand guard duty that night. He said that S-3 would have several spike teams leaving camp early to set up ambushes outside FOB 1 for additional security and early warning. ST Idaho and MacIntyre's team got stuck filling sandbags for several hours during the morning. By 0900, it was stifling. It was downright awful. Filling and stacking sand bags only compounded the misery.

After lunch, MacIntyre showered before going to his room to adjust his equipment. S-3 told him that a new One-Zero would be assigned to his team who was familiar with the indigenous troops. That meant the team would remain fully operational and it would pull a new mission within days. I went to my room to catch a few winks of sleep. Sergeant Major Harris's early morning warning made it sound like the Fourth of July was going to be a long night.

I had been asleep a short while when Hiep came running into the room to tell me that MacIntyre had cut himself while working on his web gear. He was worried because the cut appeared as though it had hit his right eye. We bolted toward MacIntyre's room. To my horror, two SF troops had him on a stretcher and were carrying him toward the dispensary. He had a large bandage over the right side of his face. MacIntyre was both angry and scared. I asked the medics how bad it was. They were unsure. MacIntyre assured me that he'd be back in the club after the medics patched up his upper right cheek. As we walked toward the dispensary, MacIntyre lifted the large bandage to reveal the cut. At first glance it didn't appear too serious to me. He explained that he was cutting a piece of web gear, when the blade cut through it easier than he had anticipated. The force of the blade struck the metal bedpost on his new bunk. The blade caromed off of the metal post and arched upwards toward his face, first cutting a perpendicular slice under his right eye—which was not too deep—and continued upward, slicing through the upper portion of his eyelid and through the eyebrow. The blade's upward arc made one additional shallow slice on his forehead.

What wasn't evident to us was that the knife had cut his eye. The incident had happened so quickly that the eyelid hadn't been able to close in time. SF Medic Doc Martin told us the bad news and ordered MacIntyre to the nearby Navy hospital for an eye specialist to inspect the cut cornea. As we lifted MacIntyre into the ambulance, he made a quip about returning in time for dinner and to watch the Fourth of July fireworks. Martin gave me a look that indicated MacIntyre wasn't returning to FOB 1 that night, or in the near future. I was crestfallen. When Martin returned to FOB 1, he wasn't optimistic. He said the Navy doctors would take care of him. The rest of us returned to getting ready for the night. After dinner, we all went to the club, as the regular base security kept an eye on the perimeter. Around 2100, the club was closed and we all went to the trenches because S-2 allegedly had an intelligence report that the bad guys were going to make a move on the Fourth of July. By midnight, the mortarmen in camp were completely bored and lit up the sky with a display of fireworks that were pretty good by combat standards. By 0100, many of us were joking back and forth at the accuracy of the latest "intel" report. A short while later most of the spike teams retired to their rooms for a quiet night's sleep.

At the morning formation, Martin had more bad news: a Marine captain had looked at MacIntyre's eye briefly, and told him that they would take care of it in the morning, as they had a Fourth of July celebration for the officers to attend. During the night, infection set in and MacIntyre was going to be shipped to Japan as soon as possible. We were in a rage. Had inter-service rivalry hurt MacIntyre? Martin opined that the cut may have been deep enough that no surgeon could save MacIntyre's eye. A short while later, we were told to begin packing all of MacIntyre's belongings for shipment back to the States. Packing my best friend's personal stuff was difficult. Twenty-four hours earlier we had been talking about running Prairie

Even though this photo is slightly out of focus, it reflects the varied uniforms for FOB 1 football games and the intensity of the games. From left, is Ron Zaiss looking at Ray Kahn, in fatigues and John S. Meyer defending against him. The football had some scars from one of the dogs in camp chewing on it.

Fire missions together. Now I didn't know when I would see him again. The good news was, although MacIntyre may have been hurt, he left the country alive. Personally, I wondered how MacIntyre would handle going home with a non-combat injury, because he had wanted to show his combat veteran father that he was a good soldier, too. I tried to get MacIntyre's CAR-15, but the "friendly" supply sergeant intervened before Spider could take direct action.

As if losing my best friend wasn't enough, a few days later, amoebic dysentery gripped my body. It started as diarrhea. Then vomiting. Then both at the same time, a life experience I had managed to avoid until that moment in South Vietnam. When the bug first hit me, I weighed more than 170 pounds. Before it ended, I had lost nearly 40 pounds. There was a morning when I made 26 trips to the latrine before 1200. I stopped counting after that. Each trip would involve bowel-twisting diarrhea and gut-wrenching vomiting. I was so sick that the smell of the latrines didn't offend my nose as much as usual. Normally, I tried to hold my breath for as long as possible while using it. The latrines were pieces of plywood with holes cut in them. The human waste landed in a crude metal drum beneath. The drums were pulled out from under the plywood daily and their effluent was burned in some sort of liquid combination of oil and kerosene. The stench from those dark fires was revolting.

All things considered, I was grateful that while having diarrhea, I could lean over and puke into the dirty hole to my right without making a mess on the floor or the plywood. The short walk between our room and the latrine became an ordeal in my weakened state. After each visit, I'd stumble back to my room where I'd collapse on the bed, if only until the next trip. If MacIntyre had been there, he would have told me how full of crap I was and then offered some sort of assistance. Instead, I could only wonder where my friend was—Japan or stateside? The medics keeping an eye on me told me that he was going to be shipped back to the states to an eye specialist, but that he'd never return to SF or any combat role in the Vietnam War. Spider checked on me often and after a few days, the churning slowed down. My body ached all over and I was so weak that I missed playing in the two-hand touch football games at Phu Bai.

Because Spider and I were on ST Idaho, I always played on his team. One of our favorite pass patterns was a deep route where I'd run west full speed, then cut hard left, right in front of the S-4 shop, hoping to peel off my defender on the building. On one pass pattern, I faked the S-4 route and continued straight ahead at full speed. My arms were extended to the max as Spider delivered the ball for a touchdown. Spider was a wizard with the pigskin. Of course, if he was unhappy with me, he'd throw the ball in such a fashion that when I caught it, my momentum would carry me into the S-4 building. Athletic footwear was a scarcity. Some men played barefooted. Some wore jungle boots. A lucky few had sneakers of some sort.

The games were played in front of the club and they were always intense. Several players were injured. One medic, John Walton, hurt his foot and was out of action for more than a week. Another troop had a broken finger. One evening after dinner, we had an older SF troop playing quarterback. By our standards, anyone over 30 was considered old and called "Pops" or "Gramps." He was moving the team east towards our goal line. His short passes were slowly gaining ground. We ran a hard blitz at him from our right. Our end had a clean shot at the older quarterback, who had his back to our rushing lineman. When the rushing end was a couple of feet away, the SF veteran's combat experience kicked in. Quicker than a cat, he turned toward the hard-charging lineman and grabbed him by the shirt. The quarterback spun the huge lineman and turned him upside down, driving his head into the ground with a blow that is designed to kill a man by breaking his neck. Fortunately, the sand and dirt of our football field was soft enough that it absorbed the killing blow. The lineman was hurt, but alive. The quarterback and the older lineman quit and never returned to the game. The image of the quarterback driving the big guy into the ground at a perfect, perpendicular angle was permanently etched in my mind.

One fact remained, regardless of what happened on the football field, or anywhere else in camp, the SOG missions continued. And while going across the fence might get you killed, it was the little things, the everyday things—the big feet, the green bombers, the sharp knives and the tiny amoeba—it was the little things that left their scars in the meantime.

For some reason Maj. Bill Shelton is all smiles as he walks west on the northern side of the football field. Behind him are three men standing in front of the Green Beret Lounge. The field wasn't too wide and sometimes S-4 personnel would leave their forklifts too close to it, adding another obstacle to the field. The building in the background is the U.S. Mess Hall that featured a chef who fled from a hotel in Hanoi in 1954 when the communists gained full control of North Vietnam.

CHAPTER FOUR

ONE DAY IN THE A SHAU VALLEY

Wilbur "Pete" Boggs had a problem: he was a man short and the S-3 brass had given him a target in the A Shau Valley designated A Shau 2. During the middle of July, Boggs, the One-Zero, had taken ST Louisiana on a practice mission to give the entire team a chance to prepare for going to the Prairie Fire Area of Operation (AO). Instead of the mission simply being a chance to practice contingency drills, live-fire weapons training and night security while in the field, the team made contact with some Viet Cong and North Vietnamese Army troops. The skirmish was quick and deadly, and for the One-Two it was unsettling. Near the end of July, one of the senior NCOs in the FOB 1 communications center asked the One-Two if he would be interested in transferring from the spike team to the commo shack. He accepted the offer.

The next day, 1 August, Boggs flew a VR (visual reconnaissance) over the target area and found a primary and alternate LZ. When he returned to camp, he was introduced to Tom Cunningham, his new One-Two.

Tom Cunningham was like every Special Forces soldier at FOB 1; he had volunteered to join Special Forces, volunteered to go to

From left, John S. Meyer and Tony Herrell, at Camp Eagle, the home of the 101st Airborne Division in Phu Bai. C&C had a launch site within the 101st compound and tents for waiting teams. Herrell was a member of ST Louisiana with John MacIntyre before Pete Boggs and John T. Walton joined the team. (Photo courtesy of John S. Meyer)

South Vietnam, and after arriving in Southeast Asia, volunteered for C&C. Cunningham's route to SF and SOG, however, was unique.

While attending Advanced Infantry Training at Ft. Ord, California, his orders to proceed to Officer Candidate School upon graduation changed. The Army told the OCS candidates that they had to re-qualify for OCS based on new criteria. To Cunningham, it appeared as though the Army had changed those rules in order to get more men to go to South Vietnam. When the rule changes were announced, Cunningham was among approximately 200 men who went to the SF recruiter, volunteering to join the Green Berets. He was one of seven men selected from that group.

After completing the first phase of training he went on to Phase II, as he was preparing to become a communications specialist. It was there Cunningham found that commo drove him nuts so he switched to demolitions.

During Phase II he met John Walton, an SF medic from Bentonville, Arkansas. Walton shipped out to Vietnam while Cunningham wrapped up his SF training in Phase III.

When he landed Cam Ranh Bay, Cunningham learned there were orders shipping him to a conventional Army unit. He wasn't impressed. The SF liaison told him the only other option open for SF troops at the time was C&C. Cunningham went through the MACV Recondo School at Nha Trang. The training was invaluable. It helped new arrivals adjust to being in-country and got them out into the bush. When the training cadre at Recondo School learned that Cunningham and a few other SF troops were heading to Phu Bai, they gave them extra instruction in immediate action drills and escape and evasion tactics. Cunningham flew to Da Nang, where he and his fellow new arrivals boarded an H-34 Sikorsky. The trip to Phu Bai was unforgettable. The pilots, knowing that Cunningham and his peers were new in-country, flew a few feet above the road, popping up over trucks, dikes and hills along the way to FOB 1. That got everybody's attention. But it wasn't over yet.

After flying past the Phu Bai Airport and the Second ARVN training compound, which were located to the east of Highway 1, the H-34 suddenly surged upwards and abruptly rolled to its right in a hard turn, which left the right door of the helicopter facing straight down toward the ground. Before the startled newbies could recover, the Kingbees swooped toward FOB 1, sometimes hitting trees in camp with the front struts of the piston-driven choppers. The Kingbees pulled one more hard right turn and flared dramatically onto the helicopter pad for FOB 1.

Boggs gave Cunningham a tour of the camp and introduced him to the team as the new radio operator. Cunningham talked to the interpreter and met the rest of the indigenous personnel. Phu Bai was everything he had imagined. Boggs took him to S-4 to get his weapon and equipment and announced that the team would be going on a mission soon—very soon. Cunningham was surprised. He hadn't had a lot of time, but then again, he figured that was the way things operated at FOB 1. That afternoon he was reunited with his friend John Walton, team medic and One-One for ST Louisiana. Boggs told them that he wanted to insert into the target that night at last light. Boggs said the target was a rough mission and he told them to load up on ammo and to carry extra hand grenades. For the next two days the last-light insertions were unsuccessful, due to the weather. On the morning of 3 August, there was a briefing at S-3 for an early morning insertion.

The briefing officer provided a lot of details and history of the target. Cunningham's impression was that previous missions hadn't been too successful. Boggs felt they'd be lucky if they got into the target, and if they did, he predicted they'd probably make contact not long after getting on the ground.

Because the mountains were so high and the morning air was clear and heating up, the Kingbee pilots said they would insert ST Louisiana with three helicopters, two men per Kingbee. As the third H-34 was spiraling down to the LZ, the door gunner told Walton that the first Sikorsky had taken some small arms fire. Walton wondered why they were going in if they had already been compromised. The question resurfaced a few seconds later when a few NVA opened fire on his chopper as it flared into the LZ. As far as Cunningham, in the second Kingbee, was concerned, the insert went fine. He assumed

Boggs kept the air resources on station a little longer than usual because it was an A Shau target.

The H-34s dropped ST Louisiana on a ridge with a wooded knoll on one end, an open area around it, and jungle on the other side. Boggs headed the team toward the wooded knoll. Walton was next to the tail gunner for the team while Cunningham was behind Boggs in the formation. Because Walton was still pretty green, having only two or three missions under his belt, he kept his questions to himself. But he did wonder why they went to the knoll instead of the jungle.

Shortly after the team reached the wooded knoll, Boggs told Cunningham to give a team okay, which released all of the air assets assigned to that target. At that point, they hadn't heard anything. When ST Louisiana moved farther up the knoll Cunningham was amazed at what he saw. There were numerous booby-traps and punji pits set up, he assumed, for spike teams. Fortunately, the traps were old and the team could see each and every one. The team continued to move for a few more minutes before settling into a thickly wooded area on the knoll. Cunningham had difficulty making radio contact with the Covey that was flying several miles away from the area of operation. He finally made contact with an aircraft that had the call sign "Alexander" just as an NVA unit moved past on a trail that cut through the middle of the wooded knoll.

"You're whispering. Why are you whispering?" Alexander asked.

While Cunningham whispered into his PRC-25, Walton checked out the wooded knoll. It was covered with dense jungle foliage. He observed the point man give a hand sign that there were NVA soldiers in the jungle at the opposite end of the short ridge near the team's LZ. Walton was sitting at the end of the formation in the thick jungle vegetation with the tail gunner; they both were surprised to hear numerous NVA soldiers moving along the trail.

The noise got the tail gunner's attention. He focused on the area to his right. Walton was sitting in front of the him, with the remaining four team members spread out in front of the two of them. As the tail gunner continued to concentrate on the woods to the right, Walton

An A1-E Skyraider lauching in support of a Prairie Fire mission. The A1-E first came into service at the end of WW II, and served throughout the Korean War and was highly sought because it was a weapons platform which could remain on station for several hours while delivering many forms of ordnance—Cluster Bomb Units, napalm, 20 mm ammo, and 500–2000 pound bombs. The A1-Es had code names and nicks names which included: Spads, Sandy, Hobo and Zorro. (Photo courtesy of Doug LeTourneau)

looked past him and saw the bushes shake about ten feet away. One of the NVA soldiers was crawling up their back trail. As Walton swung his CAR-15 toward the enemy soldier, the NVA popped up, AK-47 tucked under his arm. He had a big Cheshire cat grin on his face, knowing he had ST Louisiana dead to rights. The grinning soldier opened fire on full automatic while Walton was still turning.

Four of the NVA's rounds struck the tail gunner, wounding him severely. Walton's CAR-15 rounds hit the NVA soldier and drove his body backward into the jungle. With the threat temporarily at bay, he began to patch up the tail gunner. Walton dragged him six feet up the hill towards Boggs, got him stabilized, and started an IV (intravenous) drip of blood expander. Walton asked Boggs for permission to crawl back to the dead NVA to search for documents and anything of intelligence value. Boggs rightfully declined the offer. Moments later, the first NVA wave attack slammed into ST Louisiana. The six-man team repulsed it without taking any further casualties.

Fortunately for ST Louisiana, a flight of 101st Airborne Division gunships was diverted from a target in South Vietnam toward the A Shau Valley. The arrival of the 101st took the pressure off of the team for a few minutes as Boggs popped a smoke grenade and directed several gun runs around the team's perimeter. Every time they flew past on a gun run, the NVA on the ridgeline would jump up and fire at them. Cunningham crawled to a knoll to get a better view because it was his first contact with the NVA. The dirt in front of his face exploded several times from enemy rounds. Cunningham suddenly thought maybe this wasn't such a good idea, so he backed up. Real fast. After a few more close gun runs, the helicopters had expended all of their ordnance and returned to their base of operations at Phu Bai. Cunningham jokingly asked the 101st gunners if they could just come on down and pull them out. They declined, saying the extraction choppers were on the way.

A few minutes later, Cunningham was told the A-1E Skyraiders (Spads) were on station. Boggs had asked for a napalm run. Walton was sitting next to Cunningham, on his right, and had just finished patching up the last of the tail gunner's wounds. Both men were near a clearing. Boggs directed the napalm run, which struck the ground at the far end of the open area and moved toward ST Louisiana on the knoll. Walton didn't think anything about it. Off in the distance he could see the Spad making its run, saw the canister come loose from the aircraft and tumble toward the earth. After the napalm canister hit the ground and exploded, its forward momentum carried a one-foot hunk of burning metal up the knoll and over the open area toward Walton and the team. It stopped right between Walton's feet. He sat there staring at the burning metal between his legs for several long seconds. Cunningham was amazed at how close the napalm had come without any of it landing on him, even though he and Walton were just a few feet apart. The napalm run forced the NVA to pull back momentarily, but another wave of NVA soon assaulted the team to Cunningham's left. No one else on the team was wounded. Boggs became concerned about the vacant tail gunner position becoming a vulnerable spot and he ordered Walton to crawl back to where he had killed the first NVA. As Walton moved out in a low crawl, a Vietnamese team member moved into his position next to Cunningham.

Walton moved to the other side of the perimeter. He had crawled about eight feet, down a slight slope, when a second NVA wave attack hit the team from Bogg's side near the point. Again, ST Louisiana held. As another wave of NVA moved toward the team, Boggs began to yell to his men that they were being overrun. From his position, only eight feet away, Walton couldn't see Boggs or Cunningham or the Vietnamese team member who had filled the slot he had vacated. The jungle vegetation was so thick he could only see one or two feet around him. In fact, the foliage was so thick Walton would see the leaves move first to announce an incoming enemy soldier.

During that NVA wave attack, Boggs called in an air strike. He told the Spads to hit ST Louisiana to break the charge. The first 20mm gun run ripped into the NVA and through ST Louisiana's perimeter. Cunningham was in a world of shit and there was nothing he could do about it. The next thing he knew he was 100 yards away, watching himself get hit twice. One round went through his right leg; one went through the radio on his back. Although the radio was destroyed, it saved Cunningham's life. Boggs got hit with shrapnel from the exploding PRC-25. The Vietnamese team member who was sitting where Walton had been was killed instantly. The rounds detonated the frag, smoke and CS tear gas grenades on the dead indig. More shrapnel knocked Boggs into semi-consciousness.

The gun run broke the NVA wave attacks against ST Louisiana. It also left the team in a plume of tear gas, and smoke from smoke-grenades, weapons fire and the earlier napalm run. The NVA probably felt the conditions around the team perimeter were far more deadly than facing the gun runs from the Spads and gunships. Walton performed a quick triage on Boggs and Cunningham. He found that while the explosion of the 20mm round had left only a single piece of flesh holding the leg together, it had seared a good portion of Cunningham's wounded right leg, actually helping the situation by keeping the loss of blood to a minimum. The medic pulled out a green cravat for a tourniquet. He used his knife to twist the bandage tight above the stump to stem any further bleeding. Walton also treated Cunningham for severe throat burn from the CS gas.

Realizing the PRC-25 had been destroyed, Walton reached into his pocket and pulled out the URC-10 emergency ultra-high frequency radio and called Covey. He reported one dead, three wounded and that if Covey was going to get them out, he had to do it ASAP. Walton didn't have the luxury of spare seconds to think about the short distance he had crawled earlier. Those eight to ten feet had saved his life.

Cunningham, still watching himself from far away, heard someone on a radio calling Covey saying there were two dead. He thought he'd better find out whether or not he was alive. The Green Beret had a unique test to find out. He yelled. It sounded like it was far, far away, but he knew that he was alive. The yell also ended Cunningham's out-of-body experience. He returned to his body

From left, at FOB 1 Phu Bai outside S-2 shop, John S. Meyer, Pete Boggs and John T. Walton. This photo was taken a few weeks after the Aug. 3 mission which is why Boggs is wearing civilian clothes. (Photo courtesy of Doug LeTourneau)

lying on the ground. Cunningham knew that he had to help himself. The more he did, the better it would be for everyone.

While Walton worked to save Cunningham's life, Covey directed a series of deadly air strikes around the knoll where ST Louisiana was fighting for its life. Walton returned to the UCR-10 to tell Covey that two of the three wounded were in serious condition and requested an immediate extraction. Covey rider Pat Watkins told Walton to move the remainder of the team closer to the open area along the ridge.

Back at FOB 1, most of the spike team members were either huddled around their PRC-25s listening to Covey talking to ST Louisiana members, or in the comm center, where they monitored more frequencies. When the first reports rolled in from Covey about ST Louisiana's situation, the team sounded doomed.

In the A Shau Valley, the air strikes gave ST Louisiana a brief lull in the fighting, enabling Walton and the one remaining unwounded Vietnamese team member to move the wounded closer to the clearing. Watkins told Walton that he was going to direct a series of strafing runs by Air Force F-4 Phantom jets and that the first Kingbee would land to pick up the most seriously wounded and that a second and third H-34 would extract the remainder of the team.

Walton and the Vietnamese team member moved the tail gunner out from the tree line into the grassy area, while Boggs assisted Cunningham. As soon as the NVA heard the Kingbee, the activity picked up again. The wounded were moved out to the open area where the grass was only six inches tall. There were constant dirt spurts kicking up all around from enemy gunfire. Captain Thinh piloted the first Kingbee and landed with the right strut only a few feet from the wounded members of ST Louisiana.

There were only three times Cunningham really felt pain that day: the first time was when he got hit. He said later that his body felt like one of those huge Chinese gongs as the shock waves reverberated throughout it. The second time was when Boggs was helping him back to the landing zone. The wounded leg got caught on a tree. He immediately knew what they meant when they said pain has colors. Cunningham saw a rainbow of color. The third time occurred at the H-34. Boggs assisted Cunningham to the steps of the Kingbee, but he turned around to fire at the charging NVA. Cunningham didn't want to get shot in the back, so he used his stump to climb aboard the H-34. He crawled to the back of the chopper, thinking he was finally safe. The Kingbee lifted off.

About the same time, Walton realized that the second Kingbee wasn't heading toward the LZ as planned and that the NVA continued to pour heavy small arms fire toward Walton, Boggs and their brave Vietnamese counterpart. Walton knew why the plan called for using three Kingbees for extraction; the weather was hot and the LZ was on a mountain range in the A Shau Valley. The heat and the height of the mountains reduced the lift capabilities of the helicopters, especially in the hot morning sun. Because of this, the first chopper took only two team members—the most seriously wounded—Cunningham and the tail gunner. Walton radioed Watkins, asking where the second Kingbee was and Watkins told him the pilot wouldn't go into the LZ because there was too much enemy ground fire.

Walton felt sick. The question of weight had forced the team to leave the dead Vietnamese team member behind. His added weight might hinder the chances of the living team members being successfully exfiltrated. Walton and his counterpart scanned the sky for a helicopter. None were in sight. The NVA continued to maneuver toward the exposed trio from ST Louisiana. Walton knew the situation looked pretty bleak.

"Kingbee go down." It was Captain Thinh! He already had their wounded aboard and Walton knew there was no way he could pull them all out. But the Kingbee came spiraling down on full autorotation before flaring into the LZ. Thinh plunked it down on the ground right next to the remaining members of ST Louisiana.

Walton and the Vietnamese lifted Boggs aboard the Kingbee and then moved to the open windows on the starboard and port sides to fire at the NVA, some of whom rushed the aircraft.

Sure enough, the load was too heavy and Thinh couldn't lift

off. So he lifted the back wheel off the ground and started rolling downhill, gaining as much air speed as possible, while the NVA fired at the chopper. At the last possible moment, Thinh nursed the aging Sikorsky over the trees. Unfortunately, the chopper didn't have enough speed to gain the altitude needed to fly out of the mountains so Captain Thinh dipped down into a valley to build up more. Finally, he got the transitional lift he needed to climb out of the mountains and out of the A Shau Valley.

Because Cunningham had used the stump to get aboard the helicopter, it had started to bleed heavily. He began to fade in and out of shock, never fully passing out. It was obvious he would have to tough it out. Walton used another cravat as a tourniquet to stop the bleeding. Walton had only carried one IV with him that day and he had used that one on the wounded tail gunner. From that day forward, Walton always carried several IVs on all targets.

When the Kingbee landed at the medical facilities in Phu Bai, Cunningham was taken out of the chopper, as he put it, bare-assed naked. He remembered some doctor saying the tourniquet was too high. Cunningham couldn't believe it. His leg had been blown off above the knee and they were worried about a tourniquet being too high. When Walton and the Vietnamese team member carried the wounded Vietnamese team member into the Army medical facility, someone told Walton that they didn't treat Vietnamese. Walton told them to treat that Vietnamese or there would be hell to pay.

For Walton, the drama continued. When they got Cunningham inside, he was barely hanging on, due to the loss of blood and trauma from the amputation. One of the young doctors got nervous. He had never had a dirty, sweaty grunt from just out of the field sticking his nose into his business. When Cunningham's blood pressure was so low they couldn't get an IV into him, Walton told the doctor to do a cutdown: cut into the vein, expose it, stick a catheter into it and tie it off with a suture. The doctor soon realized the medic wasn't leaving.

Later that night, after Walton had showered and shaved, he was playing poker in the Green Beret Lounge at FOB 1. Being left-handed, when Walton dealt a hand of poker he held the deck in his

Wearing their Silver Star awards, from left: Pete Boggs, Charles Borg and John T. Walton, at FOB 1. Boggs' & Walton's awards were for combat on Aug. 3, 1968. (Photo courtesy of Charles Borg)

right hand. As he dealt the cards around the table, someone noticed a flesh wound across his right wrist. Walton was asked what had caused the wound. As Walton puzzled over the crease in his wrist, the poker game came to a temporary halt. Most of the men playing that night were on spike teams or were Covey riders and had spent time on the ground. Finally, Walton said that during contact with the grinning NVA soldier who shot the ST Louisiana tail gunner, one of the rounds from his AK-47 had creased Walton's wrist as he was turning his body toward the NVA soldier to kill him. Everyone sat there for a second, amazed at how close Walton had come to being shot and just how fortunate he was that the NVA's round hadn't inflicted a more serious wound. Walton just shrugged his shoulders and the game continued.

Early Sunday morning, several of the guys from FOB 1 drove over to the hospital area to visit Boggs, Cunningham and the tail gunner. Cunningham was asleep, but Boggs wanted to get back to work, although he had many bandages on his face, arms and chest. They slipped him a bottle of his favorite whiskey and talked in general terms about what had happened on Saturday. Boggs focused on Walton's efforts, Cunningham's stoicism and Kingbee pilot Captain Thinh's fearless and amazing extraction. Later, Colonel Jack Warren, the commander of C&C and FOB 4, and several other SOG officials visited the survivors. They asked Cunningham if there was anything he needed. They left him cigarettes, and Gordon Martin, a SF medic from FOB 1, gave him his lighter. That was one of the few things that went with Cunningham when he finally left Nam.

* * *

During an interview in July 2002, Cunningham said, "You can do everything right or wrong and it doesn't matter. Life's a matter of inches." During his morning in the A Shau Valley, he was carrying an extra pouch of hand grenades, just as Boggs had instructed him. It hung below the pouches attached to his web gear, down the side of his leg. The 20mm round that severed his leg missed it by only a few inches. "Had that round hit those grenades, Pete and I would have been history that day, right there in the A Shau Valley."

Chapter Five

DOWN IN THE DUMPS

Keeping SOG reconnaissance teams trained, operational and running top-secret missions across the fence was becoming increasingly difficult by the middle of 1968. Enemy prowess in the field improved daily, while the North Vietnamese Army committed a huge amount of manpower to combat SOG teams.

In early spring of 1968, Spike Team Alabama was devastated when several team members were killed or wounded during a rope extraction in Laos. There were no Americans available to run the team. At the end of July, Specialist 4th Class Lynne M. Black, Jr., a veteran of the 173rd Airborne Brigade, and another American were assigned to the team. However, because neither had any experience running SOG missions and there were no team leaders available, Alabama found itself on permanent garbage detail.

Garbage detail at Phu Bai consisted of getting an old deuce-and-a-half truck, picking up the trash in camp and driving to the dump, northwest of FOB 1. The garbage run was a sobering experience for most of the Americans because they saw many Vietnamese sifting through the garbage, looking for food and things to sell. And there were prostitutes at the dump who would occasionally cause delays in returning to base.

The boredom of the trash run worsened when team members pulled the detail during the heavy, seasonal rains that hit the area during August and September. Additionally, the team was stuck doing the permanent rice run, driving south to Da Nang from Phu Bai on Highway 1. This included driving over the treacherous Hai Van pass, one of the most dangerous places in South Vietnam due to enemy ambushes.

Finally, around the middle of September, Sergeant Tim Schaff was appointed One-Zero of Spike Team Alabama. Black became the One-Two. He came to Phu Bai as a qualified Green Beret with one combat tour of duty under his belt with the 173rd Airborne Brigade. A third American was appointed One-One. Schaff was a veteran SOG operative, having run recon missions from FOB 3 in Khe Sanh, FOB 2 at Kontum, and out of the Kham Duc A Team site.

When Schaff's appointment was announced, Black asked around about him. One story about Schaff told how, during a break for lunch on a recent mission, he had fallen asleep. The team ate, got their equipment together and moved on through the jungle, leaving the sleeping Green Beret behind. Soon the team realized Schaff was missing, returned to the break site and woke him. Several people started calling him "Sleepy" after that.

As humorous as that might have been, the story did not inspire respect and confidence in Black regarding Schaff's leadership abilities at the time. All that changed when he saw the way Schaff handled himself during their training mission.

Training missions were commonly conducted by FOB 1 troops on a peninsula southeast of Phu Bai—complete with helicopter insertion, team movement, contingency drills and rest security procedures. Schaff took the entire team. The new Special Forces men on ST Alabama had not trained together under operational conditions with the new Vietnamese members. The team needed time on the ground.

Prior to leaving FOB 1, there was a short, quick briefing. Intel told the Americans that there was a battalion of Viet Cong on the peninsula. A few weeks earlier a Marine or a U.S. Army Airborne unit had been run out of the area. Thus, the spike team was training in an area where regular forces couldn't hold the ground. It was no cakewalk.

The training mission was conducted as though Spike Team Alabama was being inserted into a regular target. Two Kingbees inserted the team without incident.

The team found itself in an area of operation that was so open, Schaff was forced to move mostly at dawn and dusk, or during the night if there was enough moonlight.

During the first day on the ground the team did a lot of sleeping, which didn't seem to bother Schaff. However, it bugged the hell out of Black. There was little ground cover and vegetation. Additionally, he didn't sleep well because it was the first time out with a spike team. In Special Forces Training Group at Ft. Bragg, North Carolina, he had heard about the secret missions run out of an operation simply called C&C. SOG wasn't yet a common term. Now, he was on the ground with a C&C team. For Black the combat veteran, moving through unfamiliar terrain with little sleep heightened his state of mild anxiety. His anxiety was not eased when the Vietnamese team members observed some women working in the fields off in the distance. Their minds drifted to making contact, a man-meets-woman type of contact, while thinking about the women they had spent time and money on during the garbage runs at Phu Bai.

When the team did move during that first day, it moved down into the peninsula and started to move up into the foothills where there were a few trees and a lot of low brush and rock. The rocks were smooth. They seemed to roll up out of the soil like furrows overturned from a plow's shire. These rows of furrowed rock were several feet high and stacked at an angle, creating tiers reminiscent of a bleacher area at a stadium in the United States. As the team moved over the folds from one rock furrow to another, they found old fighting positions, spent shell casings and C-ration containers.

As the day went on the team's security became lax. Black felt like he was on a hunting trip with a bunch of his friends, back in the States. Thoughts of war, thoughts of bitter combat at Dak To during his first tour of duty in Vietnam with the 173rd Airborne Brigade, were far from his mind. It was almost like goofing off. Even when

From left, Tony Herrell, John Driscoll, Chuck Willowby, Henry King, Joe "Pigpen" Conlon and Sgt. Maj. Harvey Harris. The six men gathered on the landing zone at FOB 1 shortly after they were transferred from FOB 3 to Phu Bai, following the closure of FOB 3 in June 1968. Maj. Clyde Sincere later opened a launch site at Mai Loc which was called FOB 3. (Photo courtesy of John S. Meyer)

the point man got stung in the head three times and became delirious, requiring a medevac, Black's mind still drifted.

By the second day, all of the Vietnamese team members wanted to be extracted and returned to FOB 1. They argued with Schaff sporadically throughout the afternoon. For Black, this was his first experience on the ground with the Vietnamese, so he pulled back and watched Schaff. He didn't have a clue about team protocol or what was right or wrong, so he kept his mouth shut while quietly moving out of any possible lines of fire...just in case.

Schaff didn't relent. He had run plenty of missions as a One-Zero team leader. He knew that before this team went to the field, it had to become a cohesive unit that moved with stealth and didn't argue with him once they entered enemy territory.

He hated the in-country training as much as they did, but he wanted to get the team operational. He had heard good things about his Vietnamese counterpart, the Vietnamese team leader Tho (Zero-One), and the interpreter Khanh (Zero-Two), whom all of the Americans called "Cowboy." Schaff knew that with those two experienced Vietnamese, he could go to the field sooner than later. But he wanted to see how Black, the One-One, and the remaining Vietnamese worked in the field. He wasn't going to listen to any whining about returning to FOB 1.

He ordered the team to move again that night. Again, there was dissention among the Vietnamese. Schaff took charge. He told them to shut the hell up or he would fire all of them and leave them there while the U.S. troops returned to Phu Bai. The Vietnamese mumbled among themselves for the remainder of the night. They didn't talk to the SF troops. Privately, Black worried about whether the tough-talking, no-nonsense Vietnamese would turn on the SF troops. He wondered what he had gotten himself into.

By the morning of the third day, the team had arrived at the backside of the peninsula. Black marveled at the high rolling rock formations to the team's back. On both sides were mostly open fields stretching down to the peninsula into the China Sea. It was a calm, peaceful, bucolic sight. There were rice paddies reaching out about 150 to 300 yards into the water, with the bay arching around them to the right. The steeper hills climbed to the team's left. The rising sun glinted across the water with translucent wafts of fog drifting across the paddies. In another time, this would be a slice of paradise. Black dreamed of building a house there.

By the afternoon, the team was sitting between the rice paddies, little dikes and the foothills that led to the steep mountain behind the team. Again, the debate surfaced, leave or continue. Team members were so bored they talked about taking some target practice. Privately, Black felt that the friendly environs were too beautiful to spoil with gunfire. Ho hum.

Just then the indig reported three or four guys observing the team, walking around the rocks in dark pajamas just out of rifle range, about 1,200 to 1,500 meters away. Alabama team members had seen women working in the paddies during the previous two days, but had seen no men. Black had assumed they were paddy workers. The Vietnamese men on Alabama had other thoughts and began again to talk in earnest with Schaff.

As Schaff was watching the men in the distance, he observed movement to his left. There was a line of foliage that ran from left to right for about 150 yards. It was pretty dense, about five to six feet high. One spot in the foliage dipped down. In that dip, Schaff saw three or four heads moving right to left, as the rest of the team was looking at the men in the distance.

Schaff began to get edgy. He told Black to call Phu Bai and to give them a Situation Report, using the portable PRC-25 FM radio. Schaff crawled away from the team, toward the foliage where he had seen the VC. As he crawled over a dike, Schaff observed that the VC had weapons.

The remainder of ST Alabama didn't know what Schaff had seen. The closest team member was 60 to 80 yards away from him. Black, unaware of Schaff's observation, was talking to FOB 1, telling the base radio operator how beautiful it was on the peninsula and how he hoped to have many more training missions in such scenic settings.

Schaff crawled back to Black, told him about the VC and ordered Black to call for an extraction, ASAP, because the enemy was setting up an ambush for ST Alabama. Black hadn't seen the three VC and thought Schaff was simply looking for a way to go back to FOB 1 instead of staying in the field for two more days to complete the planned five-day training cycle. "This guy doesn't have a clue what he's doing," Black muttered to himself.

Black dutifully called his commo buddy at FOB 1 and informed him of Schaff's request for an extraction. The radio operator thought Black was kidding and laughed before terminating the commo exchange. Schaff crawled back to initiate contact without realizing that the FOB 1 commo man had told Black that the choppers weren't flying and that there would be no extraction on day three.

Schaff saw one of the three VC start to walk toward him. He flipped his CAR-15 selector switch to "on" and shot him. Two more VC popped up. Schaff flipped it to full automatic and opened fire on them.

ST Alabama's M-79 man, Quang, hit them with a round of 40mm high explosive from the single-shot grenade launcher. Then the whole line of foliage opened up on ST Alabama.

"Base, this is Blackjack! We are under fire, over!!"

"Yeah, right. A fake firefight to come home. And it's steak night."

"Base! Blackjack! I'm serious, over!" The radio operator's voice was replaced with the voice of an FOB-1 officer. He told Black it was too late in the day for extraction. The H-34s had returned to their home base in Da Nang and the U.S. UH-1E's, or Hueys, didn't fly this late in the day. He told Black that it would be dark by the time they flew to ST Alabama's beleaguered location. Besides, he noted, it's against Army regulations for them to fly at night.

After the initial burst of gunfire between the VC and ST Alabama, there was a sudden lull. Cowboy and the Vietnamese team members on ST Alabama got on line and charged forward toward the VC in the foliage. Black was amazed and impressed with the boldness of their tactics. They didn't wait for Schaff. They charged!

As they were running across the relatively open area, a machine

From left, Lynne M. Black Jr., the One-One for ST Alabama, with Tim Schaaf, the One-Zero for ST Alabama during the summer of 1968 inside a Kingbee. (Photo courtesy of Rick Howard)

gun opened fire on them from the rear. The ST Alabama Vietnamese men stopped their charge and returned to the team's first position. Miraculously, no one was wounded.

Schaff asked Black about the extraction. Black told him there were no choppers. Schaff remembered that Black had spent a tour of duty with the 173rd Airborne Brigade where radio procedures were strict. He told the new One-Two in no uncertain terms what he thought of his radio etiquette.

"You are the guy getting shot at—not that asshole back in camp! Take charge of getting us a ride home and get us some air cover! I don't care how you do it, just do it!" Schaff was Black's first encounter with a motivational speaker.

Black got back on the radio and told the radio operator that ST Alabama was under attack and that if he didn't get an extraction for the team, Black would personally shoot him when he returned to FOB 1. Commo ended abruptly.

Now Schaff was pissed at Black for the commo glitch and at himself for allowing the team to move into a position where it was surrounded on three sides by enemy troops firing at them, leaving ST Alabama with nowhere to go, except to fall back to the China Sea.

Black called FOB 1 for fire support, inquiring if any was available, either from the Navy or regular Army or Marine troops in the I Corps area of South Vietnam. FOB 1 asked Black if they could hold out until the morning. Right.

As Black talked to FOB 1, the firefight roared on, and the volume of hostile fire directed toward ST Alabama increased.

Black remembered a Navy frequency he had picked up from one of the Marines he was drinking with at the FOB 1 club a few days before the training mission. He dialed in the frequency and found a guy who said he was the Navy captain of two armed airboats and that they were about twenty minutes from the peninsula. Black asked Schaff if the team could hold out for another 20 minutes. Schaff scowled at Black with one of those "that's a stupid question" looks. Schaff knew that several of his team members were getting low on ammo.

Black's long shot paid off. Team members could hear the gunboats roaring into the bay. Black gave the captain his location. Moments later the gunboats' quad 50s and 20mm cannons and two M-60s opened fire on the enemy positions, successfully bracketing the team. The Navy firepower directed against the VC mountain positions slowed down the enemy fire on the team.

Then the question arose: how would Schaff move his team 150 yards or so through the rice paddies out to the boats? He asked for volunteers to run to the boats. The silence was deafening. With daylight running out, Schaff shrugged his shoulders and ran to the first boat in a zigzag pattern.

Now the Vietnamese members of ST Alabama, Black and the One-One moved toward the gunboats. In a matter of minutes, they were chest deep in the China Sea while the Navy gunners kept firing into the enemy positions.

One of the airboats moved into a rice paddy and toward the foothills, directing heavy gunfire on the mountains as it moved. When it passed the fleeing team, the ST Alabama men were hit with a huge wave of mist blown over them by the turbines under the large latex skirt that provides an air cushion for the gunboat to ride on.

The second craft idled to ST Alabama. Climbing over the skirt to the deck was difficult. Nowhere in any SOG camp did recon teams train for boarding gunboats. Finally, it settled in the water, all the while firing suppressing fusillades to cover the team's extraction.

When the last team member struggled aboard the huge gunboat, the pilot applied the power, the huge deck raised up several feet, and the boat turned and joined the other, heading out to sea enroute to a Navy base. Uncle Sam's Navy saved Alabama's bacon that night.

Two days later, ST Alabama made a dump run. No one complained.

Chapter Six

YOU SHOT ME THREE TIMES

Near the end of September, the brass asked Schaff if he'd mind becoming the One-One, or assistant team leader. The brass wanted to put an overweight Special Forces sergeant from Germany who had a previous tour of duty with a Green Beret A Team, but no experience in Laos, in the One-Zero slot simply because he had more rank. Schaff objected. He was quietly removed from the team and the senior SF Sergeant took command.

At that time, FOB 1 teams were being pushed hard to get on the ground. Thus, there was little or no time for social niceties. More important, with the new One-Zero, there was no dress rehearsal. No practice mission. And he had little or no respect for ST Alabama's Vietnamese team members. He dismissed veteran SOG recon sergeants who tried to offer him advice about running missions across the fence. Among those who tried to talk to him were Spider Parks and Pat Watkins. Both were experienced One-Zeroes; both had been to Laos and both were respected SOG members at FOB 1. When asked later about the team leader, Spider simply said he had "shunned experienced counsel."

The brass assigned ST Alabama to run a target just southwest of the A Shau Valley. Black, unaware of Schaff's earlier discussions with the brass, was introduced to the new One-Zero and they were

Lynne M. Black Jr., posing at the range in Phu Bai. Note his unique vest, which he designed and a few others duplicated. (Photo courtesy of John S. Meyer)

ordered to fly a visual reconnaissance over the target.

VRs were flown as close to the launch date as possible and usually in a small, single-engine observation aircraft flown by two Vietnamese pilots. In this case, the VR was a day or two before the target launch date of 5 October 1968. Black and the new One-Zero flew in the rear seat of the small aircraft. The primary and secondary landing zones had been selected when the aircraft was hit by 12.7mm heavy machine gun fire.

Suddenly the cabin was sprayed with blood. A 12.7mm round had ripped through the floor, struck the co-pilot under the chin, hitting with such force that his helmet slammed against the ceiling and ricocheted into Black's lap—still containing part of the co-pilot's bloody head.

The pilot slammed the small aircraft down to treetop level and returned to South Vietnam. Black, unable to move or open a window, puked into the helmet. That night, there were a fair share of jokes in camp about Black's "puke and brain" salad.

Saturday morning, 5 October, there was no laughing when the Vietnamese-piloted Kingbees flew west across South Vietnam from Phu Bai, near the China Sea, to the A Shau Valley into the target area. The weather was clear in Phu Bai, but cloudy over the AO.

During that flight, Black remembered how the launch commander had said this mission would be a cakewalk. Spider and Watkins, however, knew that it was a tough target where the NVA had previously run out FOB 1 teams and there were no new landing zones for the team insertion. For this target, Watkins was the Covey rider in the Air Force O-2 Cessna, piloted by Captain Hartness.

ST Alabama's insertion started smoothly, as the first Kingbee landed quickly with the One-Zero, One-One and three Vietnamese team members quickly exiting the aircraft.

As Black's Kingbee spiraled downward toward the LZ, he observed an NVA flag planted atop a nearby knoll. From his days in the 173rd Airborne Brigade, Black knew that the presence of an NVA flag meant that there was at least a regiment of NVA soldiers in the area. The knoll was surrounded by jungle. On the west side there was a 1,000-foot drop to the valley floor below.

The numbers didn't compute for Black—approximately 3,000 NVA against nine ST Alabama men?

Several AK-47s opened fire before the Kingbee's wheels touched down. Nonetheless, Black and the remaining three Vietnamese ST Alabama team members exited the H-34. As the Kingbee lifted off, the NVA gunfire increased significantly and moments later, the laboring Sikorsky H-34 crashed.

Although this was Black's first SOG mission into Prairie Fire, he knew the odds were stacked against ST Alabama. He and Cowboy argued vigorously for an immediate extraction. The team had been compromised. The element of surprise was gone. The other American, who had not gone through the Special Forces qualification courses at Ft. Bragg, remained silent.

"No!" said the new One-Zero. "I'm an American. No slant-eyed SOB is going to run me off!" Watkins offered the One-Zero a chance to extract. The offer was declined. The team was to continue.

The team leader ordered the point man to walk down a well-traveled trail away from the LZ into the jungle. Black, Cowboy and the point man, Hoa, argued against heading down the trail. The first rule of recon was to never use trails, especially well-traveled ones.

The One-Zero pulled rank and ordered the team to move down the trail, with Hoa leading the way and the elder Green Beret following a short distance behind him. The trail wound into the jungle, and curved to the left. ST Alabama moved cautiously. As the team went down the trail, it moved parallel to a small rise on its right that was about 10 to 20 feet above the team. On it, an NVA colonel had quickly assembled a force of 50 NVA soldiers, who set up a classic L-shaped ambush.

The quiet of the early morning jungle was shattered when the NVA troops opened fire with their AK-47s and SKS rifles.

The AK rounds ripped into the point man's chest and face. The fatal impact of those rounds lifted the canteen covers around his waist, appearing to keep his body suspended in air. What had been a human body milliseconds earlier was being chewed into an amorphous form that hit the ground with a sickening thud. Arterial blood spurted high into the air.

Three rounds slammed into the One-Zero's head, blowing off the right side of his face, killing him instantly. Nothing in the months of pulling garbage detail could prepare ST Alabama for the grisly horror unfolding at that moment. The One-One buried his face in the dirt and started praying.

Black and the remaining ST Alabama team members returned fire. The Green Beret stood there, firing on single shot, picking off NVA soldiers on top of the rise. He reloaded his CAR-15 and went down the line, shooting them one after another. Sometimes they spun and he shot them a second or third time.

As the NVA continued to fire on the team, Black and Cowboy formed the team into a circle and directed a barrage of M-79 grenade rounds and CAR-15 fire into the surrounding jungle.

Then startling, eerie silence. Black thought he was in his grave. ST Alabama was in a low spot with the ground rising 10 to 20 feet on both the left and right.

Both the NVA and ST Alabama tended to their wounded while the living combatants slammed loaded magazines into their hot weapons. There was moaning and groaning, human suffering on both sides. Black got on the PRC-25 to tell Covey about ST Alabama's tragic turn of events. Black and Tho scavenged weapons and ammo from the dead ST Alabama team members.

Fortunately, Covey was still airborne. Black reported that he had two KIAs and two WIAs and was surrounded by NVA troops.

Covey responded, "You're not a doctor, nor for that fact, a medic. You can't determine who's dead or alive! Bring out all bodies for verification of death."

Their argument was drowned out when more than 100 NVA regulars opened fire on ST Alabama, as enemy troops had reinforced the initial ambush unit. By now, the NVA were two rows deep: the front row fired AK-47s, the second row threw grenades or fired

Kingbee pilot, Capt. Nguyen Van Tuong, of the South Vietnamese Air Force 219th Special Operations Squadron, getting ready to take off from Quang Tri launch site into an FOB 1 mission in Laos. (Photo courtesy of John S. Meyer)

RPGs (rocket-propelled grenades).

Another Vietnamese ST Alabama team member was wounded. The team had to get out of the hole or die in it.

The bold NVA told the ST Alabama members to "Chieu hoi," or "surrender," speaking first in French, English and finally, Vietnamese. ST Alabama's weapons drowned out further Chieu Hoi requests. The One-One continued to pray. Black couldn't believe it.

"This is no time to pray…do unto others before they do unto you!" he yelled. Whether or not the NVA soldiers were praying, they continued to move around ST Alabama, some climbing into the trees. Cowboy and Black crawled 15 feet toward them, close enough so that Cowboy heard the NVA commander tell his troops to prepare to charge ST Alabama's position. The commander also told his troops on the long side of the "L" ambush not to fire. Black quickly rigged a claymore mine in the direction of the pending charge.

The fearless NVA mounted a charge toward ST Alabama with AK-47s on full automatic. Black detonated the claymore mine. It blew a huge hole in the NVA ranks.

Before the smoke cleared, ST Alabama ran through the human carnage, firing CAR-15s on full automatic and throwing M-26 frag grenades while dragging their three, wounded team members. Miraculously, ST Alabama made it through the NVA wave of attackers and moved back toward the LZ, leaving their dead behind.

Covey had bad news for Black: the Kingbees had to return to Phu Bai to refuel. No extraction was possible for at least two to three hours. Meanwhile, the relentless and bloodied NVA ran after the spike team. Black planted a claymore mine with a five-second time-delay fuse. It wreaked havoc on the hard-charging NVA.

As the smoke cleared and the body parts settled back to earth, ST Alabama split in half and again charged through the battered and torn ranks of the NVA warriors, killing any standing enemy. They counted at least 50 NVA dead.

Again, eerie silence engulfed the team and ST Alabama regrouped. Just as suddenly, a new wave of NVA soldiers rushed the beleaguered team. ST Alabama had been pushed near the cliff. It was a thousand feet to the ground if they went over the edge. Now on line, ST Alabama charged through the weakest NVA flank, killing several more enemy soldiers.

Something hit Black on the side of his head, knocking him to his knees. He was scrambling to get up when the grenade went off. The last thing he remembered was being slammed into a tree, face first, and the CAR115 carrying handle digging into his chest.

He thought he was drowning, but then he felt feet kicking him and hands slapping him all over. It was the team. They were beating Black back into consciousness and pouring water on his face. He tried to get up, but his legs didn't work. From the knees down, there were no fatigue pants, just surface bleeding. One of the guys started smearing gelatinized rice on the injured One-Two's legs, arms and chest. Black's web gear and what was left of his fatigue jacket were lying shredded, bloody on the ground. The CAR-15 was bent where the barrel meets the receiver and the bolt couldn't be pulled back. One of the team buried it.

By 0900 hours, word of ST Alabama's precarious position had spread through FOB 1 like wildfire. Requests were made for extra assets. It was now an official Prairie Fire Emergency. All aircraft were pulled from their missions and sorties to support ST Alabama. Any gunships attached to SOG were summoned to their aid.

The first gunships to arrive were the Marine Hueys known as Scarface. With them was a CH-46 with a ladder attached for jungle extractions. When the twin-rotor helicopter entered the AO, it was hammered by heavy enemy ground fire, as were the Marine gunships. Green tracers were seen going toward the CH-46. The ground fire became too intense and the Marine chopper had to withdraw and make an emergency landing at Camp Eagle in the 101st Airborne Compound. Despite the hits, Scarface gunships made several passes, expending all ordnance, before returning to base to reload.

Kingbee officers regrouped and prepared to fly back to Laos to extract what was left of ST Alabama. S-3 asked for volunteers for a Bright Light mission and every recon man in FOB 1 volunteered.

ST Idaho was scheduled to insert into the Prairie Fire AO the next day, 6 October. Because the team was ready to go, there was some initial discussion about Idaho being the Bright Light team. As the day dragged on, however, and the perilous nature of ST Alabama's situation worsened, the Bright Light option faded because the original LZ was now too deadly for any helicopter to attempt an extraction.

When Watkins returned to FOB 1 for the Cessna to refuel, he told the others that it didn't look good. He wasn't sure if they'd be able to get them out. He explained the low, sunken area in the LZ, the spotty weather and how smoke from expended ordnance hung over the LZ, making it more difficult to spot the team and to deliver air strikes accurately.

A resupply of ammo, grenades, claymore mines, M-79 rounds, water, bandages and morphine was placed on a Kingbee and launched toward ST Alabama.

In Laos, Cowboy worked on Black's legs. He told Black the last wave of NVA had continued onto the LZ. Cowboy and Black heard more U.S. Marine Huey gunships arrive overhead and witnessed the NVA on the LZ open fire, hammering the lead aircraft.

Again the One-One panicked, cried and shouted skyward. The Vietnamese team members, speaking through Cowboy, told Black that they were going to kill the One-One if he didn't shut up. Black agreed.

"I'll pull the trigger on him, myself."

"God forgive you!" the One-One responded tearfully.

"You and your God have no place here!" Black retorted. Cowboy grabbed a startled Black by the throat and lifted a Catholic crucifix from his neck and shoved it to his lips.

"It's the gods who have allowed us to get this far, Round Eyes!" he whispered.

The sound of approaching Kingbees ended the religious debate as the realities of surviving an A Shau hell became center focus. The able-bodied picked up the wounded and moved toward the LZ. Spider, the Covey rider at this time, told Black that the first

Kingbee was enroute to the LZ, but they planned to work the area surrounding ST Alabama with tactical air support first. In this case, a F-4 Phantom jet pilot told Black to "key your handset for 10 seconds. Put your heads in the dirt, over."

Black acknowledged his radio transmission and told his teammates to put their heads down. As he looked into the sun, he observed the slowest moving full-flapped Phantom he had ever seen. The glide path ratio was critical. Seconds later he saw the tree line across the LZ explode into sheets of white, yellow and orange flames, setting the jungle on fire with napalm. The ship banked sharply, appearing to stand its wing tip on the ground. The pilot cranked on the burners, dropped down into the valley below and then began a vertical climb.

NVA small arms opened up on all sides of the valley. The F-4 took numerous hits on its armor-plated underbelly. Among those shooting at the fast mover were several NVA troops about 20 feet from ST Alabama's perimeter. As the napalm torched the jungle, dozens of NVA soldiers scurried into the open field to escape the instant inferno that had engulfed their comrades.

As a second jet rolled in for a gun run, the NVA initiated what they called "getting close to the belt." In this case, the NVA soldiers moved toward or outright charged ST Alabama to get as close to the team members as possible to avoid being hammered or burnt by Air Force, Marine or Army air ordnance.

Firing on single shot, ST Alabama picked off each of them as they came out of the burning jungle. The Phantoms returned with two cannon and minigun runs along the team's perimeter. Before the dust settled, the Vietnamese team leader, Tho, and Cowboy crawled out and recovered several AK-47s and precious ammunition from the dead enemy soldiers, as their CAR-15 ammo was dwindling to a few precious rounds.

Two of the 9-cylinder Kingbees came chugging up the valley toward ST Alabama. Black popped a green smoke marker. The NVA popped an identical smoke marker, confusing the pilots with devastating results.

The first Kingbee followed the NVA's smoke marker, and took

a direct hit from a rocket, which toppled it on its side, smashing each rotor blade into the ground. The approaching ST Alabama team members narrowly missed getting hit with shrapnel from the crash.

Black, Cowboy and another team member charged the rocket position, killing three NVA before a hail of NVA fire drove them back to the team perimeter. The second H-34 hit an outcropping of rock on the western side of the knoll after taking heavy enemy gunfire. It exploded and fell 1,000 feet to the valley floor below, taking with it ST Alabama's resupply.

Covey barked, "Nice going, Blackjack!"

"Fuck you, Covey," he replied. Cowboy told the One-One to pray for everyone except Black because he was on the "devil's side." Black broke into laughter as he assessed ST Alabama's predicament: ammo was desperately low; the blood trails looked like slug slime, the F-4 Phantoms had expended their ordnance and Covey was belligerent. His nerves were shot. Training and man's basic survival instinct had completely taken over. Then the NVA bugles sounded.

Waves of NVA troops carrying SKSs with fixed bayonets advanced on ST Alabama. When they were 15 feet away ST Alabama opened fire. The semi-automatic SKSs were no match for the fully automatic firepower of the spike team. After the first burst of full automatic fire, the team went to single shot. It was another turkey shoot. Without a word, a look or a plan, acting solely on instinct, all of them, except the One-One, scurried forward and dragged back dead NVA, placing the bodies in a circle around them and stacking them high.

The deadly skirmishing continued for several hours before Covey told Black that more gunships and five Jolly Green Giants, the heavily armored Sikorsky HH-3Es, were en route.

"Blackjack, Covey. What you're up against is the regiment you were sent to find, over."

"Is that all, only 3,000 of the bastards? Well, I think we made a dent in 'em. Who's winning?"

"They are," Covey responded. As Black finished his commo, he saw a sight he would never forget. The NVA formed a front line of NVA troops who were firing their AK-47s. Behind them were several NVA soldiers swinging thongs made of leather and cloth, which held three to five hand grenades each, and with a jerk of their collective wrists, the NVA hurlers launched more than two dozen communist-manufactured grenades at ST Alabama.

The sky was full of grenades. Fortunately, they weren't U.S. grenades. They hit the ground and threw dirt, smoke and dust all over the place. ST Alabama looked up just as the AKs started again, and behind them, the thongs whirling overhead like helicopter blades. When the AKs stopped, the grenades were released. ST Alabama fired. More grenades were released; Alabama threw some back.

ST Alabama was caught in a deadly version of the kid game "Pop Goes the Weasel." The AK-47s continued to roar. Alabama ducked. The grenades were launched. Alabama rocked. Catch, throw, duck, rock. Catch, throw, duck, rock!

The NVA advanced. Grenade shrapnel severed the antenna on the PRC-25 portable radio Black carried. He quickly rigged an impromptu antenna from wire. The relentless NVA continued to advance, inch by bloody inch.

Cowboy took two Vietnamese team members over the cadaver-walled perimeter, seeking to get another line of fire to direct at the advancing NVA. The advance continued, despite firing from Black and the remaining Vietnamese team members. The NVA were now merely feet away from the team's perimeter.

At the last moment, with the NVA a few body lengths away from the perimeter, two Huey gunships from the Americal Division, 176th Aviation Company, the Minute Men Muskets of 36-C, arrived. The UH-1B pilots were code-named "The Judge" and "The Executioner." They roared into the battle, first with a minigun blast, followed seconds later with several 2.75mm rockets placed in the NVA ranks. Alabama was saved, if only for a little while. The NVA backed off for a few moments, briefly licking their collective wounds, although they were far from whipped. New assault lines of NVA troops formed. Before the NVA opened fire on ST Alabama, however, the Executioner confronted the NVA head on. With both door gunners blazing away with their hand-held M-60 machine guns, he hovered inches off of the ground, between the team and the front of the NVA, and skipped several 2.75mm rockets off the ground into the NVA. Before the bleeding, startled NVA could respond, the pilot lifted the old UH 1B model gunship over the tree line and ducked down into the canyon, regaining enough air speed to return for another pass at the ST Alabama perimeter.

Before ST Alabama could celebrate, the NVA charged again. Three more dead NVA were added to the cadaver wall.

Silence dominated the battlefield. No bird chirps, no speaking, no noise of any type. Even the aircraft over the scene had flown far enough away that their absence amplified the empty air. The One-One, who hadn't fired a single shot, continued to pray.

Black patched up a bleeding Cowboy. He gave some him morphine before bandaging a wound on his right side from an AK-47 round.

"Where's John Wayne when you need him?" Cowboy asked. The others laughed.

"Chieu Hoi, du maa (Give up, motherfuckers)!" an enemy soldier yelled. Another NVA told Black to "Chieu Hoi" in English. Black flipped him the bird as a sniper shot Alabama's tail gunner, Cuong, in the crotch, hitting an artery.

As Tho applied direct pressure to Cuong's wound, an A-1E Skyraider lumbered into the AO. Flown by a pilot code-named "Snoopy," he roared in from Black's left, brushing the treetops, full flaps, working his throttle. The aircraft was so close to the team that Black could hear the distinctive, metallic click-click of the napalm canisters being released from the old Korean War era plane. The Skyraider appeared to be falling, but actually it slipped down into the valley to escape NVA gunfire, as the Americal UH-1B gunships and fast movers had maneuvered earlier in the day.

His wingman appeared and as he flew over the team they could hear the nuts and bolts and God knows what creaking and groaning as he salvoed the rockets. The NVA were pissed. Again, the hot shell casings from the airborne warships rained down on ST Alabama.

Then three small mortars opened fire. Black knew there was no way in hell any of the team could catch mortars and throw them back. He and the Vietnamese team leader, Tho, rolled over the cadaver wall toward the mortars, cautiously picking their way through the charred NVA bodies and carnage from the previous airborne assaults. They moved into the jungle, within 20 feet of the first mortar tube. Tho drew a plan in the ground. He would hit tube one, Black would hit tube three and they'd combine on tube two.

After the mortarmen launched three salvos, Tho opened fire on his target while Black attacked his targeted tube and several nearby NVA soldiers.

The survivors chased Black. In the confusion, the NVA opened fire on each other as Black headed toward tube one—with NVA soldiers still chasing him—where Tho was pinned down. Black threw a hand grenade and killed at least three NVA with a blast of gunfire to free Tho. They turned on the NVA chasing Black and dealt with them. Then he and Tho wiped out the NVA at the second tube before they quickly returned to the team, all the while picking up ammo and loaded AK-47 magazines from dead or wounded NVA soldiers.

By now, Watkins had returned to flying Covey rider above ST Alabama. Spider had called the U.S. Air Force's 37th Air Rescue and Recovery Group in Da Nang to attempt a rescue of ST Alabama. During the Vietnam War, when pilots were shot down in North Vietnam or Laos, and all else failed, the Jolly Green Giants were called. The Sikorsky HH-3E weighed 22,050 pounds loaded, had two General Electric T58-GE-5 turboshaft 1,500-hp engines, extra armament and firepower, and they were manned by remarkable Air Force pilots and crews.

The first heavily armored Jolly Green Giant HH-3E, code-named JG 28, started its descent to the LZ from 4,000 feet. As it approached, the JG 28 crew was looking for an orange panel on the southeast side of the LZ. However, as the aircraft was about to touch down, crewmembers noticed a second panel. The NVA had an identical panel. The momentary pause was nearly fatal for JG 28, as the NVA opened fire on it from several sides. The heavy gunfire severed the main fuel line, causing a massive fuel leak inside the HH-3E.

JG 28 had to withdraw from the LZ. In a matter of seconds, there were two to three inches of aviation fuel on the aircraft's cabin floor. The fumes temporarily blinded the crewmembers. The pilot was able to stabilize the rugged HH-3E and returned to Da Nang, escorted by Spad 11.

As JG 10 hovered a safe distance away from the LZ, Watkins directed a few more air strikes around ST Alabama, with the hope that the communist soldiers would put their heads down long enough to get the team out.

After a few air strikes, JG 10, piloted by Air Force Major Vernon R. "Sam" Granier, was called to attempt the extraction. For Granier, this was his first assignment in the Prairie Fire AO as a Jolly Green Giant pilot.

When the call from Covey came, Granier knew that there were two U.S. Green Berets on the ground with their Vietnamese team members and that the majority of the team was wounded. He didn't hesitate. Granier piloted the Jolly Green Giant toward the LZ. Unlike JG 28, Granier knew which side of the LZ ST Alabama was on. As he approached the LZ, NVA gunfire again reached a deafening roar, despite ST Alabama directing firepower at the communist soldiers.

As Granier began to hover over the LZ, JG 10 was hammered by enemy gunfire. His crew chief reported that one NVA round had torn a six-inch hole through the floor. The round apparently slammed into one of the engines. Both engine-warning lights went on. Both engines were on fire.

Granier did a 180-degree turn and moved the damaged aircraft away from the deadly enemy fire, away from the team, struggling to keep it airborne, calling upon all of the training he had received to continue flying. Both crewmembers continued firing their machine guns as Granier battled to keep the ship in the air.

Time ran out for JG 10. After traveling several hundred yards, Granier warned his crew to brace themselves for a crash landing. Both crewmembers continued firing their weapons until the burning

HH-3E slammed into the jungle.

ST Alabama was stunned. Covey and all of the men flying over the target area viewed the horror in grim silence.

The men back at FOB 1 monitored the radio transmissions on their PRC-25s as Covey talked to Black. Spike Team Alabama's radio signal was too weak to hear any response. The word spread through camp about the latest horrific turn of events surrounding ST Alabama. The usual hustle/bustle of a Saturday at FOB 1 was replaced by quiet, hushed tones as the entire compound feared the worst, but continued to pray for the men of ST Alabama. Word of a proposed Arc Light mission reinforced the gravity of ST Alabama's situation. An Arc Light was a strike by a B-52 bomber from more than 25,000 feet.

Back in Laos, the stunned members of ST Alabama returned to their cadaver perimeter once again, nearly out of ammo. One-One was face down, muttering, "The Lord is my shepherd..." One of the Vietnamese went about collecting AK-47s and ammo from the dead NVA as Spider and Watkins directed more air strikes around the team.

Within 10 to 15 minutes after Granier's burning HH-3E crashed into the jungle, Covey learned that there were two survivors from the Jolly Green Giant and asked ST Alabama if they could locate the remaining crewmembers. Granier had broken his back, but somehow had pulled himself from the burning HH-3E. The other Jolly Green Giant survivor, Sergeant Earnest Dean Casbeer, had been thrown clear of the crash. Neither knew the location of the other.

Watkins told Black where the Air Force survivors were and that they'd run a daisy chain between his position and the men, hopefully to clear the area enough for the team to get to both of the survivors.

The NVA threw one more curve at ST Alabama. When Black tried to talk to Covey, he found the primary, secondary and alternate FM frequencies jammed by the NVA. Frustrated, Black smashed the PRC-25 and pulled out his URC-10 high frequency survival radio. He was told that an Arc

Light strike was being planned for this area as soon as possible.

By now all the air assets, Navy, Marine and Air Force, which had been scheduled to fly sorties into North Vietnam, were diverted to the Prairie Fire Emergency surrounding ST Alabama.

Covey directed numerous air strikes, including more gun and rocket runs from helicopter gunships. Scarface, the Hueys from the Marine Light Helicopter Squadron 367, returned to make several runs. After refueling and reloading in Phu Bai, the Minute Men Muskets returned to wreak havoc on the persistent NVA troops. They pounded the jungle area between ST Alabama and the Air Force survivors.

Around 1800 hours, a Jolly Green pilot, Air Force Major Don Olsen, called over the radio, "Blackjack, JG 32, over. I'm parked down in the draw, in the trees from you. You have 20 minutes of fuel before I leave…the first person we MUST see is an American… Hurry! We're taking heavy ground fire."

Anything that couldn't be carried was thrown over the side of the cliff. As quickly as the wounded could move, they headed toward the Jolly Green Giant. The chopper had literally cut away treetops and branches to nestle into the thick dark green foliage, thus reducing its profile to enemy gunners. Olsen had to keep the aircraft stable as there were large trees on all sides of the aircraft. The trees were large enough that they could severely damage the five rotor blades and cause the chopper to crash if he hit any of them.

Covey directed more air strikes in a daisy chain fashion in the portion of the jungle between ST Alabama and the hovering Jolly Green Giant. Watkins hoped this would drive out or kill the NVA in the zone. Even that task became more difficult, as smoke from all of the ordnance continued to hang above the trees, decreasing the visibility for pilots and helicopter gunners.

As they moved toward the hovering HH-3E, ST Alabama entered a cool ravine before climbing the final hill to the chopper. There they encountered a village with hooches built on 10-foot stilts, complete with large pots cooking rice and vegetables. Instead of NVA troops, Black found an American taking food from one of the pots. He was the Flight Engineer, Sergeant Earnest Dean Casbeer, one of the two Air Force survivors from the crashed HH-3E. Soon they found Granier, who had assisted in directing the hovering Jolly Green Giant to this area in the jungle, despite his broken back.

The NVA focused heavily on the chopper, easing the pressure on ST Alabama. As they neared the Jolly Green, Black thought it felt like they were moving closer to the gates of hell itself. The NVA were pouring small arms fire and RPGs at the hovering ship while the door gunners and pilots intermittently fired the mini-gun, M-79s and M-60s, and helicopter gunships and Skyraiders made gun runs around it.

Time was against them. The weather began to close in. The smoke from previous air strikes hung over the area for longer and longer periods of time before clearing enough for the next attack from the air.

On the ground, the men of ST Alabama heard NVA running through the bushes around them. Fortunately the NVA failed to spot the spike team or the Air Force crewmen. Desperate, Black had to move his team onto a trail so it could move to the hovering HH-3E more quickly. As the team moved up the trail, the tail gunner was shaking violently and had turned a pasty white. Team members set Cuong down and proceeded to the aircraft. At the crest of the trail, they saw the HH-3E taking hits and dealing out its own; its M-60 was red hot. Black saw someone firing an M-16 out of one of the windows.

As Black moved to the chopper, the intensity of gunfire seemed to multiply. The air was so full of lead he could see it. Fuel and bits of metal skin fell from the aircraft as they reached its underside.

The jungle penetrator smashed to the ground next to him and raised three feet before he put three team members on the first load. Granier, the Air Force Flight Engineer and a wounded ST Alabama team member were on the second hoist lift. The wounded Vietnamese became entangled in jungle vines while he was being hoisted upwards. The Air Force hoist operator had to stop the hoist, lower it and give him time to untangle himself. When the hoist moved up toward the aircraft, the Vietnamese was not sitting in the seat, but hanging on, with assistance from Air Force Sergeant Casbeer.

Despite the NVA gunfire, Black ran back to the bamboo thicket where he had left the remainder of the team. Cuong, the dying tail gunner, pointed his .45 cal. pistol at the advancing NVA and said, "Toi kiet (I die)." He motioned Black to return to the HH-3E before shooting himself.

Black was running back to the ship when two NVA stepped onto the trail and pointed their AK-47s at him.

"Chieu hoi!" one of the soldiers shouted. Black stretched out his arms and continued walking toward them.

When he was only a few feet away, he said, "Chieu hoi!" The young NVA soldiers appeared surprised. Before they could react, Black grabbed the AK-47s by their searing barrels and stripped them from the soldiers. He backhanded the soldier on his right and smashed the other soldier in the face with one of the weapons.

He left the stunned soldiers lying there as he sprinted to the chopper, where he found the praying One-One. The rest of the team was on board, firing any weapon they could get their hands on. As the jungle penetrator lifted Black and the One-One upward, they were showered with hot spent casings from the M-60 and other weapons being fired from inside the aircraft.

The entire team fired out the windows and from the back door as the overloaded HH-3E began to lift out of the jungle. Major Olsen told Covey he was at maximum power.

As the Jolly Green Giant slowly rose, Black felt the ship making upward surges from the B-40 rockets slamming into the armor-plated underside of the aircraft. It felt like a giant slugging the ship in the stomach, boosting it upward with each rocket blast. From his view above the fray, Watkins couldn't believe the bird kept flying. Somehow the pilot got the Jolly Green out of there.

Once clear of the jungle hole, the ship began its ascent out of the valley and the shadow of death. The door gunner removed his helmet and placed it on Black's head. The pilot told him, "We're on our way home." Not quite.

From above, Watkins saw the crippled ship catch fire and try to make it out of the killing zone. It crossed two ridgelines before descending into a clearing where it crash-landed. Olsen had gotten them out of the killing zone, but JG 32 had flown its last rescue mission. Everyone except Black and the One-One were transferred to another Jolly Green Giant, piloted by a Coast Guard exchange pilot, Lieutenant Commander Lonnie Mixon. Mixon took over 30 hits picking up ST Alabama and the others.

After everyone knew that Black, the remaining personnel from ST Alabama, and the Air Force survivors from JG 10 were cleared from the original target area, they hammered it with everything they had, including more napalm, bombs and gun runs. Captain Hartness, the pilot of Watkin's FAC plane, was so mad that he flew the 0-2 down into small arms fire range and fired 2.75mm rockets into the area where the NVA had knocked down JG 10. He and Watkins took a hit to the front and the engine died. Hartness somehow got the Skymaster 0-2 up, out of the area and back to Phu Bai. There was no engine pressure when he landed.

A Cobra gunship landed and opened the armament compartment doors, which had seatbelts attached to them. Black and the One-One buckled up and were soon airborne alongside the Jolly Green Giant, returning to Da Nang. They were flying so fast that Black had to turn his bloodstained face away in order to breathe. Within minutes, he was so cold he was shivering uncontrollably. The Cobra landed at a Marine medevac site, where the Americans were wrapped in poncho liners and helicoptered to Da Nang.

At the Da Nang infirmary, everyone was getting patched up. When Tho saw Black, he raised his right hand in a fist above his head.

"CHIEU HOI, DU MAA!" he yelled. The One-One, who was not wounded, stood up on a chair.

"Listen up, men! I want to commend each and every one of you for a job well done. As the team leader of ST Alabama, I want you to know I personally am going to put each of you in for the Medal of Honor. You medics take care of my people." He stepped down and left the room. The wounded, exhausted members of ST Alabama looked at Black, aghast.

Black couldn't believe what he had heard the One-One say, but because Alabama was his team and since they were in another unit's facility, he wouldn't do anything that would reflect poorly on the entire team. That night, Black was so mad he knocked the pills out of the medic's hand and instead of lying down for treatment, he went with a Jolly Green medic to his Air Force barracks for a show. There, the medic applied bandages and compresses to the numerous bleeding abrasions and shrapnel holes in his chest, back, arms and legs, and to the burns on his hands from the AK-47s.

While walking to the club, they passed a line of parked Jolly Greens. "So That Others May Live" was printed on the side of one HH-3E. Indeed, two members of the U.S. Air Force's 3rd Air Rescue and Recovery Group in Da Nang had paid the ultimate price while attempting to extract ST Alabama from Laos. Not far from Black, HH-3E pilot Granier was being treated for his broken back.

When they entered the club, every man present rose and started clapping. Everyone crowded in and started shaking hands and slapping Black on the back. The pain was excruciating, but Black thought about how a few hours earlier, ST Alabama appeared to be doomed, fighting for its life. Now he was in a club with men lined up to buy him drinks. The pain was bearable.

The clock said 2200 hours. At Phu Bai, a subdued gathering in the club celebrated ST Alabama's survival and quietly chalked up the deaths of several good Vietnamese team members to poor leadership. Little was said about the arrogant, dead One-Zero. Recon members talked to Watkins and Spider, looking for lessons learned during that long day. Both of them concurred on at least one point; Lynne Black was the reason that the team came home. When the Covey riders had made recommendations, he listened. It hadn't been easy, but he didn't argue; he didn't challenge. He listened.

The overall commander of C&C in I Corps, Col. Jack Warren, presents the Silver Star to Lynne M. Black Jr., at an awards and decorations ceremony held at FOB 4 in Da Nang in late 1968. The Silver Star was awarded for combat action on Oct. 5, 1968. (Photo courtesy of Lynne M. Black Jr.)

Both Spider and Watkins also agreed that without Black's leadership and heroic effort that day, the prospects of anyone on ST Alabama surviving that hellhole had been bleak.

Black and the medics drank until dawn of 6 October 1968. They recounted the story to all who asked and to those who didn't, but were within earshot. Black finally lay down on a cot in the medic's room. A medic told him about the Jolly Green crewmember Greg Lawrence that died in the earlier rescue attempts. Black was lying on his cot.

Back in Phu Bai, Black learned that ST Idaho had been inserted into target E-4 early that morning to search for an American POW camp, which was a few klicks from ST Alabama's target. The secret war in Laos marched on.

* * *

Thirty-one years later, Black cooperated with the Army and Air Force recovery teams searching for and returning the remains of SOG members and all pilots and aircrews who crashed in the Prairie Fire Area of Operation. He assisted the Army personnel in locating and returning the Special Forces sergeant who had walked ST Alabama into the deadly ambush that cost him his life.

A few months after the recovery attempt successfully located and returned the team leader's remains to the US, Black received a phone call from a man who identified himself as an NVA general. He said he was the colonel who led the first 50 NVA troops into battle from the long side of the L-shaped ambush, atop the rise, which was on Black's right side on 5 October 1968. The NVA general said he had given the order that triggered the deadly ambush.

"We had an honest discussion about that day. The general told me that when they heard the Kingbees come in, he assembled 50 men and set up the ambush along that trail," Black said. "He asked me who the American was on the recon team who didn't lie down on the ground during the ambush. He told me that the man standing had the radio on his back. I told him that it was me; I was the radio operator. Then he said, 'You shot me three times that day.'"

Black explained that he remembered shooting single shots into the NVA soldiers who stood to his right, firing on ST Alabama. "When he told me that, I remembered that I had shot a few of them more than once. I remember spinning them around when I shot them. Apparently, he was one of them.

"Then he told me, 'The worst thing about having you shoot me was the fact that I was lying there, watching you kill my men, and there was nothing I could do about it.'"

Black said he and the NVA general chatted a few more minutes about the events of 5 October 1968, before Black mentioned that the NVA had inflicted heavy casualties on ST Alabama, killing three team members and wounding five of the remaining six survivors. "The NVA general told me that his unit had suffered 90 percent casualties that day."

The general explained to Black the NVA were killed or wounded either in direct combat with ST Alabama or from the numerous air strikes that Black and Covey directed around ST Alabama the entire day and after the Jolly Green Giant lifted clear of the jungle.

Black then told the general that when he observed the NVA flag flying in the middle of the knoll, he assumed that the intelligence estimates of an NVA battalion of approximately 3,000 troops was accurate. The general's response ensured ST Alabama's place in SOG history.

"No," the general corrected Black, "It was a division. We had about 10,000 soldiers of the Army of North Vietnam there that day."

CHAPTER SEVEN

LAST BULLET

For several days prior to 6 October 1968, the weather had been cloudy and uncertain. However that began to change on Saturday, 5 October 1968, when ST Alabama was inserted during the early morning hours into an A Shau Valley target. And while ST Alabama was fighting for its life, Spike Team Idaho One-Zero Don Wolken was flying a VR over our target area, code-named Echo Four, or E-4. While Wolken was gone, Sau, the Zero-One, and I inspected the team. At one point during that Saturday, there was some discussion about ST Idaho running a Bright Light mission to rescue ST Alabama and we had gone so far as to draw an M-60 machine gun and thousands of rounds for it, should we be ordered to run the mission. A combination of spotty weather in the AO, the limited options for an LZ and the vast amount of NVA troops in the area resulted in the Bright Light being scratched. ST Idaho again prepared for E-4.

When Wolken returned, he and Sau quickly inspected the team again. This was the first mission where Wolken was the One-Zero. In September, Spider had been promoted to Covey rider and Wolken and I had moved up, respectively. This would be my third official mission in C&C.

With Spider as the One-Zero, we had run a practice mission east of the A Shau. ST Idaho was inserted shortly after another spike team was inserted and the two teams moved parallel to each other. I was introduced to "wait-a-minute" vines, vines with long, sharp stickers that caught on a person's clothing and took a minute or two to work free. The practice mission was otherwise uneventful.

A few days later S-3 told us to gear up to place Air Force seismic sensors in the middle of the A Shau Valley. For several days prior to the mission, Spider, Wolken and Sergeant First Class Bob Ross from S-3 practiced installing the devices.

The decision was made to augment ST Idaho with Ross and the One-Zero from ST Rhode Island, Lester Daniels. They would join Spider, Wolken, myself, Sau, Hiep and Phuoc from ST Idaho. Sau was the Vietnamese team leader, Hiep, the interpreter, and Phuoc, our new point man who Sau had been training for several months. Finally, S-3 told us that we were going to insert into the A Shau the next day. That night, at the FOB 1 clubhouse, Wolken and I sat there, worried about our collective fates in the A Shau Valley. Basically, we thought it would be our last night on earth. Wolken ordered several bottles of champagne and we started drinking. He had his bottle and I had mine. By the time we started drinking from our second bottles, we were pathetic.

"Tilt, we're going to die tomorrow."

"You're right, Don. We're going to die. I'll drink to that." Hell, he was older and had more years in the army than me—who was I to argue? As the night progressed and we crawled deeper into our champagne bottles, the commentary became more morose. After the club closed, we drank some more before Spider finally told us to get our sorry butts into bed. Fortunately, the next morning the weather was heavily overcast. I had a pounding headache. Wolken complained of the same. When they trucked us out to the launch pad, Wolken looked at me and placed his hands together as though he were praying.

"Please, God. Hold those clouds. We can't go to the A Shau like this."

I told him, "Don, I want to die. I'm in too much pain." We

were hurtin' for certain. Thankfully, the mission was scratched and Wolken and I returned to bed to recoup and regroup.

By the next morning the weather had broken and we were inserted smack dab in the middle of the biggest road running north to south through the A Shau Valley. The insertion was quick and smooth. Within minutes, we moved off the trail and set up security. Because I was the rookie on this mission, I had rear security with Hiep. The Air Force sensor had three components to it. A long thick electrical cord ran from the center sensor with a separate cord reaching to each of the two smaller units. Everything had to be covered. As Ross and Spider worked on burying the first device, I looked around the A Shau Valley, almost imagining that I could hear the spirits of Green Berets killed there warning us to get out before the NVA kicked us out. In short order, Spider moved the team out toward the second insertion point, while Wolken, Ross and Daniels buried the cable. The theory behind the sensors was simple: insert them off the trail and they would detect any movement down the main road through the A Shau Valley and report it to Air Force transmitters and receivers. Sophisticated, state-of-the-art equipment would monitor traffic in the valley instead of people. We were told the sensors were so sensitive that they could determine the difference between trucks and tanks and personnel, thus they could report how many NVA and supplies were moving down the road.

As Hiep and I sat on the tail gunner position, we looked around the desolate valley floor. Along this road there were no big trees. There was no jungle. There were, however, hundreds of bomb craters of varying sizes. But what surprised me the most was the number of punji pits that we passed. Some were huge, large enough for animals. The majority of them, however, were in poor repair from the heavy monsoon rains that had pelted the area in recent weeks. As Spider and Ross finished inserting the main sensor, we slowly moved south along the road, carefully burying the cable. Hiep and I simply looked at each other and shrugged our shoulders. I assumed that by this stage of the mission, the NVA would be on us or at least lobbing mortar or rocket fire at us from the surrounding

From left: Sgt. Les Daniels, Sgt. Don Wolken, Nguyen Cong Hiep, Sp. 4 John S. Meyer, Nguyen Van Sau, Staff Sgt. Robert J. Parks, Master Sgt. Bob Ross prior to Aug. 1968 mission to insert Air Force sensors into the A Shau Valley. (Photo courtesy of John S. Meyer)

mountains. Soon we inserted the third sensor and Spider gave me the signal to call for an extraction. Within minutes the slicks landed and lifted us out of the valley. As we gained altitude, heading east, an NVA gunner opened up on us with a 12.7mm heavy machine gun. However, he was so far north of our flight pattern that he had no effect. Since we had anticipated needing a lot of TAC Air, we immediately called in air strikes on the 12.7 position. Wolken and I looked at each other in complete disbelief. We had just walked down into the valley of the shadow of death without seeing one NVA soldier. The most serious problem encountered was heavy mud on our jungle boots. The next day, Spider told us that the sensors had detected and reported enemy activity along that road.

A few weeks later on my second mission, we inserted another set of sensors along the main road at Khe Sahn. This was the base where the Marines gained national attention battling the NVA earlier in 1968. Because of that recent history in that area, we went in very heavy, all guns, bullets and grenades. And again, the NVA wasn't to be seen. Both of these missions were surprising because we anticipated getting hammered. Spider joked with me, saying that I was one of the few people in the history of C&C to have run a practice mission and two missions and still not have a Combat Infantryman's Badge—the award given to soldiers who have seen combat with the enemy or were under direct hostile fire. I kept telling myself that this was a fluke, and I remembered what the Special Forces trainers told us at Ft. Bragg; the NVA and the Viet Cong guerrillas will fight when they want to, no sooner.

After Spider left the team, Wolken met James Davison and brought him on because the thin, quick-witted Louisiana native had a previous tour of duty in Vietnam with the 173rd Airborne Brigade and had survived the battle of Dak To. The lengthy cycle to train Green Berets wasn't cranking out enough SF qualified personnel, so the SOG brass recruited combat veterans from mostly airborne units such as the 101st Airborne Division, the 173rd, the 82nd Airborne Brigade or the First Air Cavalry. Davison was recruited through that program. During the live-fire drills and other aspects of training,

ST Idaho, Oct. 6, 1968, at FOB 1 in the early morning hours prior to launching into Echo 4. From left, kneeling, Phouc—who ran point on that mission, Nguyen Cong Hiep—interpreter, Nguyen Van Sau. Standing from left, Jim Davidson, Don Wolken and John S. Meyer. (Photo courtesy of John S. Meyer)

Davison proved to be as quick with a CAR-15 as he was with his mouth. He was sharp. To round out the six-man team for the Echo Four target, Wolken picked Sau, Hiep, and the young, tough, savvy pointman, Phuoc.

Each American carried a minimum of 25 magazines for his CAR-15; the Vietnamese carried at least 20. At that time, no one could get the new 30 or 36-round magazines for the CAR-15. We were stuck with the 20-round magazines, which we only packed with 18 rounds. Any more bullets would put too much pressure on the spring that pushed the rounds up and could cause a malfunction. Wolken and I both carried sawed-off M-79s with 21 HE (high explosive) rounds and one tear gas round each. We also carried several smoke grenades in yellow, purple, violet and red, plus the smaller smoke canisters that gave off white smoke. Wolken also carried a .22 caliber semiautomatic pistol with a suppressor. I carried the PRC-25 radio and a bunch of hand grenades, while Davison and the Vietnamese carried several claymore mines and extra batteries for the PRC-25. Sau and all the Americans carried URC-10 emergency radios. Every team member carried signal mirrors, colored panels and hand grenades, both the old M-26 grenades and baseball grenades. Because intelligence reports said there was water in the area, I added a few more hand grenades in an extra canteen holder, in lieu of water. We also carried iodine water purification pills for any jungle water we used. On this target, I went in light on water, but packed an extra C-ration of fruit.

At first light on 6 October, the weather was crystal clear. In the morning, most spike team members looked west toward the mountains to check out the weather. When Wolken and I looked west, there was no question about it; the weather had broken and it was ST Idaho's turn to cross the fence into the Prairie Fire AO. The weather was so brilliantly clear that it reminded me of the perfect day to go down to the shore in New Jersey. As I looked west on that Sunday morning, I wondered what my family and friends were doing in Covenant Presbyterian Church in Trenton, New Jersey. The fact that it was Sunday appeared not to register with anyone in FOB 1. During a quick briefing in the S-3 Operations Room, Wolken pointed out the LZs he had selected and S-3 reminded us that intelligence reports stated that there was an NVA POW camp which contained U.S. troops within our target area, at the extreme western edge of it. Were there any men from MACV-SOG in there? American airmen?

Shortly before we left FOB 1, the team posed for two photographs over the strong, bitter protests of Sau, Hiep and Phuoc. They said we'd jinx the mission. A few minutes later, ST Idaho was loaded into a three-quarter ton truck, driven the short distance across Highway 1 and onto the helicopter pad. Soon the Kingbees were flying west on the hour-plus flight to Laos. Those long flights to the target area were peaceful and memorable because we were flying high where the air was cooler and cleaner, as there was no pungent odor of human excrement coming from the rice paddies.

In addition, from 4,000 feet, South Vietnam, Laos and Cambodia were beautiful. During these flights, I often thought about my grandfather's and my cousins' farms in Belle Mead, New Jersey. In October they would be plowing and harrowing the fields, preparing for winter and harvesting any late crops. Smelling whiffs of aviation exhaust from the Kingbee reminded me of driving my cousins' Farmall tractors across the Garden State farmland in more peaceful times. As the H-34s churned westward, my vision always seemed better, aided by the adrenaline that was flowing in anticipation of the unknown. Once over Laos, the door gunners test-fired their ancient, Browning .30 caliber machine guns. The terrain below became more mountainous. The A Shau Valley's crater-pocked valley floor ended all visions of farmland. As we flew into our target area and Covey showed the Vietnamese helicopter pilots where the LZ was located, the morning calm spent enjoying the landscape ended. The adrenaline started dripping into the blood stream at a higher volume as our Kingbee went into a diving spiral, spinning madly toward the earth.

Instead of the churning sound that the Kingbee's piston engine usually made, it was kicked into neutral and the pilot auto-rotated in a downward spiral. The G-force pushed my stomach upward into my chest. While descending, Wolken sat in the door, looking at the

LZ itself for any troop movement or suspicious activities. I squatted behind him, my hand on his left shoulder, watching the perimeter of the LZ for any enemy movement. Now the blood was pounding through our veins. At the last second, the pilot engaged the engine and the helicopter flared out, quickly coming to hover a few feet off the ground. The Kingbee pilot brought the right side of the aircraft close to a bomb crater that had been blasted out of the side of a mountain. By the size of the crater, it appeared as though the bomb had been at least a 500-pounder. Before Wolken could jump out, the Kingbee lurched upwards a few feet. The Vietnamese door gunner tapped me on the shoulder, urging me to tell Wolken to exit the Kingbee. There was a lot of elephant grass, some of it 12 feet tall, on the outside of the crater and other jungle vegetation inside the crater, making it difficult to see the ground. At first, I wondered why Wolken hadn't jumped, when I thought he could have exited the chopper. The Kingbee dropped down several more feet and much to my surprise, as the rotor wash from the Sikorsky separated the thick, tall elephant grass, it revealed a steep drop on both sides of the crater lip. The door gunner tapped Wolken on the shoulder, trying to nudge him into exiting the chopper. Wolken sat there as calm as he did during poker games. He was not going to exit the Kingbee until he was ready. Even I became impatient with Wolken, but I didn't say anything. He had more experience than me and from where I was squatting I couldn't see the ground. Finally, the right wheel of the Kingbee touched the bomb crater that was our LZ.

As the Kingbee wheel touched the lip of the bomb crater again, Wolken jumped out and promptly disappeared in the elephant grass on the outside of the crater. The Kingbee skipped up several feet. I couldn't see Wolken; hell, I couldn't see the ground! Now the harried door gunner was nudging me. As the Kingbee settled downward toward the crater, I thought I could jump from the lower step on the Kingbee, a distance that appeared to be of only two or three feet, and land on the crater. I jumped. But I didn't land on top of the crater. I didn't jump far at all. The weight of all the equipment, weapons and ammo carried me nearly straight down so I didn't land squarely atop the crater as I had envisioned. Instead, I slipped down the outside lip. Damn, why had I jumped? I still hadn't seen Wolken. The hillside was much steeper than I had realized and the ground was muddy and slippery. I kept rolling down the hill, in the same direction as Wolken. Sau jumped out of the chopper and landed atop the crater as the Kingbee quickly left the area and the second bird moved in toward the bomb crater. Davison, Hiep and Phuoc quickly exited the Kingbee and successfully landed on the crater's lip. The four of them straddled the crater's lip and silently mocked Wolken and me as we struggled up the slippery slope, trying to return to the top of the crater. It took us several minutes to rejoin the team. By the time I reached the top, I was ready for an extraction. I was exhausted.

As I stood in the sweltering morning sun, I radioed Spider, who was flying overhead in the O-2 Covey, and gave him a team okay. (Back in S-3, a major would mark on a board that ST Idaho was on the ground. A radio-teletype Special Forces troop would send a coded message to MACV-SOG headquarters in Saigon giving the exact hour of insertion in the AO.) Spider said he'd stand by for 10 more minutes before releasing the air assets that were flying in a holding pattern a short distance away. Ten minutes later I broke squelch three times for the final team okay. Spider told me to be careful. As we moved away from the LZ, Phuoc was walking point with Sau behind him. Wolken was third. I was behind him, Davison was behind me and Hiep brought up the rear. We patrolled for 10 minutes and then paused for 10 minutes to listen. This was the time frame of movement we strived for while on the ground. During the listening pause, I noted how much cooler the triple-canopy jungle felt than the hot, open area around the bomb crater. We couldn't see the sky because there was so much jungle growth above us, and the trees appeared to have no end as they reached skyward. The contrast between the bomb crater in the sun and the darker, cooler jungle was startling. I liked it in the jungle, and we were finally on the ground. We had good weather, too. If we made contact with the NVA, Spider and his fellow Covey rider, Pat Watkins, would round up as many air assets as we needed. There would be none of the weather-related problems that ST Alabama had experienced on Saturday.

Ten minutes later we moved out. Although our primary mission was general reconnaissance of the AO, Wolken and I wanted to get as close as we could to the NVA-operated POW camp. In recent months, we were told that there had been several attempts by SOG teams and "other assets" to get as close to the POW camp as possible. At least one spike team had reported smelling food cooking in the area, but before it could get near enough to confirm the POW camp, the NVA drove them out. In those POW camps, we knew the Americans would be abused and beaten relentlessly by their captors. As I was mulling this over in my mind, I heard a muffled expletive and a second expletive from the front of our team. Phuoc suddenly moved to the right, Sau moved to the left and Wolken ducked down.

"Bees!" Wolken said, through gritted teeth. I signaled Davison and Hiep and backed up toward them. I didn't want to get stung under normal circumstances, and certainly not during the middle of a mission. Bees! Were they NVA commando bees? My respect for Phuoc grew in leaps and bounds because he had been stung several times, yet kept his cool under fire, so to speak. After we moved away from the bees, Wolken called a quick break so he, Sau and Phuoc could apply mud to their bee stings. I silently thanked the bee gods for sparing me.

After the trio finished tending to their stings, we moved out, returning to the move-10-minutes, wait-10-minutes pace through the jungle, the principle being that in the jungle, you can occasionally learn more from hearing than seeing. As always, we stayed away from trails, avoided open areas and moved with great caution. We knew the NVA and any indigenous personnel consigned to work for them would have an intimate knowledge of the land and its animals and we went to extreme measures to avoid any contact with them. Whenever we paused for our 10 minute listening break, the bird and animal sounds would gain more volume, as though when humans moved, they feared the two-legged animal. Half an hour after the bees, Phuoc signaled that he heard a lot of activity in front of him.

Soon we all heard it.

Whatever it was, it was headed toward us and it was moving fast. At first, we thought it was an NVA regiment charging toward us. For a few gut-wrenching moments, I recalled a One-Zero talking about how the NVA had recently overrun his spike team minutes after landing in an A Shau Valley target. He said the first rounds fired by the NVA were shocking because of the volume of fire and the AK-47s being so close to him. The sound kept moving toward us. The jungle was so thick the team didn't have time to get on line to face the direction of the noise. I got behind a log, pulled a pin from an M-26 frag grenade and placed my CAR-15 on full automatic. And then we were overrun…by hordes of chattering monkeys swinging through the trees. It looked like a scene from an early Tarzan movie. Phuoc pointed his CAR-15 at the retreating monkeys, pretending to fire on full automatic at them. The comic relief garnered exaggerated laughs as the team collectively regrouped and returned to the business at hand.

Around noon, we heard the first shot fired by an enemy tracker. Just a single, solitary shot. It sounded far away, yet it was unnerving. Wolken glanced at me. We both looked at Sau. Sau was unhappy. Had they found our trail? Were they NVA or local trackers? By 1400 they had located our trail. There were several shots from different positions behind us. During the next few hours, there were several times that shots rang out. The team moved with more urgency, more concern. We were the hunted. By dusk, the trackers had moved through the thick jungle quicker than we had and were gaining on us. We kept moving until last light when we set up our RON (Remain Over Night) site.

Due to the dense jungle, our RON was linear instead of the preferred circular configuration. We were close enough to each other that every team member could touch another team member. I moved out of the RON to place a claymore mine on our eastern perimeter. I was in the middle of a growth of ferns when the tracker startled us. He fired one round, which echoed through the jungle and sounded as though he was less than 10 meters from our southern perimeter. How did he get so close, so fast, so quietly? That shot sent a chill through my body that was hard to shake. I continued moving through the jungle to place the claymore on our perimeter. It took a lot of time in the growing darkness. I finally found a tree that was far enough away from our RON that it would protect the team from the claymore's back blast, yet give us a line of defense against attack. I placed a few pieces of black electrical tape to it, anchoring it to the tree. During Green Beret training at the Special Forces Training Group in Ft. Bragg, SF instructors always cautioned us about the enemy turning claymore mines around. When they turned them around, the full force of the plastic explosive and 700 steel ball bearings would hit the SF troops instead of the enemy. I hoped the tape would prevent or at least hinder any effort to turn the claymore mine toward ST Idaho.

As the night slipped deeper into darkness, the trackers dominated my mind. I couldn't get over how close the last gunshot had been to our team. Around 2000 hours, I thought I heard movement from the spot where the tracker had fired the last shot. The first few times he moved, the sound of his movement was barely audible. Because the tracker was so close, no one on the team ate immediately after setting up our RON. Time seemed to slow down as the jungle became pitch black. I could move my hand in front of my face and not see it. Several times, I looked at my watch's luminescent dial, tucked under my black contact gloves, and the hands seemed to be moving in slow motion. I thought the calendar date would never change to 7 October. With the jungle so dark, so quiet, and with the tracker so close, all of us were on edge. Again, I thought I heard the tracker move around toward our eastern perimeter. The movements were slow, almost silent, almost imperceptible. Was it my imagination? Around midnight, each team member was in various stages of preparing some sort of food, which was a challenge in the darkness. Also, I radioed a team okay to the airborne command center that flew over Southeast Asia 24 hours a day. Because it was so quiet, I only had a limited commo check, breaking squelch on the PRC-25 at the appointed hour. I didn't go into detail about the trackers because they were so near to us and I was worried about the NVA's RDF (radio direction finder) capabilities, which we were told were improving.

After chow, Sau and Hiep went to sleep. Both men had been working with SF and MACV-SOG for four years and they were pros. They got their sleep when they could. Phuoc remained alert. Later they'd rotate the watch. The tracker had Wolken, Davison and me on edge. It was the first time we had encountered a tracker so uncomfortably close to the team. I couldn't sleep. Between 0100 and 0200 hours, I listened to the tracker continue to skirt our team's perimeter. Around 0200 hours, it sounded as though he had stopped in front of my claymore mine. Had the NVA soldier found it? And if he had, was he trying to turn it around toward ST Idaho?

I wasn't 100 percent sure, so I turned to Wolken and whispered that I thought the NVA was in front of my claymore mine. Because Wolken was hard of hearing in one ear, I repeated my suspicions and my fear of him turning the claymore around toward us. I asked him if I could detonate it. He said no. I thought I heard movement in front of it again. Other than that slight sound, the jungle was deadly quiet. I asked Wolken again about the claymore. I couldn't tell what his answer was, so I detonated it. The magnitude of noise, light and debris flying through the air seemed doubled, because the night had been so dark and quiet before. I was amazed. The blast woke up the team and half the jungle.

As the debris was settling, Wolken said, "What the hell did you do that for?"

"I thought you said to do it."

"No, I said don't do it!"

"Well, if that was an NVA tracker or one of those sappers we've heard about, he's no threat to us anymore." From the hissing that came from Sau's direction, I could tell he was unhappy, too. Regardless, for the remainder of the night, there was no more movement around our perimeter. Wolken, Davison and I took turns sleeping.

A short while before sunrise, a tiny sound woke me. All my life I had been a heavy sleeper, now it was a different story. I heard the slight noise again. I didn't move. I knew I had heard something, but I couldn't distinguish the sound. As I lay there motionless, I heard it again. It was above me, not on the ground. The sound was too small to be monkeys and to calm to be angry bees. Now I was fully awake. I slid my thumb over the selector switch on my CAR-15 for peace of mind. If needed, it would be ready to fire in less than a second. I checked my rucksack. Because we slept with at least one arm in our rucksacks, I knew it was ready to go in the event of enemy contact. All the while, I remained motionless. The only part of my body moving was my eyelids. I opened them carefully as an additional precaution. It took a few minutes before it dawned on me that I had heard tiny droplets of morning dew landing on the leaves above us. Six months ago, I wouldn't have heard a freight train roll past me. Now, dewdrops were my wake-up call.

Before first light, the entire team was alert and ready for an attack. In recent months, a few SOG spike teams in the C&C operation had reported being attacked by NVA troops shortly after dawn. Several of the team members placed claymores outside our perimeter for added firepower in the event of attack. First light and sunset were dangerous times for spike teams. After the previous night's scare from the tracker, we didn't know what to expect. As morning's first light began to penetrate the jungle's dark blanket, we prepared to move out. The claymores were pulled back in. The first 10 minutes of movement were extremely cautious. During the first listening break we heard no unusual noises, although there seemed to be less animal and bird noise throughout the jungle than we had heard on Sunday. If I listened closely, I could still hear dewdrops landing on jungle leaves. During the pause, several of the men began to put water and seasoning into plastic bags used to prepare the new, state-of-the-culinary-art rations we carried to the field. Most Americans carried LRPs, the freeze-dried rations of chicken and rice, beef or chicken and vegetables, and chili, while the Vietnamese team members had a plastic pouch filled with rice, flavoring, meat and spices that were designed specifically for indigenous troops. The men would take turns seasoning the rations and wrapping them tightly before placing the cold plastic bag next to their body, usually around the stomach. The bag would remain there for an hour or two, until the body heat made the ration more palatable. During the later listening breaks, the men would take turns eating, while the others remained on full alert.

Off in the distance I could hear the Cessna with the Covey pilot and Spider. I gave him a quick SITREP including the tracker being close to our perimeter at last light. As usual, Spider urged caution while moving through the jungle and to not take any chances that would expose the team to extra risk.

At some point during the morning, we moved down a hillside and crossed a small brook. The water was refreshingly cold and remarkably clear, reminding me of the water we used to drink in the White Mountains of New Hampshire. I could see the bottom as clear as day. Several of us refilled our canteens and placed iodine pills in the plastic containers before moving out and before drinking the water. I had had a bout with amoebic dysentery and didn't want to take a chance on it happening again. Each team member filled his canteens one at a time while the remaining five men remained alert for contact with the enemy. Throughout the morning we heard no more tracker shots or any obvious enemy movement in our vicinity. We heard no trucks, no tanks and had not crossed any major trails. The only thing that concerned me was the fact that Sau's eyes began to get bigger as the day progressed. But when Sau said there was "beaucoup VC, beaucoup VC," it surprised me. Actually, it scared me, because I hadn't heard or seen anything. Wolken had heard Sau and was concerned as well. What had we missed that Sau hadn't?

At noontime Spider returned to the AO, never flying directly over the team, but close enough where I could hear the twin engines of the little push-pull aircraft. Deep in the heart of the Prairie Fire AO and far away from any friendly ground support, just hearing the Covey and Spider's voice was comforting. I gave Spider a team okay, but told him Sau was nervous. Spider told me to trust Sau's instincts. Before he left, he asked if we could hit him with a mirror signal. Making visual contact with an aircraft from the middle of the jungle reminded me of finding a needle in a haystack. Sometimes the process could take a long time. We were fortunate because we were near a clearing on the side of the hill. I started to talk Spider towards us. I told Spider that he was north of my location. After a few wrong turns, I told Spider that we were located at his nine o'clock, with the O-2's engine being 12 o'clock. The pilot changed course and shortly he passed over our position.

"Bingo." I said. Then the pilot turned away and they looked for our mirror signal. Phuoc flashed his mirror when I gave him a signal.

Finally, Spider said, "Roger on your location. You've covered some territory. There aren't many LZs down there, so keep that in mind. Look for possible LZ sites in case Charlie hits you." He said he'd return at 1600 hours, as another C&C team was on the ground closer to the DMZ river.

Wolken had Sau and Hiep swap places in the team's line of march. Sau was now in the rear tail gunner slot, I was in front of Sau in the fifth slot, and Hiep was in the second slot, behind the point man, Phuoc. Around 1300 hours, ST Idaho broke out of the thick triple canopy jungle and emerged onto a grassy field. It felt odd being out in the open. We moved cautiously through the field, with thick jungle on our right and a steep drop on our left. The grassy area descended gently and wound to the right, before taking a sharp switchback about 130 degrees to the left. After the switchback, we started climbing up a fairly steep hill. In a few minutes we covered a lot of ground because there was no thick jungle. And then I heard Sau hiss like a snake. I turned with a start and saw Sau crouched, his CAR-15 tucked under his arm, ready to fire. He pointed across to the hill we had just descended, to the narrow grassy area, a short distance from where we had emerged from the jungle. We stood looking across the ravine at two NVA soldiers armed with AK-47s and smiles.

Smiles?

It appeared as if they had emerged from the jungle at the same spot we had. What the hell was going on? I had never seen NVA soldiers so close. I had never seen them out in the open. The fact that they were standing there, looking cocky as hell, was mind-boggling. I had assumed that in the Prairie Fire AO, such a meeting would be a fight to the death, but they didn't raise their weapons or make any hostile moves. They just stood there with their arms crossed and smiled at Sau and me. And they looked much bigger and much stronger than I had imagined the average NVA soldier. They looked to be taller than Phuoc, who, by Vietnamese standards, was a tall man. Because they were no more than 45 to 60 yards away, I pulled out my sawed-off M-79, indicating to Sau I'd like to permanently wipe the smiles off those smirking faces.

"No! Beaucoup VC, di, di (go, go)!" I turned to catch up to Wolken. Sau was moving backwards up the hill just as quickly as I was advancing toward the remainder of the team, which had continued moving up the grassy area without realizing that Sau and I had stopped. All the while, Sau's eyes were locked on the NVA until the grassy area we were climbing wound toward the right. When I finally caught up to Wolken, I told him what had happened. Immediately we headed up the high, steep ground to our right and into the jungle. The vegetation became thick again, although not as thick as the triple canopy cover we were under earlier in the morning. Within an hour, we were atop a knoll big enough to hold ST Idaho. It was an ideal spot for a team break. Wolken had pushed the team hard. We moved for intervals of time much longer than 10 minutes. Wolken had wanted to get to high ground as soon as possible. He told me to get out the PRC-25 and to get Spider back over us ASAP. Heeding Spider's advice, we had searched for potential LZs without finding one. Then Wolken and I looked at Sau.

By now, Sau's eyes were bigger than saucers. "If you raise Spider," Wolken said, "tell him I'm declaring a Prairie Fire Emergency. If he says anything about not hearing any gunshots, tell him to fuck off, I'll explain later. Sau's never been wrong. Look at him." As we spoke, Sau looked at us.

"Beaucoup VC. Beaucoup VC. Call Kingbees now!" he whispered. I put the long antenna on the PRC-25 and made several calls on the primary, secondary and alternate frequencies. For a brief moment I wondered to myself if Sau was overreacting. From the time we had sighted the two brash NVA, I had heard nothing. We had heard no tracker gunshots. Nothing. My attempts to reach someone with the PRC-25 were fruitless.

Worried that the battery might be low, I replaced it and tried again, but to no avail. I turned on the emergency beeper on the URC-10. The distress signal was on an ultra-high frequency channel that was supposed to be monitored at all times by any aircraft flying over the Prairie Fire AO. The radio had two modes: one for voice communications and one for the emergency signal that was supposed to carry for miles. Some aircraft had homing devices that could vector the pilots to our signal. We weren't on a mountaintop, but at least we were higher than we had been an hour earlier when Sau spotted the smiling NVA. I turned to the voice channel on the URC-10.

"I have a Prairie Fire Emergency. Team in distress. I have a Prairie Fire Emergency. Can anyone hear me?" I spoke in a hushed tone with my hand cupped over my mouth and the radio. I looked at my watch. We still had more than 100 minutes before our next scheduled commo check with Spider at 1600 hours. I thought of an old lumberjack's line from the summer I worked in Yosemite National Park: "If no one hears you yell timber, they won't know the tree is falling." No one responded. I returned to the PRC-25 and made several more attempts, again with the same results. Hot and sweaty from the arduous pace that Wolken had forced on us, and frustrated with the inability to raise anyone on the radios, I sat down with my back against the PRC-25 and opened a can of apricots.

I was facing south and just starting to sip the sweet apricot nectar when all hell broke loose. The green jungle around us erupted with deafening full-automatic blasts from NVA AK-47s and our CAR-15s. Because my back was to them, I hadn't seen Sau's warning gestures or watched him get the jump on the approaching NVA. I remember spilling apricot nectar on the stock of my CAR-15 as I turned to my left where the majority of the NVA gunfire was coming from. Foolishly, my first thoughts were that I'd have to clean the nectar off of my weapon and not to spill the entire can of apricots because I had waited so damned long to eat them. They were always a treat in the jungle.

During the initial seconds of the firefight, I remember Sau and Phuoc yelling profanities at the NVA as they fired on full automatic. The crack of AK-47 rounds had never sounded louder or closer. All I could see from our perimeter was gun smoke, the red and orange blasts coming from the darker-than-ever green jungle, and green AK-47 tracers flying over our heads. In an odd sort of way, there was an eerie beauty to the scene. The thunderous fury of dozens of men blasting away at each other on full automatic, within 10 feet of each other, killed all other sounds. The eardrums were numbed. Adrenaline had slammed into our bloodstreams and was now screaming through our systems. It heightened all senses. It extended time. For example, a CAR-15 fires 20 rounds of 5.56mm high velocity ammunition in less than one and a half seconds. Yet those first opening moments of combat with the NVA seemed much longer than a second and a half. Ordinarily, when firing on full automatic, the weapon expended rounds quickly and we trained ourselves to try and gauge when that last round in the magazine was slamming into the receiver. Some men placed a tracer round in their magazine as a visual cue. During that firefight, it seemed as though I counted the rounds leaving the CAR-15 and knew exactly when the 18th and last round was exiting the weapon. Also during that first exchange, Phuoc was slightly behind me to my right, and since I was on the ground, he was firing over my shoulder. That exposed my right ear to an almost full blast from his CAR-15. The explosions were painful, but Phuoc saved my life. I had aimed my CAR-15 down the hill toward the largest number of AK-47 muzzle flashes that I could see to my left. What I hadn't seen were a handful of NVA soldiers who broke out of the jungle to the right and had opened fire on us. Phuoc realized I hadn't seen the NVA troops coming up the hill. So he got to my right and blasted them back into the jungle. I was so focused on the first muzzle flashes that I had completely missed the others. If those NVA soldiers had advanced a few more feet, I would have been history and the remainder of the team, which was on my left, would have been at risk.

That time warp continued when everybody ran out of bullets simultaneously. The only sounds audible were the metallic clicks of cold magazines being slammed into hot machine guns and bolts slamming shut to resume the firefight. A key element in any firefight is the race to reload after the initial contact. On 7 October 1968, ST Idaho won the race. Nobody was faster than Sau, Hiep and Phuoc at getting the first magazine out, the second one in and returning full-automatic gunfire on the enemy. Within seconds we had gained fire superiority. The months and months of training on the range under the tutelage of Spider and Wolken, all of the live-fire drills, all of the live-fire races to see who finished reloading first, paid off. All other games in life were frivolous and irrelevant. In this deadly game, if you missed hitting the target, you died.

The majority of the enemy fire was coming at us from the east and south sides of the small knoll. Wolken and I chucked a couple of M-26s down the side of the knoll, in between blasts of full auto on our CAR-15s. As soon as we gained complete fire superiority, I turned on the URC-10 beeper and started screaming into the PRC-25, "I have a fucking Prairie Fire Emergency!" That bitter, fear-laced plea was greeted by complete silence.

Wolken was less than subtle. "Keep yelling until you get someone."

A key factor in ST Idaho's favor that day was the small knoll that Wolken had driven us to. The jungle was so thick and the knoll so small, that only a score of NVA could rush us at once. They weren't the fast-moving, fear-inspiring charges that the NVA were known for successfully executing, either. Here, the jungle worked against them, but the NVA kept coming. At one point, Wolken pulled me over, pointed into the jungle and said, "Look. They're stacking up the dead bodies to get to us. Hiep showed me. Can you believe it? And they keep coming. Hell, if we kill enough of them, the body stack will be as high as we are." Because the jungle area was so dark, at first I couldn't tell exactly what I was looking at, but Wolken was right, the NVA were stacking bodies and firing at us from behind their dead comrades. A lot of NVA soldiers died in those first few minutes of hell on earth.

For more than an hour, my cries and screams into the radio and the URC-10 beeper went unanswered as the NVA mounted more attacks. There was no need for radio secure procedures now. The hide and seek portion of the game was over. Now it was simply a matter of survival. My respect for the NVA's tenacity grew that day, but the hill, the jungle and our CAR-15s worked against them as they continued to pile up or drag away more bodies. With no help around, conserving ammo while keeping the enemy back became a top priority. There were no more full automatic blasts from us. Although we had been in contact less than two hours, it felt like we had been fighting for several. As the team anxiously waited for help from above the few team members pitted against the many NVA seemed ludicrous in terms of survival. The enormity of the jungle hit home. I had never seen trees that grew so tall. My 23rd birthday seemed a thousand years away. Obviously, when a spike team made contact with the NVA and then had to wait for Covey, or any airborne asset, there was some mental anguish involved. Any time a team got help in less than an hour or two, people boasted about it as though it were a minor miracle because the AO was so far from Vietnam.

Finally I heard the Texas drawl of Spider on the radio. An F-4 Phantom jet returning from a bombing run in Northern Laos had heard the beeper and called him. I told Spider we had a "Prairie Fire Emergency." Spider said that he had also called the Judge and the Executioner. Thankfully, we had made the mirror contact with Spider earlier and he was able to pinpoint our location in a matter of minutes. Soon Spider was over us. He told me to pop smoke. Our SOP was not to say what color of smoke grenade we would use, assuming the NVA were monitoring our FM frequency. I popped a yellow smoke. He said he saw two yellows, which meant the NVA were monitoring our frequency and had guessed what color we would use.

We changed frequencies and I popped a violet smoke. A few minutes later, the first A-1E Skyraider arrived on target and made a gun run on our eastern perimeter. His wingman made the first napalm run on the south side.

"Put your heads down. I'm going to make you sweat," he said. He brought it so close we could feel the heat from the deadly jelly. A few seconds later we smelled burning flesh. As he dived toward us a third time, the pilot drawled, "It's crispy critter time." The napalm run was so close we could feel the air being sucked away from us by the exploding material. If the jelly landed on a person's skin, it would continue to burn either until it burned itself out, or was deprived of air by mud or some other substance. The Spads' arrival changed the tempo of the firefight. When the NVA heard the old World War II plane making another run, they charged us in a desperate attempt to get as close to us as they could in order to avoid the Skyraider's deadly ordnance. The NVA were getting close to the belt.

Their urge for survival and drive to get at us combined for a surreal rhythm to the communists' movements: the A-1E Skyraider would strike, and as it roared toward the earth the NVA would push toward us. Then we'd blast away and push them back down the hill. Again, they'd hear the Skyraider and its pending arrival pushed them back toward us in a bizarre death dance.

Then an Air Force pilot in an F-4 Phantom arrived on station. "Tell your people the ordnance will arrive on target before you hear me or the rounds," the pilot said. I told the team to put their heads down. The phenomenon of having bullets tearing into a target before anyone could hear the aircraft which delivered them was unbelievable. The jungle in front of us was shredded by the F¬4's gun run. Within a minute or two, his wingman dropped two 500-pound bombs. The change in aircraft staggered the NVA for a few moments. Right then and there, I thanked the Lord for Uncle Sam's Air Force.

The Judge and the Executioner rolled in right behind the fast mover. The Judge's minigun run was real close to our perimeter. Seconds later, the Executioner followed behind him, firing several 2.75 mm rockets while his door gunners blasted away with their M-60 machine guns. Because we hadn't expended any ordnance to our west, we ran the gunships over the western edge of our perimeter.

They drew no enemy fire either.

By now, each team member had developed lanes of fire down the hill through the jungle vegetation and grass, and vice versa; the NVA weapons had cut away jungle vegetation in small swaths, too. During the early contact I had fired my M-79 twice into what sounded like several NVA troops advancing toward me in the jungle. I couldn't see them, but I could hear them. Each blast had cleared some vegetation at ground level. At one point, while I was talking to Spider, I thought I saw something moving in my lane of fire, slowly advancing up the hill. I was anchoring the southern end of the line of defense. At first, I wasn't sure what it was or if the heat of the day was giving me optical illusions, but we were between air strikes when I saw the movement again. I watched it closely. Finally, I figured it out. It was the ass of an NVA soldier crawling up the hill through the grass. I was talking to Spider about the next series of air strikes, so I casually kept an eye on this soldier's progress through the grass for a few minutes. He moved slowly and when he did, all I could see was his butt. All the while, I had my CAR-15 pointed at him while I was talking to Spider.

"Wait one," I told Spider. The NVA had started to raise his head. He appeared to be trying to pinpoint where he was. Because the F-4 strikes had hit so fast and hard, no one on ST Idaho had fired their weapon in the last few minutes, thus he probably wasn't sure of where we were. Although he was still some distance away from me and he was crawling through the grass, I fired one round from my CAR-15 and hit him in the head.

"Damn, Tilt, what happened?! You just blew off my ear! The next time you fire your weapon, tell me, or at least don't hold down the transmission button." When I fired the round from my CAR-15, I didn't realize it, but I had held down the rubber-covered transmission button on the handset, keying an open microphone to Spider's poor ears.

For the next few hours, Spider and I worked numerous fast movers and A-1Es, hitting the southern and eastern perimeters hard. The Air Force poured thousands of 7.62mm minigun rounds, 20mm rounds, several 500-pound bombs and numerous napalm and CBU

(Cluster Bomb Unit) canisters on the dauntless NVA troops. In between gun runs, Wolken and I would fire our M-79s upward, like mortars, through one small opening in the jungle canopy toward the NVA positions. Directing the air strikes made me feel as though I brought some inherent value to the team. For months, Hiep, Sau and Phuoc had complained about my feet being too big, thus making too much noise in the jungle and me being too tall. Since the NVA had hit us, no one complained about my big feet or the fact that I was yelling too loud into the radio.

About a half hour before dusk, Spider told us the Kingbees were on their way. By that time the Judge and Executioner had refueled, reloaded and were returning a few minutes in front of them. Everyone on ST Idaho was dangerously low on ammo, grenades and M-79 rounds. We also knew that as soon as the NVA heard the choppers heading in for us, the enemy soldiers would muster all of the firepower that they could bring to bear on the helicopters. The only problem was that we had no immediate LZ in sight. The NVA gunfire was too intense to be extracted on ropes. The vegetation surrounding us was too thick for a landing. We had to get to a location where the helicopters could at least hover for us. About ten minutes before the Kingbees arrived, Spider was running F-4s and Spads around our perimeter like a master conductor. The tactical air strikes were constant and allowed us to reduce the amount of ammo and grenades we fired at the enemy. And sure enough, as soon as the helicopter's props were audible from our perimeter, the NVA stepped up the attacks against us. I remember thinking that if it were me in the NVA uniform, I'd back off and let the choppers take us out, but the persistent NVA launched one more wave attack, although it lacked the fury and surprise of the earlier ones.

Before the Kingbees moved in to attempt to pick us up, Spider had the Judge and the Executioner make gun runs so close to our perimeter that we could hear the expended shell casings from the gunship's M-60s and minigun falling to earth. Through all of the excitement, I told Wolken that Spider had spotted an area west of our perimeter where a Kingbee might be able to settle into some elephant grass for us. Wolken and Hiep passed the word to the team and we started moving toward the area. From our location, we couldn't see the elephant grass and I had assumed we were locked into double or triple-canopy jungle. Again, the Judge and the Executioner hammered our eastern flank as we moved toward the tentative LZ.

Spider was right. Within a matter of minutes, we were out of the jungle and into the elephant grass as the Kingbee moved toward the small area about 10 to 15 yards west from our perimeter. The Kingbee could not land, but Captain Thinh roared in, chopping the tops off several small trees, and hovered 10 feet off the ground, waiting for ST Idaho. As had happened earlier in the day, each movement, each breath, each thought unfolded in slow motion, similar to the action scenes in a Sam Peckinpah movie. And as ST Idaho moved to the chopper, Mother Nature threw us a new curve: 10 yards of elephant grass.

The elephant grass was between 6 and 12 feet tall, and the ground was muddy and slippery. I went first, trying to blaze a trail through it. I tried using my machete-like blade, which had a savage hook on the end of it. But the grass was so thick, I could not hack through it quickly enough. After a few moments, I fell. As I landed, Wolken ran over me and plowed forward. The only good thing about the fall was that my body pushed through some more elephant grass. Phuoc stepped on me, too. When Wolken fell, I returned the favor. Again, I fell and again, I was his stepping-stone. The progress toward the hovering Kingbee was painstakingly, maddeningly slow. At one point, I felt as though I was stuck in a living horror show; salvation, the Kingbee, was only feet away, but Mother Nature held us back while the NVA tried to kill us. As we inched slowly toward the Kingbee, the helicopter's rotor wash pushed the tall elephant grass down, bending it toward us, adding one more to the number of roadblocks Mother Nature had in store for us.

As we moved slowly toward the camouflage-painted Sikorsky, the cacophony of noise surrounding us reached a new level of madness. The NVA knew why the Kingbee was there and they knew we were vulnerable. If they were going to collect any bounty for killing an American, especially a SOG One-Zero, this was the moment to strike. Again, Spider directed the Judge and Executioner through gun runs along the eastern and southern perimeters while the Kingbee hovered on the western edge. The noise was almost overwhelming; as we got closer to the chopper, its piston engine and the sound of the rotor wash became more dominating. Meanwhile the gunships roared past, attempting to hold back the NVA, who were now mounting one last attack. Someone, possibly Davison, had stretched out a claymore mine and detonated it, adding to the pandemonium.

Sau and Hiep covered our frantic, desperate drive to the chopper. After taking 10 minutes to cover those last 10 yards, we reached the hovering Kingbee, which was about eight feet above the ground. Phuoc set up an impromptu security watch on the western side of the rotor wash. A quick check of my ammunition revealed I was down to one frag grenade, one white phosphorous grenade and two magazines of CAR-15 rounds. If I didn't get extracted, that last frag grenade would be mine. There was no way in hell I was going to be a POW, especially after all of the NVA ST Idaho and TAC Air had killed. If I had to use it, I'd take as many NVA with me as I could.

The rotor wash began to work a little bit in our favor once we were under the helicopter. That small change gave me a glimmer of hope as it was pushing the elephant grass down slightly from directly under the helicopter. Wolken arrived and stood across from me with his back facing north, or toward the front of the aircraft. I stood facing him. When Davison moved toward Wolken and I, we lifted him into the hovering bird. Then we threw Hiep and Sau in. They joined the Kingbee door gunner, firing their weapons from the chopper toward the NVA. The ST Idaho members followed team SOP; each member fired out of one Kingbee window. The old chopper had windows, actually window frames, and once we entered the aircraft, the first man into the bird went to the nearest window on the port side of the aircraft. The second man joined him at the next window. The third man went to the starboard side of the helicopter.

That way, there would be two people firing from each side of the aircraft. The port side was the most vulnerable on the H-34 because there were no door gunners on that side of the aircraft. Wolken and I grabbed Phuoc and tossed him into the Kingbee.

At some point during the craziness, I looked up at the pilot of the Kingbee, Captain Thinh. He was above all of the madness on the ground, completely calm and collected, while his aircraft took numerous hits from enemy rounds. What made his demeanor all the more extraordinary was how it contrasted with our adrenaline-hyped, frantic behavior on the ground. We had been fighting for hours. We were dirty, we were sweaty and we were exhausted. And there sat Captain Thinh, cool as a Rocky Mountain breeze, giving the impression that it was just another milk run. It was as though he said, "No sweat, boys. I've got all day. You just take your time. The stewardess will break out the beverages after you're secured in your seats." Looking at Captain Thinh for that brief moment generated a mental image I'd carry with me forever. Frankly, I never understood how one man could be so steady under so much enemy fire, and keep the chopper hovering.

Finally, Wolken and I were the last two ST Idaho men on the ground. Darkness was closing in, along with the NVA. As the One-Zero, Wolken told me to get into the Kingbee. SOP dictated that the One-Zero was the last man off the ground. He bent down, linking his hands together, in an effort to boost me into the Kingbee. My foot slipped out. By now, my adrenaline was roaring like a runaway subway. I grabbed Wolken by his fatigue jacket and threw the 220-pound staff sergeant into the hovering Kingbee. Before I threw my rucksack up and into the Kingbee, I emptied a magazine into the elephant grass. I tossed my rucksack up and jumped up onto the first rung of the ladder, where Wolken grabbed me by the shoulder and pulled me into the aircraft while yelling into the gunner's ear to get the hell out of there. Captain Thinh wasted no time. He lifted the Kingbee out of its hover as Hiep and Sau blasted away out of the port windows. Phuoc and Davison fired out of the starboard window while Wolken and I emptied our last magazines, directing our last bullets toward the dozens, if not hundreds, of enemy muzzle flashes lighting up the darkness. They were reminiscent of tiny Christmas tree lights. As we ascended skyward, I fired my last M-79 round and dropped my white phosphorous grenade toward the enemy. Its explosion looked spectacular against the dark, deep green jungle. Wolken and Hiep said they heard enemy rounds going through the Kingbee. I couldn't hear anything. They pointed to bullet holes in the walls of the aircraft. For a few brief moments I feared that some of those bullets would damage the old Sikorsky and that we'd crash into the jungle with no ammo, no grenades and no claymore mines. Fortunately, the 7.62 mm NVA rounds hit no vital part on the helicopter or any person onboard.

The hell and fury of the LZ were suddenly behind us. My ears were so numb from the firefight and the gunfire from inside the helicopter that all sound was heavily dampened. The usual noise of the helicopter's rotors was muted. Wolken said something, but I couldn't hear him. Actually, I didn't care about what he said, as I didn't care about any communication unless it was a matter of life or death.

As Captain Thinh's Kingbee climbed upward, the cool night air hit us. Its chill was welcome. There was no giddy celebration. There were no cheers. There may have been some weak smiles at first, acknowledging the fact that ST Idaho had just survived an NVA-dominated hell in the Prairie Fire AO, but there was no celebrating. For a few moments, the Kingbee gained altitude while heading straight south, giving Wolken and me a front-row seat to the final fleeting moments of the sweetest sunset we had ever seen in our lives. Only a few short minutes earlier, I had wondered if I'd ever see another sunset, live another day or eat another meal. For a few moments, I focused on my last hand grenade. Had Captain Thinh not pulled us out of there…I pulled the pin and threw it down toward the jungle.

The unbelievable contrast between the maelstrom on the LZ and the stunning beauty of dusk over Laos and the lush, deep emerald jungle below was overwhelming. As the bird turned east toward Phu Bai, Sau looked at me with a slight smile and gave me a thumbs up.

That moment of respect from the fearless warrior meant more to me than anything anybody would say to me about this mission. I felt as though I had earned my spurs with ST Idaho in Echo Four. I only hoped the next target wouldn't be this rough. One thing was sure; we had survived. How many NVA hadn't? During that ride back to Phu Bai, I took a swallow of warm, iodine-tainted water from my canteen. Ah, it was the sweetest water I had tasted in a long time. The little pleasures in life seemed exaggerated. Of course, I was just happy to be able to drink water because I was somehow still alive to drink it. The chilly air cooled the sweat and gave me the shivers. The last half of the ride was so cold, at one point my teeth were chattering.

When Captain Thinh's Kingbee reached Phu Bai, the dusk had given way to evening darkness. As he began his descent, we moved through warmer air. When he landed, there was no ceremonial circling of FOB 1 before landing on the launch pad. Captain Thinh flew the old bird straight in and landed. As ST Idaho exited the chopper, I climbed up to the pilot's seat and thanked him for saving our lives. I told him he never had to pay for another drink in the FOB 1 Green Beret Lounge again. Never. He smiled and politely said thank you in Vietnamese. His fuel was low and he had no time to socialize. His family was waiting for him in Da Nang. Quickly, Captain Thinh lifted the Kingbee off the ground and gained altitude for his flight south to the 219th Vietnamese Air Force base at Da Nang, showering me with another layer of dirt and grime. I didn't care. It felt good. I looked around the landing pad; there were only a couple of medics who wanted to make sure we had no wounds or serious injuries. Two days earlier, the entire compound was on edge when ST Alabama was in a world of trouble in the A Shau Valley, thus I thought there would be some fellow spike team brothers to greet us. But I had forgotten that an Australian floorshow, complete with what was promised to be some lovely lasses from Down Under, was booked for that Monday night at FOB 1. A short truck ride from the landing pad and across Highway 1 took us down the sandy road and through the puddles to S-3. Wolken went inside for his initial debriefing. Davison asked if I needed any help. I said thanks and asked him to reconnoiter the floorshow for us while I took care of the team. I told him that he had performed well under heavy enemy fire.

"Man, I've never seen anything like that," he said, shaking his head as he walked away.

Because it was late, I went to the mess hall and got some chow for Sau, Hiep and Phuoc. While returning from there, I stopped by the club to get a case of cold sodas for the team. The club was packed, so I asked one of the guys to get the soda. Loaded with soda and chow, I headed to the ST Idaho team room to eat with them. When I entered the small team hootch, Sau appeared as though nothing unusual had happened. Somehow he had already showered. I had never been so close to thunderous death before and I felt numb. Hiep and Sau were more concerned about getting an overnight pass to Phu Luong, the small village just north of FOB 1. As I started eating, I realized how dirty my face was, but didn't care. Phuoc talked about the bees getting him and Sau. Then he regaled the team with the story of us getting overrun by monkeys. Asked how many NVA were out there, he simply replied; "Beaucoup. Beaucoup NVA." Because I was out of ammo, I asked Cau if I could borrow a magazine for my CAR-15. With all of the excitement in camp due to the floorshow, it would be a perfect night for a VC attack. If anything happened during the short walk back to my room in the U.S. billets, I didn't want to be unarmed. Only a few days earlier, one of the SF troops found a marker on the roof of the clubhouse as a target for VC mortar men. To date, the VC mortar men were poor shots.

Thanks to the floorshow, the shower was empty and there was plenty of water. Washing away the day's crud felt good. As I was returning to my room, I saw Spider. I gave him a hug and thanked him for getting us out of Echo Four.

"You done good today, Tilt," he said. But then he reminded me about firing a round from my CAR-15 while the mike was open on my PRC-25, and that I hadn't radioed him with a team okay once Captain Thinh's Kingbee left the LZ. Uncertain of the team's status, he had sent a second Kingbee into the LZ. "Think what would have happened had the NVA shot down that second chopper. How would you feel?" Last but not least, he asked me if I was the guy who threw a hand grenade from the Kingbee long after leaving the LZ. Sheepishly I answered yes. "Don't you realize what that does to pilots? At first, we couldn't tell if it was a late hand grenade or if the NVA were opening up on your Kingbee with anti-aircraft gunfire. Next time, don't throw a hand grenade that late in the extraction." I told Spider I thought it might get down to an NVA and Spider simply frowned and said, "Don't do it, damn it. We were all on edge for hours getting you out of there today and the pilots don't need that shit, comprendé?" Then he told me I had done well on the radio, working the TAC Air with him. "You and Wolken brought the team back in one piece."

"We couldn't have done it without you, Spider. We owe our lives to you."

Finally, I went to the club where the Australian floorshow was in full swing. I met Wolken outside. He told me he had completed his initial intelligence report, but that in the morning he and I would have to return to S-3 to complete a detailed After Action Report. Then we took a minute to quietly acknowledge that each other had performed well under fire.

"That was too close today," Wolken said. "I still can't believe you ran over my ass."

"I was just returning the favor." As we entered the club, the act was between songs and someone yelled that Wolken was entering the club. Someone else grabbed the microphone and reported that Wolken and ST Idaho had been in contact several hours and that we needed a cold drink. I stayed behind Wolken and followed his lead. The man with the mic led a quick "hip, hip, hooray," two or three times. Then he said the show had to go on. The small club was packed and it was sweltering. Since the A Shau Valley sensor mission, I had stopped drinking alcohol, but I was thrilled to get a cold Coke, finally. The floorshow's impromptu stage was small and the dancers certainly weren't as beautiful as we had been led to believe. As with any floorshow, however, a lot of the guys wanted sex and a few guys made fools out of themselves, but no one got hurt. I was just happy to be alive.

Finally, I found a small table where ST Louisiana medic John Walton was sitting. Although he was only a Specialist 4th Class, Walton had run some rough missions. I simply liked the Arkansas native. He was a rock-solid poker player who won thousands of dollars playing pot-limit poker on paydays and he had introduced me to the intricacies of poker. When we weren't in the field, Walton and I would play poker every night. Once the club closed at 2300, he and I would step outside and review the night's hands, personalities and how the cards flowed. Many nights we would sit outside the club talking about poker for hours. He was six-foot-two, always seemed to hold his head to the side a bit, had a good sense of humor and enjoyed the two-hand touch football games we played in camp. We were becoming friends. At Phu Bai in 1968, there was no set course or program for training spike team members. As with many SF operations, the veterans in camp worked with the rookies. I always felt like a sponge, trying to absorb all I could from fellow SF troops. Men running reconnaissance missions usually talked to each other after a mission, whether it was successful or one fraught with problems. The reason was simple: to learn as much as possible about what had happened while that team was on the ground and to pick up any lessons that the team had learned. Of course, there were some missions where the horrors of combat were so severe or human errors so egregious, that some men couldn't or wouldn't talk about them.

Walton fired a series of questions at me about the trackers and NVA tactics. He was an intent listener. Walton said all of the spike team SF troops were keeping tabs on ST Idaho after they had heard that we made heavy contact with the NVA. He said people at FOB 1 were afraid that darkness would settle in before the Kingbees could reach us. From listening to Spider talk to us, they could tell that we were getting low on ammo and hand grenades. I explained how I emptied my last magazine and fired my last CAR-15 bullet as we exited the LZ.

St Idaho, a few days after Echo 4 mission, eating steak behind the Green Beret Lounge. Front row from left: Cau, Minh, Nguyen Cong Hiep, Son and Chau. Back row from left, Nguyen Van Sau, Jim Davidson, Don Wolken, Tuan, and John S. Meyer. (Photo courtesy of John S. Meyer)

"That's too close, Tilt." As we talked, John realized that this was the first mission where I had experienced an extended period of combat with the NVA. "Did you kill any NVA today?" he asked. I paused for the longest time before answering. His very direct question sent me back to that moment when I was talking to Spider on the PRC-25 and I had fired one round, striking the NVA in the head. The clarity sent a chill through me. For some reason, I remember seeing some of the yellow fatty brain tissue exploding when I shot that soldier. I don't remember how long it took me to answer Walton.

"Yeah, John. Now that you mention it, I did. I hadn't thought much about it 'til now. John, I've been in-country six months and it's the first time that I can definitely say that I killed one of those bastards. I've never killed anyone before today." Walton reminded me that if I hadn't shot him, he would have killed me in a New York minute. "If I had to do it over again, I would do the same thing," I told him. "But you know, John, it isn't something I'm proud of."

I was sure I had killed other enemy soldiers during the wave attacks where they'd open fire on us before they would break out of the thick jungle. We'd shoot them back into the heavy jungle vegetation before seeing a face, uniform or weapon. A line from a Doors song The Unknown Soldier surfaced in my mind: "The war is over for the unknown soldier...bullet struck the helmeted head." What madness! Had I not shot him, he, or one of his buddies, would have killed me. Still, Walton's question had hit me hard. Later, I saw Spider and mentioned to him that it was the first time that I could say that I had shot and killed an enemy soldier.

"Do unto others before they do unto you. Remember those words, son," Spider said in that Texas drawl. "Hell, if you had let him shoot you, I'd never talk to you again."

I stepped outside for some fresh air and sat in the dark, reflecting on how lucky ST Idaho had been in Echo Four. I sat there for awhile, alone with my thoughts, amazed at the day's turn of events, including those two big NVA soldiers who just stood there and smiled at Sau and me. I thought about Sergeant First Class Glen Oliver Lane, the

One-Zero who disappeared with an ST Idaho team in May. How did that veteran SF troop die, and me, a rookie, survive? When the club closed, I met a young South Vietnamese woman who lived on base at FOB 1. Since the end of July, she and I had begun a quiet liaison meeting in her small room behind the new pilots' quarters. The South Vietnamese woman was from Da Nang. She was beautiful, educated and attracted to me. She worked at the club and was one of two South Vietnamese women allowed to live in the FOB. That night, she had heard men talking about Wolken. She knew that we had been in heavy combat. She never asked me a question about the team or our missions and she worked hard to maintain her distance from any tactical questions. As we chatted, she could tell I was still shaken by the day's events. In between hugs, she quickly put together one of her spicy, delicious noodle dishes. Of the day's mission, I simply told her that we ran into beaucoup VC.

"I'm glad VC no kill you." I spent the night, leaving before sunrise.

On 8 October, Wolken, Davison and I went through a detailed debriefing. Wolken gave the Vietnamese men the day off. Sau and Hiep were allowed to remain in town overnight. After we left the intel shed, we returned to our rooms to clean our equipment and get a total resupply of ammo, grenades, batteries and claymore mines.

At some point, I wanted to write a letter home to tell my parents, my sister and little brother about how I had survived a day in the Prairie Fire AO. But because the C&C operation was top secret, all I could say to them was that I had had an interesting day in the jungle and to mark down the date on the calendar for a later conversation. I knew my Dutch Reform mother was unhappy about me joining the Army and going to war, but I didn't want her or my family worrying. Had I been killed in Echo Four, the official statement would have said I died in South Vietnam. When I later received a Bronze Star with a V for valor, it read that the award was for combat in South Vietnam. The troops in camp often joked about that aspect of the secret war.

A day or two after the extraction, Captain Thinh and his crew came into FOB 1's Green Beret Lounge. I went in and thanked him again and ordered a round of drinks for all of the Kingbee pilots and crewmembers. Speaking through an interpreter, Captain Thinh said the Kingbee he flew to extract us from Echo Four had 48 holes in it from enemy ordnance. Sitting at the bar, Captain Thinh appeared to be just as cool and above the fray of daily life as he had on 7 October. Thinh said that an enemy round had torn a baseball-sized hole through one of the rotor blades. I asked him how he could hover so long. He told me that when he piloted a helicopter, he thought only about flying, nothing else; no enemy bullets, weather or anything, only flying.

"If it's my turn to die, I die. That day wasn't my turn to die."

A couple of days later, Wolken pulled me aside and said he had been offered a position flying as the Covey rider. It was a dangerous job, but one that was better than being on the ground. He asked me if I was ready to become the One-Zero of ST Idaho. I didn't think I was ready yet. On the other hand, the thought of having a new man come onto the team and give us orders didn't sit well with me either. So I said yes. I tracked down Davison and told him about Wolken's decision. He said he could easily understand Wolken's decision and he gave me a look that didn't register at the time. So we went to the team, got a truck and drove out to the firing range for some live-fire drills. The next morning after formation, I told Davison I wanted to have a short team meeting and that I had a few prospects to fill Wolken's slot on the team.

"Tilt, I have to tell you something, brother, I don't think I can do this. I survived Dak To, brother, but I ain't never seen shit like that before in my life. We were real lucky to survive that mission. I don't think I can go on. I hate to desert you, brother, but I think I want off of the team." Now I understood that look on his face from the previous day. I told Davison that I respected his decision and that I appreciated his frankness. I thought it took more courage to be honest in camp than to not say anything and go to the field. A man unsure in the field could get other team members hurt. I reiterated that he had performed well under fire in Echo Four. He hadn't run, he hadn't quit and he had demonstrated exemplary courage during the entire mission. As we walked and talked, I put my hand on his shoulder.

"James, you and I and Wolken did something few men in America will ever do; we survived Echo Four and all that the NVA could throw at us. There were six of us against hundreds of North Vietnam's finest. We will always have a special bond, something no one can ever take away from us. Thanks again for your honesty." I asked him if he wanted me to talk to the sergeant major, or did he want to do it. Because he had only been in camp a short while, he asked me if I wouldn't mind speaking to the sergeant major first. I agreed and asked him what sort of assignment he preferred.

"I don't know, brother. I'll need some time to get my head straight."

* * *

Thirty-two years later, I talked to James Davison in New Orleans on the telephone. One of the things he said was, "Brother, I've never been the same since those two days in Laos…"

CHAPTER 8

FOUR BULLETS IN HIS BOOTS

A few days after returning from the Echo 4 target, I talked to Spider Parks and Pat Watkins about the many changes that were swirling around the American component of ST Idaho and whether or not I was ready to be a One-Zero. Spider provided brotherly advice and reminded me that I had been on the team more than four months and that he and Wolken had trained ST Idaho hard after the old ST Idaho team disappeared in May. “Talk to Sau and Hiep. See what they say,” he advised.

I walked over to the indig team room and talked with Sau and Hiep. After a few more jokes from Hiep about my feet being too big and me being too tall a target, he said that he and Sau thought I would be okay as a One-Zero. Besides, he added, he and Sau didn’t want any strangers taking over our team, like what had happened to ST Alabama. Hiep ended the brief chat by telling me that I might not be the brightest American in camp but I did okay calling in air strikes.

I went back to Spider, and he had that “I-know-what-happened” grin on his face. We went to the S-3 shop and made it official: I would be the ST Idaho One-Zero. I was pleased that Spider, Sau and

From left, Don Wolken and John McGovern take off in Kingbee heading to Quang Tri. Although they are smiling here, both had volunteered for a special mission. (Photo courtesy of Stephen Bayliss)

Hiep had faith in me. But, at the same time, the invisible weight of being a One-Zero landed on me mentally—their safety now rested squarely on my shoulders. There was no celebration. We simply went about our business. I asked S-3 about replacements. The sergeant said there were a few new SF troops slated to arrive at FOB 1 any day. With that, I packed up the team and headed to the range for live-fire drills.

While we trained in Phu Bai, the replacements arrived in Da Nang. Among the newly-minted Special Forces soldiers were Douglas L. LeTourneau, a skinny, 135-pound California cowboy, John Shore, a blond-haired, slightly overweight, baby-faced kid from Georgia, and Frank McCloskey, a tough, combat-hardened veteran of the 101st Airborne Division. McCloskey arrived sporting seepage from a wound in the back of his head.

This trio of Green Berets had completed their Special Forces in-country training program in Nha Trang, the 5th Special Forces Group Headquarters. When a sergeant in Nha Trang asked for Special Forces soldiers to volunteer for a "secret project" they raised their hands. In short order they were flown to FOB 4, in the northern sector of South Vietnam—I Corps. Upon reporting in, they were told camp commander Col. Jack Warren would brief them in the morning on the C&C mission in Southeast Asia.

Finally, after more than a year of training for LeTourneau, the game was on. How much better could this get? It seems all his life he'd been preparing for this moment, from riding rodeo broncs and breaking nearly every bone in his body to wrangling animals for television shows like Daktari and Cowboy in Africa, starring Chuck Connors, LeTourneau knew a little bit about taking a calculated risk. And after he had gotten his hands on Robin Moore's book The Green Berets he knew this was for him. Guerilla warfare? Check. Counterinsurgency training? Check. Unconventional warfare? Check. LeTourneau couldn't wait to write his own story that he could someday share with his dad, a WWII B-17 pilot and former POW.

Nothing, however, could have prepared him for the sight that greeted him as he entered the transient barracks. There, etched into the concrete floor, and forever in his memory, was the charred outline of a man's body, a grisly reminder of the 23 August 1968 attack on FOB 4. That fateful evening, North Vietnamese sappers and Viet Cong operatives killed 18 Green Berets in a carefully executed sneak attack.

The deadly side of guerrilla warfare was brought home to him right there. He was in a war zone. The enemy didn't play by any set rules. It was an unsettling evening.

The next morning after breakfast, the trio walked over to S-3 and chose their codenames. LeTourneau, McCloskey, and Shore now became "The Frenchman," "Namu," and "Bubba"—names that would stick with them far beyond their tours of duty in Vietnam.

Because S-3 was temporarily located in the headquarters section of FOB 4 since the attack it was a quick shuffle into the briefing room with everyone else. An intense, short, black-haired man wearing pajamas, slippers and a bathrobe walked in smoking a cigarette. Before a word was spoken, Col. Warren abruptly pulled a white sheet off a large map with a flourish, tossed it aside, and announced, "Welcome to C&C, men."

Turning to the large map that had black-tape, boxed target designators on it in Laos, the DMZ and North Vietnam, he continued. "This is what you volunteered for. This is why this is a top-secret project. If anybody asks, the president can say we have no men stationed in the AO. That's why you'll wear sterile fatigues and carry no form of identification of any kind on your missions. That's why you agreed not to talk to anyone about this operation for at least 20 years. Our intel reports land in the White House. Any questions?"

Not waiting for a response, Warren continued to explain the difference between spike teams and hatchet force elements, where the different FOBs were located, how FOB 3 at Khe Sanh was closed after the siege earlier in the year, and how Major Clyde Sincere, Jr. had opened a site at Mai Loc now designated FOB 3.

Following an update on intelligence reports in the respective Areas of Operations, Col. Warren asked if anyone had any questions. LeTourneau raised his hand. "Where do you need help, sir?"

"We need men at FOB 1. We lost a One-Zero on October fifth and some of the First Special Forces TDY (temporary duty teams) troops from Okinawa are returning back to the island."

LeTourneau turned to Shore and McCloskey and asked, "How about it? FOB 1?" Shore nodded in the affirmative.

McCloskey said, "No. I think I'll stay here."

LeTourneau turned back to Warren and said, "We'll go," nodding toward Shore, surprised at McCloskey's response.

Without missing a beat, Warren told the remainder of the SF troops in the room that he'd be right back. He turned to LeTourneau and Shore and said, "Follow me," as he headed out of the briefing room and into the S-3 Operations Center. He told the Center staff to get a Kingbee to FOB 4 in an hour to transport LeTourneau and Shore to FOB 1 ASAP. Next he headed to S-1 and told the clerk that the newbies were to be processed and cleared to go to Phu Bai.

An hour later, PFC LeTourneau and Spec. 4 Shore were in a Kingbee heading north over the Hai Van Pass that crossed the rugged Troung Son Mountain. As they flew parallel to Highway 1, the door gunner nodded to LeTourneau and Shore, indicating they should sit in the doorway that was on the right side of the chopper, thus setting them up for the typical newbie welcome to FOB 1. Unaware, they sat on the floor and enjoyed the ride, dangling their feet outside as the Kingbee pilot did some nap-of-the-earth flying.

After they passed the Hue/Phu Bai Airport on the eastern side of Highway 1 in Phu Bai, the Kingbee pilot abruptly rolled the chopper on its right side, providing LeTourneau and Shore with a heart-stopping look at the ground. Both leaped to grab something that was attached to the aircraft, anything that didn't move as the crew quietly laughed at their expense.

When they landed, the rookies quickly jumped off the chopper, grabbed their gear made their way across Highway 1 to the long road that led to the command center. A truck carrying a recon team drove past the jittery pair, heading to the landing zone.

When they finally reached the S-3 shop, it was a beehive of activity. They were told to step outside and that someone would take them to their billets once things calmed down. The departing recon team had a Brightlight mission. That meant a team on the ground was in trouble. LeTourneau and Shore were not a priority.

As they stood outside, Pat Watkins walked up and introduced himself. He then promptly asked LeTourneau if he had been demoted to PFC before shipping out for South Vietnam. Watkins had done his homework. Before LeTourneau and Shore landed at FOB 1, Watkins had gone into S-1 to learn about the new men being sent to Phu Bai. The Frenchman was listed as a PFC and his MOS (Military Occupational Specialty) was listed as weapons. At that time, in Special Forces, no one below the rank of E-5 received that SF MOS when going through Special Forces Training Group. When he saw LeTourneau's MOS and rank, he thought either LeTourneau was a badass who'd been demoted or he was lying.

LeTourneau explained that when he went through Training Group, he had requested the weapons MOS, pointing out that he had joined SF to go to 'Nam and that he wanted to go as a weapons man. Somehow he convinced the review board to allow a private E-2 to go through that training, thus setting a new precedent. He was one of, if not the first, E-2s to get that training. On that day, every E-2 that came after LeTourneau alphabetically had the option to elect for SF weapons training.

SFC John McGovern walked by and Watkins introduced LeTourneau to the veteran SF trooper. McGovern had run several missions with the Hatchet Force before being transferred to Recon Company, where he eventually became the One-Zero of ST Virginia. By October, McGovern was one of the senior enlisted men in camp. All of the recon men respected him due to his experience running missions and his ability to work with indig troops. In short, McGovern epitomized the quiet professional, the experienced combat-veteran Green Beret who quietly performed his missions without pomp and circumstance.

Watkins told McGovern about LeTourneau's MOS and that he wanted to run recon. McGovern said ST Virginia could use a weapons trained troop. He said he was getting short in country and that he was going to be transferred to the S-2 shed for his remaining time during this tour of duty in South Vietnam.

"Let me introduce you to the new One-Zero of ST Virginia Spec 5 Childress," McGovern said. Childress had run several missions and McGovern described him as a good man. McGovern explained that the recon teams needed SF-qualified men to replenish the recon team ranks. Back in May, there were 30 recon teams in camp. By mid-October, only a few teams were fully operational. "We've lost some good men in recent months."

Meanwhile, Watkins told Shore ST Idaho had an opening because the One-Zero had transferred to flying Covey.

Within 24 hours, LeTourneau and Shore were on recon teams at FOB 1 and they immediately began training: immediate reaction drills, weapons and explosives training, reviewing team SOPs, practicing helicopter extractions on strings. and practicing wire taps.

As October yielded to November, many of the members of the two recon teams began to build a rapport because they were doing so much training together on the Phu Bai range. In addition, LeTourneau and Shore also quickly learned that the veteran indigenous personnel on their teams were highly skilled and fearless warriors.

One night, while LeTourneau was recording a verbal message for his parents on his portable cassette player, Lap—the young point man on ST Virginia—came into his room and spoke into the recorder: "I want to tell you, parents of Private LeTourneau, not to worry about him. We respect him and I'll keep an eye out for him. And, don't worry; if an enemy shoots at him, I'll catch the bullets with my body. I'll protect your son. Thank you for sending him to Vietnam. He's a good soldier."

* * *

A few days before Thanksgiving, ST Virginia's One-Zero Childress announced that an operation order had come down from S-3. The team had a mission in the western section of the DMZ. Childress told them that he was going to fly a VR of the target area before the team launched for the mission. He also introduced a young lieutenant who would be assigned to ST Virginia for the

ST Virginia in 1968, drinking a "welcome home" beer at FOB 1 Phu Bai, following a successful mission in Laos. Standing from left, three unidentified South Vietnamese team members, Stephen Bayliss and John McGovern—the team One-Zero. Kneeling center is Richard Childress with two unidentified team members. (Photo courtesy of Stephen Bayliss)

mission. "We need bodies and we're glad the lieutenant volunteered to join us," he told the team.

After the team meeting, Childress told LeTourneau to help the officer obtain any gear and equipment needed for the mission. When Childress left to fly the visual reconnaissance, LeTourneau and the lieutenant walked over to the supply building, gathered all of the appropriate gear and assembled it so the officer would be comfortable under the weight of his web gear and rucksack.

Afterward, LeTourneau ran into McGovern and mentioned that ST Virginia finally had a mission, but he didn't have a CAR-15—the preferred weapon among most recon men at FOB 1—even though the lieutenant had somehow obtained one. Since he was only a PFC, LeTourneau didn't want to ruffle any feathers.

The quiet-spoken McGovern gave him a wry, half smile and said, "We can't have that. You need to have a CAR-15 for your first mission. Follow me."

The duo walked over to McGovern's room. He opened his locker and pulled out a clean CAR-15 and handed it to LeTourneau. "This is a special CAR-15," he said. "According to official Army records, this CAR-15 was written off as a combat loss at FOB 3 Khe Sanh, meaning as far as the Army's concerned this weapon doesn't exist. Some day, after a successful tour of duty in Vietnam, if you're so inclined, you can take this baby home with you because it doesn't exist. But, as you can see it does and it's a sweet weapon. It never failed me. And I know that since you're a weapons man, you'll take good care of it."

Up to this point, LeTourneau had used an M-16 for all of his training. Now, with his CAR-15 he was ready to take on the world.

That opportunity arrived on Thanksgiving Day 1968. After the weather cleared at the Quang Tri Launch Site, ST Virginia boarded the Kingbees and headed west to the target area, with three American and four South Vietnamese team members: Lap, the 17-year-old hard-core point man who had run many missions; Hoanh, the interpreter; Cho, the M-79 operator; and Khanh "Cowboy" Doan , who had fought valiantly beside Lynne M.

Black, Jr. with ST Alabama.

As the second Sikorsky churned westward, the 135-pound LeTourneau went through a mental checklist of everything that he was carrying: McGovern's CAR-15, the PRC-25 FM radio, an extra battery for it, a sawed-off M-79 grenade launcher, a .22 caliber High Standard Pistol with a silencer, ammunition for all weapons, hand grenades, a gas mask, smoke grenades, a camera and five special bags of dehydrated rice. He quickly realized that he was carrying more than 100 pounds of gear.

His inner thoughts were jarred when the door gunner test fired his 30-caliber machine gun without announcing his intention to anyone. Within a matter of seconds, the Kingbee cut power and began a tight, downward spiral into the LZ, where Childress, the lieutenant, Hoahn and Lap were already waiting. The dizzying downward spiral ended as the pilot revved the engine and landed on the LZ. Cho exited the H-34, with LeTourneau and Cowboy following him into the wood line, connecting with the remaining members of the team. The Kingbee lifted off the LZ and quickly cleared the target area.

And then there was absolute silence.

The audio contrast was startling. As LeTourneau's senses adjusted to the quiet, he scoped out the LZ, which was in a deep valley between three jungle-covered mountains. Gradually, sounds of the jungle resurfaced, birds chirping, bugs humming. After 10 minutes, Childress signaled LeTourneau to radio Covey with a "Team OK." The insertion was successful, no enemy activity evident.

Childress moved the team toward the first mountain. Movement was slowed by tall elephant grass and the only communication between team members was hand signals. The team moved in 10-minute intervals, stopping every 10 minutes to listen to what was going on around it. After more than an hour, the team finally emerged from the elephant grass as it continued to climb the first mountain.

LeTourneau was on hyper-alert, his heart pounding hard whether sitting in a long rest period or moving up the mountain. Near the top of the mountain, Lap pointed out an observation platform that had been cut into the jungle high off the ground. From that platform, anyone could observe the LZ and the valley where the team was inserted as well as other open areas that could be used for landing helicopters. Had a trail watcher been sitting on the platform when ST Virginia flew into the LZ? If so, where was he and when would the NVA hit the team?

Late in the day, the team finally reached the top of the mountain and found a wide, well-used trail. LeTourneau's first thought was, "How could any trail be out here in the middle of nowhere in this thick jungle?"

Regardless, the team set up its night perimeter, far above the trail where it could see anyone moving while remaining camouflaged and out of sight. At last light, Childress made the final commo check with Covey as the team settled in for its first night in the jungle.

It was an uneventful night. Childress did a midnight commo check with Hillsborough, the night command aircraft that flew high above the Ho Chi Minh Trail and the DMZ, and he checked in with Covey in the early morning.

After the team ate breakfast in shifts, Childress directed Lap to move parallel to the trail with Cowboy as the tail gunner in the line of march and LeTourneau walking in front of Cowboy. The team moved slowly in less than 10-minute intervals before taking breaks to listen to the surrounding sounds. They did this because moving next to a trail was fraught with inherent risks.

As ST Virginia moved up the second mountain, Cowboy and LeTourneau began to hear women's voices off of the trail. Cowboy urged LeTourneau to go explore the sounds. LeTourneau shook his head no, indicating they had to stay with the team. Cowboy, who spoke broken English, repeated the suggestion adding: "It could be a small NVA village. We could kill everyone and make the NVA beaucoup angry. We want to let them know we can hurt them the same way they attack our camps and villages."

LeTourneau again declined and gave him the hand signal to plant some M-14 Anti-Personnel Mines on the trail behind them, in case NVA soldiers were trailing them. As the team moved on, LeTourneau

Members of ST Virginia taking a photo break during training in Phu Long, outside FOB 1 in January 1969. Standing in back from left: Doug "The Frenchman" LeTourneau, an indig team member and newly appointed One-Zero, Gunther Wald, who served in the Marine Corps before joining Special Forces and an unidentified team member. Kneeling are several indig team members, including the interpreter Hoahn, last on right. (Photo courtesy of Doug LeTourneau)

planted a few more toe poppers and marked their locations on his map after covering them expertly. He laid down some powdered mustard gas on the ground for any tracker dogs that might follow their trail. The mustard gas powder was left over from WWI—how it landed at Phu Bai remained a mystery to LeTourneau. The good news was that it still worked. That fact was confirmed during the next break when the team heard a dog howl in anguish after snorting some of the old mustard gas.

Maybe it didn't work that well, because a few minutes later, the dog was back on the team's trail. Cowboy told LeTourneau to use his pistol to kill the dog. LeTourneau's mind flashed back to Special Forces Training Group where instructors had said the same thing.

LeTourneau pulled out the .22, quietly moved back down the trail, took off his rucksack and moved a few more feet before lying down on the ground, facing the trail. The dog never realized LeTourneau was there. When the dog was about 10 feet away, LeTourneau fired one shot. It struck the dog between the eyes, killing him instantly. The canine dropped in his tracks, out of LeTourneau's view.

Unaware of what had happened, the dog's handler moved up the trail. When he got near the dead dog, he stepped on a toe popper. LeTourneau and Cowboy heard the NVA screaming in pain and anguish. They left him behind, figuring he would die shortly.

The team moved further up the mountain, with LeTourneau and Cowboy providing rear security. Again LeTourneau and Cowboy heard women's voices below them. Again, Cowboy urged LeTourneau to go downhill and attack the encampment. And again, LeTourneau declined.

By the time LeTourneau completed his last radio call to Covey, the team was enveloped in darkness and team members began to set up a perimeter for the night.

Dawn broke without any enemy activity. When Covey flew over the team in the morning, he warned Childress that a team was being extracted under enemy fire and another was being inserted into a top priority target. "Sit tight," was the last instruction from Covey. ST Virginia didn't move from its quiet spot alongside the mountain. During lunch hour, each member ate in shifts and LeTourneau went out to inspect the claymore mines the team had deployed to ensure that the NVA hadn't turned the deadly explosive devices around to face toward the team. When he completed his inspection, LeTourneau found a log to sit behind.

Later in the afternoon, Childress signaled the team to pull in their claymore mines and prepare to move out. Due to the combined weight of his rucksack and web gear, LeTourneau moved to his knees and slung his rucksack on his back.

Just as it landed on his back, AK-47s opened fire. LeTourneau was slammed to the ground face first. The impact so severe he thought he had broken his nose.

Startled, LeTourneau jumped up with his CAR-15 pointing toward the AK-47 gunfire that was near the front of the team. Surprised that there were no NVA near him, LeTourneau removed the rucksack to discover that four AK-47 rounds had ripped through the 23-pound PRC-25.

He reached into an especially tailored pocket on his fatigue shirt, which was sewn with vertical zippers—one on the left side of the shirt and one on the right side, between the top and bottom pockets on the shirt—pulled out his URC-10 emergency radio and broadcast a general alert for any aircraft in the area. ST Virginia was declaring a Prairie Fire Emergency.

Then, there was sudden, complete silence. Eerily silent.

Amazed at the quietude, LeTourneau walked to Childress, who asked him what he had done with the PRC-25. LeTourneau explained that four rounds had ripped through the radio and that it was probably useless.

"Get the fucking radio," Childress yelled. "What if it's working and we leave it behind for those assholes to use?"

Stunned, LeTourneau went back, picked up the ruck sack and walked back to Childress, who grabbed the handset as NVA troops began firing at ST Virginia, and yelled into the radio, "We have a fucking Prairie Fire Emergency. Get us the fuck outta here or I promise you I'll kick your ass all the way back to Saigon."

As the firefight raged on, the remainder of the team was lying down on the ground, firing at the NVA, while Childress and LeTourneau continued to argue while standing up, oblivious to the AK-47 rounds cracking over their heads.

LeTourneau yelled back at Childress, "It don't work!" while pointing at the PRC-25 radio where the antenna had been shot off. No antenna, no commo.

LeTourneau grabbed a spare whip antenna and handed it to Childress, who screwed it into the PRC-25.

This time, Childress screamed into the radio, "We need an exfil, now! I'm declaring a Prairie Fire Emergency. Is anyone out there?"

Within a second or two there was a response: "Calm down, Childress. I realize you're under fire," said a Covey rider. Just at that moment several AK-47s opened fire from the wood line near the log where LeTourneau had been unceremoniously slammed onto his face. Lap and Cowboy returned fire.

Covey rider continued: "We heard your team declare a Prairie Fire Emergency on the Guard frequency and I've rallied the cavalry. What's your mark? Do you have an LZ in sight?"

Before Childress said a word into the radio, he turned to LeTourneau and said, "See. It works. Suppose we had left it for the NVA. Never. I say again, never, ever leave behind a radio."

As if to emphasize that point, the NVA opened fire again as Lap began looking for an LZ while he moving the team down the hill, away from the most concentrated NVA gunfire.

Cutting LeTourneau no slack, Childress roared, "Tell Covey we'll give him a fix in five minutes. We'll probably need strings to get out of here. I doubt we can make it down to the valley where a Kingbee can pick us up."

Without missing a beat, LeTourneau—who for the first time felt four burning stings in his back—repeated those words to Covey while he and Cowboy began providing covering fire as the tail element of the team. Then LeTourneau nodded to Cowboy, who ignited several claymore mines that the team had set out on its perimeter. Those mines only slowed the NVA for a few seconds.

Before the dust and debris from the blasts had settled, NVA soldiers were moving through it toward Cowboy and LeTourneau.

Without saying a word, the two men took turns firing at the enemy while moving down hill. Rotating around each other. Cowboy would fire several bursts from his CAR-15, and then reload. As he reloaded, LeTourneau would open fire, providing covering fire for the team.

During one short lull, Cowboy again planted a claymore mine in the direction of the advancing NVA and LeTourneau dug out another claymore from his ruck sack and placed a 10-second delayed fuse in it. When the NVA again advanced, Cowboy ignited his claymore mine. When the NVA moved toward the team again, LeTourneau ignited his fuse and ran down the hill with Cowboy to catch up to their team.

Before they reached the team, two B-40 anti-personnel rockets slammed into the trees above them, showering them with shrapnel. A few more exploded as LeTourneau and Cowboy moved down the hill. Then the 10-second fuse ignited another claymore. It bought precious time for the gun-and-run team of LeTourneau and Cowboy to cover ground and catch up to the remainder of ST Virginia.

As Childress called in air strikes, LeTourneau reflected on how surreal this firefight had been. It wasn't anything like he had witnessed on television or in any movie. Instead of men charging each other and killing each other in plain sight, here in triple-canopy jungle, he observed green tracers from AK-47s first, or at the most an enemy hand or foot. And, somehow the NVA found firing lanes where they could launch shoulder-held B-40 anti-personnel rockets that slammed above and around them as they raced down the hill for their lives. Again, the voices of his Special Forces instructors echoed in his mind: they had told the young aspiring Green Berets at Ft. Bragg that the NVA was a tough, resilient opponent. Many had fought against the Japanese during WWII and against the French, driving them from Vietnam in 1954 after the battle of Dien Bien Phu in North Vietnam.

The sounds of Kingbees in the distance and the crashing thunder of B-40 rockets slamming into the trees above his head shook LeTourneau out of his moment of introspection and turned his undivided attention to a crescendo of AK-47 fire from the enemy. ST Virginia responded with volley after volley of full and semi-automatic gunfire while LeTourneau and Cho fired several M-79 rounds toward the densest section of jungle where the AK-47 gunfire was emanating.

Through the gunfire, someone popped a smoke grenade, which brought the Kingbees closer to the RT Virginia's location in the jungle. Over the din of gunfire, Childress and Cowboy told everyone to put on their Swiss seats and to prepare for a string extraction.

In short order, a Kingbee was hovering over ST Virginia, more than 125 feet above the jungle floor. LeTourneau, Cowboy, Cho and Hoanh hooked their D rings into the old McGuire rig that hung from the end of the ropes and shortly were being lifted out of the jungle.

As the quartet of recon men was being lifted into the air, the NVA unleashed another salvo of AK-47 gunfire and several B-40 rockets. Shrapnel from the rockets hit them with varying degrees of size and velocity. All of them were wounded.

It was during those explosions that LeTourneau realized his CAR-15 had somehow become caught in the rope above him, just far enough away that he couldn't reach it. He pulled out his M-79 and launched a 40 mm grenade toward the NVA positions: now, all he could see of the enemy were hundreds of muzzle blasts from AK-47s and green tracers rounds eerily climbing upward toward the quartet of ST Virginia men.

Before he could reload his M-79, the Kingbee began to move away from the target area, surprising him because the men had not cleared the jungle yet. Instead of continuing to climb out of the target, moving straight up until the men cleared the jungle's triple canopy of trees and vegetation, the Kingbee was moving away from the target area due to the heavy enemy ground fire. In recent months at least two Kingbees were shot down during string extractions from hot targets, but these facts were unknown to LeTourneau at that time.

Shrapnel from the B-40 rockets exploded around the ST Virginia men stinging them with pieces of hot metal, further spooking the Kingbee crew. LeTourneau began to violently collide with the tall jungle trees. Feeling like a metal ball in a pinball machine, LeTourneau caromed off several more trees as at least one more B-40 exploded in the treetops, again showering him with shrapnel.

A tree branch hit LeTourneau from the side and turned him upside down in his rope Swiss seat. As the rope seat began to slip down from his hips, LeTourneau remembered Spider telling how a One-Zero from another team had been recently shot out of his Swiss seat during a rope extraction.

Another tree struck LeTourneau before he was able to muster a surge of strength and momentum to reach up and grab the rope above him as his body finally cleared the treetops.

The only thing between him and certain death below on the jungle floor 200 feet below was the single piece of rope tied into the Kingbee.

With one final urgent pull, LeTourneau was able to move himself upright in the Swiss seat as the Kingbee continued to climb higher into the sky, distancing itself from the fury of the exploding B-40s and AK-47 gunfire while gaining air speed.

As the Kingbee ascended, the heavily sweating LeTourneau clung to the rope as another sensation overwhelmed his body: chattering teeth. Within a matter of minutes, the Kingbee had climbed to an altitude of more than 5000 feet, where the air is thinner and much, much colder than on the jungle floor—so much colder that LeTourneau's body began shaking violently from the dipping temperatures as the Kingbee continued to climb into the safety of higher altitude.

LeTourneau would never forget that extraction. Rockets were exploding around him while he was dripping with sweat, hanging upside down, and in the next moment, he felt as though his sweat was freezing to his body.

Few people realize just how cold and terrifying it is to be hanging from a rope, freezing to death while going more than 100 miles per hour dangling under a chopper.

In ordinary circumstances, few people would ever think about freezing to death over Southeast Asia, but for the men in C&C, it was just another hurdle they had to clear.

As the Kingbee headed east, LeTourneau looked down on spots in the jungle that appeared to be good LZs, thinking "Why don't you land there?"

But, ST Virginia's collective agony continued until the Kingbees finally landed in South Vietnam. By that time, every member of ST Virginia had their circulation cut off to their legs. They couldn't stand or walk. All they could do was unhook from their Swiss seat, grab their stuff and try to get the circulation going again in their legs while the door gunner helped them get back to the Kingbee.

When the team returned to the Quang Tri launch site before heading south to Phu Bai, Childress pulled LeTourneau aside and told him, "Take good care of that radio. You're going to take it on the next mission whether you like it or not." Childress and the lieutenant returned to the S-3 tent, while LeTourneau went into the old WWII tent where the Vietnamese members sat on old stiff cots, searching each other for shrapnel wounds while bandaging the more serious wounds.

As darkness fell, the Kingbees lifted off from Quang Tri for Phu Bai. When the old war birds landed on the FOB 1 landing zone, ST Virginia was greeted by one man: Former ST Virginia One-Zero John McGovern. He greeted each of the team members as they exited the Kingbees, asking each one, "Are you okay?"

After the Kingbees departed, bathing them in the sand, dust and

LZ debris kicked up by the prop wash, McGovern asked Childress, "Did you hear about Bader, et al?"

Childress shook his head. "No, what happened?"

"November thirtieth, we lost a Kingbee with seven SF troops on it and we lost the entire Kingbee crew. They were a bunch of straphangers who volunteered to pull an Elder Son mission on the trail. But, an anti-aircraft round hit the Kingbee en route to the target. It exploded in mid-air. They never had a chance."

In silence, McGovern drove the tired, dirty and hungry team back to the team room. As the Vietnamese team members climbed off the truck, McGovern turned to LeTourneau and said, "You know what was really scary about that mission? The day before they got shot down, me, Lynne Black, Rick Howard, John Peters, Tim Schaff and a few others had volunteered and were actually on the Kingbee suited up ready to go, only to be canceled the last minute due to bad Whiskey X-Ray (weather) in the A.O. That was too close for comfort."

After a long pause he asked LeTourneau, "How did it go out there? I heard you were good on the radio. You didn't get rattled. You ain't a cherry no more. You've joined a small, unique club of SF men, C&C recon men who went across the fence."

"It was nothing like I could have ever imagined," LeTourneau responded. Looking toward the Vietnamese team members, he added, "Let me get some chow for the indig. You were right about them. They have ice in their veins. I'm beat. I'll see you in the morning."

LeTourneau walked through the white sand to the mess hall, picked up some fresh sandwiches and cold sodas for the team. After lingering with the Vietnamese team members LeTourneau returned to his room, finally taking off his rucksack and web gear.

As he started to undress, LeTourneau became aware of pain in his back, from where the four AK-47 rounds had slammed him face-first into the ground. First he peeled off his jungle fatigue shirt and was amazed to find four bullet holes in it. Then, he took off his undershirt. Ditto! Four bullet holes were in it. LeTourneau picked up the rucksack: four bullet holes were in it—both in the front and the back—something he hadn't realized during the firefight.

Then, he looked in the mirror and saw the four large welts and broken skin up his spine where the AK-47 rounds had hit his body after punching through his rucksack and PRC-25.

Only then did LeTourneau begin to comprehend just how lucky he had been hours earlier in the day when the NVA shot him in the back four times.

LeTourneau began to cut away the black electrical tape around his socks, which he pulled up and over his pant legs to keep out leeches and bugs. Then he made a startling discovery:

When he pulled his pant leg from the sock and pulled off his right boot, four AK-47 bullets fell on the ground. In the heat of battle, the Frenchman didn't realize that after he was shot in the back, the four 7.62 mm NVA rounds had fallen down through his pants and socks into his right boot.

He stood in utter amazement, staring at the four rounds on the floor, before picking them up and throwing them in the sand outside his room.

Exhausted, LeTourneau walked over to the shower room. The water stung the wounds in his back. Amazingly, the four bullets had enough energy to penetrate his skin wounding him, but not enough to get under his skin.

Too tired to treat the four bullet wounds in his back and the shrapnel wounds in his arms, LeTourneau finished his shower and went to bed.

* * *

The PRC-25 wasn't called a "Prick-25" for nothing. In addition to weighing a ton, they were famous for their inconsistency in the field. The Frenchman would use this same radio on Christmas Day to help ST Idaho avoid an NVA ambush.

CHAPTER NINE

UPSIDE DOWN OVER LAOS

November 1968 was an intense month for Spike Team Idaho and any recon team that could go across the fence. The reason: the NVA continued to push tons of supplies and thousands of soldiers down the Ho Chi Minh Trail Complex. The NVA and the communists running North Vietnam wanted that critical southward movement of materials and men to flow like Mao Tse Tung's "army of human ants." The presence of SOG recon teams and Hatchet Forces hampered that flow at an ever-increasing cost to Hanoi. Of course, the majority of the media in the United States still portrayed the Vietnam War as a conflict where peasants in North Vietnam dropped their plows at night to pick up old weapons left over from World War II and the French-Indochina War to battle the ugly American aggressors, only to return to their little rice paddies at the break of dawn. The truth about NVA involvement was underreported.

The NVA now turned its full attention to the Ho Chi Minh Trail Complex in Laos, which was not one single trail, but an ever-growing series of trails weaving through the mountains. If bombers attacked the road and destroyed it, the labor forces would rebuild it, sometimes in a day or two, depending on how extensive and

From left, Ron Zaiss, John S. Meyer and John T. Walton at Phu Bai, enjoy a few laughs after a football game of two-hand touch at FOB 1. (Photo courtesy of Ron Zaiss)

accurate the bombing had been. And the NVA continued to carve lengthy sections of road through triple-canopy jungle, making the roads invisible from the air, roads that were wide enough to handle the tanks and trucks moving south.

After I had run a few missions into Laos, there were two dominating thoughts that stuck with me while flying in the helicopters across South Vietnam toward the Prairie Fire AO: in the air over Laos, the lush, emerald green land of Southeast Asia was beautiful. Whenever we crossed the fence into Laos, I felt we were 20th century warriors, flying into a primitive land in the 12th or 13th century, where the only weapons carried by the indigenous people were spears. Modern man versus hill agrarian. The local farmers still used the slash-and-burn method of farming, burning huge chunks of land, planting and harvesting until the soil's nutrients were drained before repeating the cycle.

But on the ground in Laos, it was total warfare. The NVA forced all indigenous personnel to work with them or die. Recon team leaders were told that the NVA and local personnel along Laotian ridges sent out a wave of signals, either gunshots, drums or radio signals to warn inland troops about the westward movement of the helicopters in an azimuth. The enemy had spotters at many chopper LZs and started using two-man teams to track the SOG recon teams. By 1968, the NVA had pressed local trackers into service, area hunters and tribesmen who knew the mountainous terrain and knew how to track people or animals. The wily NVA learned from the trackers and placed their own trackers in key hotspots along the trail, such as the A Shau Valley. Additionally, the NVA formed and trained a sapper division of elite NVA soldiers for the trail. The 305th Sapper Command trained hunter-killer teams for one mission: hunt and kill SOG teams. Recon team leaders were told the sappers wore only a loincloth, an AK-47 and ammo when they attacked a recon team. Hanoi added an incentive: bounties on recon team leaders—bounties that would be collected if the team leader were dead or alive. Meanwhile, President Johnson had halted bombing of North Vietnam when he announced on 31 March that he would not seek re-election. That allowed the NVA to focus more attention and resources to the Ho Chi Minh Trail Complex.

During this month, ST Idaho had met various levels of NVA or Pathet Lao resistance at several landing zones. In the first half of the month, there were days when we would get on the H-34s, fly across South Vietnam, across the dreaded A Shau Valley into Laos, only to be shot out of the primary, secondary and alternate LZs. There were two or three days when this long, dull, uneventful flight would end with a pulsating firefight at different LZs. Privately, the One-Zeros told each other that the NVA had spies telling their troops in Laos where the recon teams were headed, although, in some target areas, there were a limited number of LZs that could handle a helicopter landing. (It would be more than a decade before it was revealed that there was a breach in U.S. Naval security and key NVA operatives in SOG offices sometimes provided LZ coordinates to NVA soldiers and LZ watchers.)

Someone in Saigon or FOB 1 finally came up with a unique strategy to get a team on the ground: have the Covey find a parcel of jungle with no LZs, bomb it with a 2000-pound Daisy Cutter bomb and, as the smoke clears, have a recon team rappel into the target from hovering helicopters. The spike teams at Phu Bai had conducted a lot of rappelling practice, both from the rappelling tower at the eastern end of camp and from H-34s. The plan sounded like a rock solid idea. The attractive aspect about it as a One-Zero was that there would be no cursed trackers in the area. The recon team could get on the ground fast and move before the NVA reacted. After hours of training, ST Idaho was confident and ready to rappel down a rope for a target insertion.

Finally, the day came when the C-130 was ready with the Daisy Cutter ordnance. Covey had found a swatch of jungle with no LZs or open areas. ST Idaho was aboard two H-34s, heading toward the target area. I felt good about having a new tactic that could get ST Idaho on the ground instead of getting shot out of LZs. Within a few minutes I was hooked onto the rope and standing in the door, waiting for the Kingbee to take us down to the bombed area. Our rappelling equipment at that time was primitive, but effective. From the choppers, we hung 150-foot long ropes. Our rope seats were called Swiss seats. They consisted of a six-foot cut of rope which was tied around the waist twice, then both pieces went under the legs and were tied on the left hip, leaving the front open for a metal D-ring. It was hooked into the Swiss seat, into the top of the D in the D-ring. The rope from the chopper fed through it with one full twist for friction, wrapping around, but not onto, the right side of the body. The left hand reached upwards to the chopper rope, while the right hand gathered the lower portion of the chopper rope and tucked it behind the back for braking. This H-34 had two or three metal steps on it and I was standing on the bottom rung, hooked into the rope, with my left hand grabbing the top portion of the rope and my right hand braking behind my back. We had circled a fair distance from the bomb target area. After the C-130 dropped the Daisy Cutter, I felt the subsequent explosion and then felt the Kingbee begin moving toward the target as planned.

Then the unexpected surfaced dramatically. Seconds after the huge bomb exploded, there was a secondary explosion and a third. The Kingbee abruptly aborted the approach, I rolled back inside the old Sikorsky and we watched in startled amazement as a series of secondary explosions continued to ignite beneath the jungle's triple canopy. We returned to FOB 1 shaking our heads, both at the damage we had inflicted on the NVA stockpiles and how a new tactic was postponed until tomorrow. Pat Watkins, a veteran One-Zero serving his second tour of duty in SOG, returned to base with a broad grin on his face. Watkins had been the Covey rider on that mission. He came up to me and said the aircrews counted several dozen, possibly as many as 100, secondary explosions triggered by the Daisy Cutter.

"Can you imagine," Watkins said, "somewhere in Hanoi right now, some general is scratching his head and wondering to himself, 'How in the hell did they learn we had that supply cache there?' They'll be conducting investigations for months without realizing it was just sheer dumb, blind luck on our part."

The next day, we tried it again. Watkins found another chunk of jungle, with no visible roads, LZs or open areas. This time, after the C-130 dropped the Daisy Cutter, there were no secondary explosions. As the Kingbee approached the smoking LZ, I again stood on the ladder, ready to rappel into Laos. I wondered if this was the first time a SOG recon team rappelled into a target. I assumed there would be no answer, as there was no military historian at FOB 1, or anywhere in SOG for that matter. There were no records such as the team that stayed in a target for the longest amount of time, the shortest amount of time, etc.

As Captain Tuong piloted the Kingbee into the smoking area, I was surprised to see several trees still standing. The center of the blast was on a hillside, in mountainous terrain. From a distance the terrain didn't look too severe, but as we approached, the rugged nature of the terrain and the number of trees still standing became apparent. As soon as Captain Tuong brought the Kingbee to a hover, I began to rappel down the rope. The hillside was still smoking. The noise of the Kingbee and the relentless rotor wash combined to drown out any other noises on the LZ. As I descended down the rope, however, the aircraft noise lessened and I heard people talking. My first thought was how in the hell did they get trackers out here already? As I neared the ground, I realized there were two voices, one on either side of the smoldering LZ. One voice emanated from the jungle area where the Kingbee's nose pointed. The second voice came from the jungle area to the rear of the Kingbee.

The second man scheduled to come down the rope was a long, lanky man from Savannah, Georgia, Henry King. I signaled King not to jump off the Kingbee until I gave him an all clear. I landed behind a smoking tree that had been knocked down. It rested on other smoldering tree trunks, tipping upwards slightly to my left. Its highest point was about five feet off of the ground. I immediately signaled abort mission to King. At first, I was afraid he didn't understand my signal, as it appeared he was about to rappel down to me. Meanwhile, because no one had opened fire, I assumed the bomb had startled the two local people I heard talking to each other. I couldn't understand a word they were saying, but neither of them appeared to have a weapon. As I looked up, I was glad to see King climbing back into the Kingbee. I got on the radio and told Covey to abort the mission, as we had been compromised again. For a few, fleeting moments I had considered trying to get the team on the ground. Frankly, I was sick and tired of getting shot out of LZs and I wanted to run a mission instead of going through a gut-wrenching firefight on the Laotian LZs.

Then I saw the helmet of an NVA soldier heading towards the bombed area. He was approaching from the area where I heard the first voice, from the jungle area in front of the helicopter, which was up the hill from where I was on the ground. As soon as I saw him, I opened fire with my CAR-15. Suddenly, the Kingbee swerved away, leaving me on the ground. Just as suddenly, it was eerily quiet. I thought I heard a round being chambered in an AK-47, from the general area where I had observed the NVA a few seconds earlier. After I had opened fire, due to the jungle and the distance, I couldn't tell if I had hit him or not. I pulled out my sawed-off M-79 grenade launcher and fired one round into the area where I had last observed the NVA. The high-explosive round sounded extraordinarily loud, shattering the spooky silence. At that moment, I was happy that the NVA didn't have those deadly M-79s. As the smoke cleared from the M-79 round, the local guy down the hill from me yelled across the LZ. At first, there was no answer. I hoped my M-79 round hadn't injured the local farmer or woodcutter. I felt no hostility toward them. The AK-47 toting NVA was another story.

Then it hit me. I was standing in the middle of a smoking LZ, in the middle of Laos, and I was alone. All of a sudden, I felt small. Very small. The trees that had survived the bomb blast were tall. The jungle surrounding the LZ was both impressive and formidable and not somewhere I wanted to travel by myself. I tried to raise Covey on the radio. There was no answer from Watkins. Even though I was the American team leader on ST Idaho, I insisted on carrying the radio because I wanted to be the person calling in air strikes around my team. The Vietnamese kept us alive in the field and I felt my end of surviving jungle warfare was to direct tactical air strikes and

Capt. Nguyen Van Tuong stands beside his Kingbee at Quang Tri launch site minutes before flying ST Idaho into a Prairie Fire target in Laos. (Photo courtesy of John S. Meyer)

helicopter gunships against the enemy. The fallen trees, all jagged edges and odd angles, gave the LZ an extra element of bizarreness.

Again, the voice behind me yelled something. This time a voice that sounded wounded answered in muted tones. I reloaded my M-79 and put a full magazine into my CAR-15. I loosened the tape on several of the M-26 frag grenades I wore on my web gear. As I busied myself, I wondered when Captain Tuong was going to return to pull me out of the LZ. Tuong was a talented, fearless pilot. He had pulled ST Idaho out of several hot LZs, regardless of the volume of enemy fire. At that moment, however, I knew he had a problem; his fuel was getting low. Time on station over the AO was always a major concern for recon teams. After an insertion, the Kingbees could only remain on station for up to 10 minutes before heading home, flying east across Laos and all the way across South Vietnam. But I knew Captain Tuong. During the monsoon season, he had allowed me to sit in the co-pilot's seat of the H-34, getting some cherished stick time. I remembered how on one rainy day, as our Kingbee was heading north to the Quang Tri launch site for a resupply run, I found myself heading straight toward a Marine Corps CH-46 Chinook. It was bigger and heavier and far uglier than our Vietnamese Air Force H-34. I was about to move to the right to get out of the path of the CH-46. Captain Tuong said, "No move!" I told him the CH-46 was much bigger than us. Tuong said, "No move!" I looked at him and he was dead serious. His boyish face had a scowl to it I hadn't seen before. Again I suggested that we get out of the way of the United States Marine Corps' big ugly helicopter. With a heightened sense of agitation, Captain Tuong repeated his mantra; "No move! We Vietnamese flying Vietnamese helicopter in Vietnam. We no move!" The moment I became aware of the sweat rising on my brow, the Marine chopper veered to the right. The proud Kingbee continued to chug north to Quang Tri.

That moment stuck in my head as I heard the H-34 returning to me. Captain Tuong brought the Kingbee into a hover as King dropped the sandbags that were attached to the bottoms of the ropes. The rope landed a few feet away. I stumbled across the burnt wood.

There were more gunshots as I started to hook myself onto the rope. I snapped my Swiss seat D-ring onto the rope. Then I had to return fire. I saw no NVA, but the weapon that was being fired had the unmistakable bark of an AK-47. I fired another M-79 round in that direction. That round's explosion must have startled Captain Tuong, because he jerked the Kingbee upward, yanking me off of the ground before I could slip the D-ring on my left shoulder around the rope. That shoulder D-ring was critical for staying in the Swiss seat. We had heard horror stories about the body desecrations the NVA performed on SOG men and I didn't want that happening to me. As Tuong lifted me into the air, I opened fire with my CAR-15 on what appeared to be a muzzle flash coming from the hilltop area. Then I became scared. I still hadn't hooked my shoulder D-ring and someone fired a few green tracer rounds at us. Captain Tuong started to pull out of the target area. As he started gaining speed, I ricocheted off of a few trees before I cleared the jungle. Having sat in the Kingbee co-pilot's seat, I understood why he pulled away from the LZ before I had cleared the trees. If the chopper gets shot down, the mission turns into an operational nightmare, while potentially injuring or killing the crew and the recon team members aboard the ship. I wasn't angry with him; hell, he came back for me. I would have been stranded down there for at least two or more hours before other choppers with ropes would have been able to extract me if he hadn't.

But being dragged through the trees hurt. The insides of my arms at the elbow joint were bloodied and sore from the rope cutting into the skin. I was lucky. I was still in the seat, out of harm's way, but I had to hold on tightly with my arms to avoid turning upside down. I remembered our rappelling instructors telling us that if the shoulder D-ring wasn't hooked, that mistake could cost us our lives. Every recon man had heard the stories about team members getting shot out of their Swiss seats on extraction or getting ripped out of their Swiss seats by trees as the helicopters pulled them through the jungle. Within minutes I was 5,000 feet above Laos. I was happy to escape from that LZ without further harm to myself or to my team, but regardless of what I tried, I couldn't get my shoulder D-ring hooked. We were now flying at more than 80 miles per hour. I had no goggles. I could feel the rope tightening around my thighs. I was ready to experience my legs going numb from the seat, as other team members and trainers had told us. Meanwhile, because my right arm was bleeding and sore from the severe rope burn, I transferred to my left arm. Between the wind and the equipment I was wearing, I couldn't get both arms firmly around the rope at the same time. Also, I couldn't get my long sleeves pulled down to protect the crook of my arms. After a few minutes, the left arm cuts were hurting and I transferred back to my right arm as the secure arm to prevent falling upside down. As I looked up to the Kingbee, I could see King hanging out the door. I gave him a sign to get the Kingbee to land. Between the cold air, the air speed of the helicopter and the bleeding arms, I feared that I wouldn't have the strength to last the entire flight across Vietnam. This was the first time that I had been extracted from a target on stings and I was angry at myself for not getting the damned D-ring hooked before I lifted off the ground. My arms were getting very sore. As I went to switch arms, I was struck by some sort of air pocket and suddenly, I was upside down at 5,000 feet.

My only physical link to life was the D-ring hooked into my rope seat and the 150-foot piece of rope hanging from the helicopter. I twisted my body to look up to King again. Thank God he was still hanging out the door. I signaled again to get the chopper to land. As I was giving King signs, I felt the rope slipping inexorably down my thighs to my knees. At the same time, my web gear was sliding from my hips, over my stomach toward my neck. In a matter of moments, the Swiss seat was at my knees. The only way I stopped it from moving farther was by spreading my legs. A few weeks before this target, I had attempted to weigh my equipment and myself. As I felt the web gear settle on my throat, I remembered that the gear, weapons, ammo, water and PRC-25 and an extra battery for it, weighed more than 80 pounds. I tried to shuck my rucksack. No luck. It was tangled in with the web gear, adding a lot of weight to my neck. I tried to signal King one more time.

The speed of the helicopter and the weight of my equipment turned into a death grip. I tried to get the equipment off my neck, but couldn't.

As the Kingbee continued flying east at the same rate of speed, I remembered reading somewhere that if a person fell a great distance, he would die before impact with the ground. The rope slipped over my knees. Actually, the rope didn't move; my upside-down body was slipping farther through the rope of my Swiss seat. I felt really stupid. After all of the training, this was going to be a dumb way to die.

There was no relief from the weight of the gear that was choking me. I could feel myself losing consciousness as my body moved downward through the rope. When the rope reached my feet, I had my legs spread apart and could feel my strength ebbing. Why hadn't I done exercises to strengthen my legs for such an emergency? Twice before during my lifetime I had passed out. Now, I could feel that familiar blackness sweeping through my mind. I was going to be dead, not from combat – from a stupid mistake! As the rope slid across my feet, I knew I was moments away from passing out, and there was no way I could keep my legs spread. Just before the end, several brief scenes from my life flashed through my mind: Dolores, my kindergarten sweetheart, why did she move to California? I saw my dad's new 1949 Chevrolet milk truck with its dark evergreen paint, with white side panels and rich gold leaf letters; my red wagon from childhood; high school football games; and to add insult to injury, I saw the front page article in my hometown paper about my death. The story was below the fold because stories about local boys dying in Nam were now commonplace. That angered me, because my family would never know where I really died. On the other hand, I didn't want them to know how I really died.

Just as I started to pass out, I felt the rope slip off my feet. My body went limp. I vaguely remember hitting elephant grass before landing hard on my back, on the ground. I had only had fallen 10 or 20 feet! The elephant grass cushioned the fall. I hadn't realized that Captain Tuong had the aircraft descending during those last frantic moments. I tried to move, but couldn't. I was barely conscious when King tried to pick me up. He said we were still in Laos. He unhooked the web gear that was around my throat. He pulled me out of the backpack. Then he picked me up, carried me to the chopper and threw me into the old Kingbee. It felt good having my head bounce off of the chopper's metal floor. I told King to get my gear. He told me to shut up as Covey and the Kingbee pilot wanted to get out of Laos as quickly as possible. Now the Kingbee was dangerously low on fuel.

I don't remember much about the ride back to Phu Bai, except that someone gave me water. I didn't even mind the taste of the iodine. I couldn't believe I was alive. Only once before had my life flashed before my eyes: I was driving fast on a rain-soaked New Jersey back road, racing some high school friends, and I took a turn too sharp. As the VW traveled sideways on the slick road, heading toward an oncoming car, I thought that it was all over for me. In both cases, I was amazed at how fast the mind worked, the clarity of detail, and yes, the taste of fear while standing at death's gate. As the Kingbee flew back to Phu Bai, I knew I'd never forget to hook the D ring on during future rope extractions, regardless of how many NVA soldiers were firing at me.

When we landed at Phu Bai, I thought there would be a greeting party of some sort after my close encounter with death, but there was no one on the landing pad across the street from FOB 1. I climbed up to the Kingbee's pilot seat to thank Captain Tuong for saving my life. He didn't realize how close I was to passing out. He said that someone told him not to land in Laos, but that King had impressed upon him how serious my situation was at the end of the rope. We walked across Highway 1 and down the narrow road which led into camp.

When I reported to S-3, the greeting was less than warm. "Why didn't you have the entire team rope in so you could continue the mission? You only saw woodcutters, right?" The S-3 major was hated by most recon team members. Apparently, he had not heard about the NVA firing on the Kingbee. Then I had to tell him the bad news, that all of my equipment, my web gear—the old BAR ammo belt which we preferred to wear, all the hand grenades and the backpack with the PRC-25—remained in Laos. "Why didn't you tell someone?" the major asked. I said that I was telling him. He then ordered me to go to S-4, get new gear and to be ready for another target the next day. Before going to S-4, I checked on the Vietnamese members of the team, told them we'd have a new mission in the morning then stopped by the club to see who was there.

Again, nobody said a word. Nobody had heard about my extraction. To me, that extraction was the closest I had come to death without being involved in a firefight and I never wanted to be that close again. Bubba Shore, the third American on our team for that insertion, came up to me in the club and put his arm around my shoulder.

"Do you want to hear the kicker to today? I've waited to tell you this, but guess what?" And he just stood there with this anxious look on his face, which seemed odd at the time. "I don't know how to tell you this, but I'm glad you and Henry didn't make it into the target today."

"Why?" I asked.

"Well, there were no ropes in our Kingbee."

"What?" I asked Shore, who had been on Idaho about a month, to repeat what he had said. The words didn't sink in right away. Bubba explained that the Kingbee he and the second half of the recon team were riding in had no ropes to rappel down. And there were no thick gloves either. That was the topper. Had King, Sau and I rappelled in, our mission would have been compromised without the second half of the team on the ground.

My brush with death seemed to go unnoticed in camp, other than in an After Action Report. All One-Zeros filed AARs after a mission, whether teams spent one minute or one week on the ground. Of course, I told any of my friends who would listen. It took me the remainder of the day to get my new equipment together, get the magazines loaded, find another sawed-off M-79 grenade launcher, tape down the rings and pins on the M-26 frag grenades and get another PRC-25 and rucksack. True to his word, S-3 sent ST Idaho out to another target in the morning.

Chapter Ten

TOUCHED BY THE NVA

Our patrol order was simple and straightforward, but it was a long way from the whole story. By early November 1968, spike teams in FOB 1 had taken a beating. Teams running missions into Laos found it harder and harder to penetrate the Prairie Fire AO.

Enemy trackers were getting better and Charlie kept installing more 37mm anti-aircraft guns, which were extremely effective against choppers. In addition, the NVA began putting spotters on LZs. Spotters were indigenous farmers, VC or NVA troops who relayed information regarding any landing in an LZ, and because the number of good LZs was limited, they'd begun to booby-trap some of them, too. These booby traps were triggered when a helicopter struck a thin, taut tripwire strung across the LZ. The trip wire was connected to firing devices in anything from hand grenades to 250-pound bombs that had failed to explode on impact—bombs the NVA repaired, activated and hid on the LZ. Nonetheless, the brass in Saigon and the S-3 boys at FOB 1 never relented in trying to get a team on the ground in the Prairie Fire AO. Because of the endless NVA activity in Laos, Saigon had an equally endless appetite to get as much intelligence from the AO as possible. So FOB 1 kept running missions and it felt like our team set a record of sorts by

Another night of poker in the Green Beret Lounge at FOB 1. With back to camera, John S. Meyer. To left is an unidentified player, Tony Herrell, Dan Cook, Muskets gunship pilot, Don Wolken and another unidentified player. Note the big sign on the wall: it's one of several that were hung in the club honoring the Special Forces soldiers detailed to FOB 1 from the 1st Special Forces Group, in Okinawa, Operation Detachment A Team 214. Those teams ran many missions before men from the 5th Special Forces Group were transferred to MACV-SOG operations in C&C. (Photo courtesy of John E. Peters)

getting shot out of more LZs than any team in Phu Bai.

Setting that record was a draining, often deadly exercise that ran like this: As the team leader, I'd get a target in the morning. Covey would pick primary, secondary and alternate LZs. The team would load up on the Kingbees, go into the primary LZ and get shot out of it. Then we'd get shot out of the secondary and alternate sites. Because the flights to the Prairie Fire AO were so long, we'd have to fly back to Phu Bai, refuel, eat lunch, get another target and try it again with identical results in the afternoon.

Gone were the days when S-3 held formal briefings in the S-3 operations room in Phu Bai. There the Covey pilot and Covey rider reported what they found in the AO that morning. If they hadn't flown over the target area, they would have the latest Air Force intelligence reports on anti-aircraft weapons in the area. S-3 would give a brief description of the target area: the terrain, the mission and the latest on anti-aircraft weapons. The One-Zero would report on the VR he had flown the prior day over the target area, including the general escape and evasion plan and the rallying points. He would tell those attending the briefing which LZs he had picked, based on his observations and after reading any updated intelligence reports from Saigon, the Air Force and various intelligence agencies. Those were the days.

After four days of being run out of LZs, ST Idaho was beat. The fatigue of being airborne for so long and then flying into an LZ and either getting shot out of it or spotting enemy personnel, which compromised the mission, took its toll. For example, as the Kingbee began to spiral downwards into the LZ, the adrenaline would begin flowing. The sluggishness wore off. As the One-Zero, my primary responsibility was looking at the LZ for any people, weapons, tripwires or anything suspicious. The One-One would have his hand on my shoulder, looking at the wooded area for spotters, trackers or armed NVA troops. On the fourth day, we were blown out of the three LZs in the morning. On the last one, the Vietnamese door gunner on the H-34 opened fire with his old 30-caliber machine gun before we were close to the LZ. He pointed to the wood line and said “VC!” I couldn’t see what he was pointing at, but the Kingbee lurched out of the area and headed east for FOB 1. The entire team nodded off during the return flight.

While the team ate lunch, the S-3 told me the target for the afternoon of 8 November would be Echo Eight. Shortly after receiving the assignment, I found our Covey rider for the target joking with a couple of guys in the club. When I told him that our afternoon target was Echo Eight, the smile drained from his face.

“Don’t forget what happened to Lane. Be extra careful out there. Charlie has his fucking act together there, and we still don’t know what happened to Lane.” Even though the fact sheet on Lane’s last day was seared into my mind, Spider promptly reminded me that Lane was inserted into Whiskey Five, a target a few klicks away from Echo Eight. After Lane’s team was inserted, the radioman gave a team okay. That was the last anyone ever heard from them. With Spider’s warning ringing in my ears, I briefed the team. Sau’s eyes lit up when I showed him the map and our latest target.

“Number fucking ten target!” he exclaimed. He had been present at Lane’s final briefing, but didn’t run that fatal mission. After we ate lunch, we boarded the Kingbees and headed west. Lane and the other missing members of ST Idaho haunted us. En route to the target, Spider radioed me that he had found a good LZ on the side of a mountain. As the One-Zero, I carried the radio on ST Idaho because there had been a few cases where young radiomen accidentally misdirected air strikes onto their teams or had not maintained proper radio security while on the ground.

I sat in the door when we neared the target area and Shore crouched behind me. When the Kingbee pilot spotted the LZ, the old H-34 suddenly went into a dying swan act as he spiraled downward several thousand feet toward the clearing. A few hundred feet from the ground the pilot revved the engine and flared for a landing. It was at this moment that the vastness of the jungle, its height, its darkness, its forbidding nature, loomed over everything.

As we descended, I searched the LZ for booby traps. Shore scanned the wood line for any NVA, trackers or anything suspicious.

For the first time in four days, there was no greeting party or booby traps. The insertion was slick. From the LZ, we found a narrow path through several giant trees into the jungle, leading to an enormous wooded area that looked more like the White Mountains of New Hampshire than a Southeast Asian jungle. We were finally on the ground. The adrenaline wiped out any fatigue. Because the wooded area was so open, I put the team on line as we advanced north up the mountain, instead of moving in the traditional linear fashion. Sau reminded everyone to cover their tracks. Because the insertion had gone so well and the vegetation was less dense than the jungle we were accustomed to moving through, I had the team advance as quickly as possible. As we moved up the mountain, I radioed Spider with a team okay. Usually, after receiving a team okay, Spider would fly out of the target area. On that day, he didn't.

"Be careful...I'm going to fly over another team and I'll be back in an hour. I'll stay over target until I hear a 'click' team okay from you." A "click" team okay was merely quickly breaking squelch three times on the PRC-25 handset. Without speaking, we minimized the NVA's radio direction finding (RDF) capabilities and enhanced our chance of staying on the ground longer.

I wanted to get as far away from the LZ as quickly as possible. For more than an hour we pushed up the hill, moving on line for at least 30 minutes before returning to the more traditional in-line formation. Because we moved without taking a break, climbing straight up, the team was sucking gas, me included. We were still a long way from the top of the mountain, which was where I hoped to establish our RON site. After about 75 minutes on the ground, Son, who was running point, and Sau, who was behind him, signaled "trail ahead." Son and Sau moved forward for a point reconnaissance while the rest of us caught our breath. This was the first time Sau had agreed to have Son run point for us. Son was one of our younger team members and had joined ST Idaho after Lane's team disappeared. Sau returned in a few minutes. Speaking through Hiep, our interpreter, he said there was good news and bad news. The good news was there were NVA walking casually along the east-west trail. Some of them had AK-47s on their shoulders without magazines in them. He didn't think they knew we were there. The bad news was the trail was wide, as wide as two lanes on an interstate. I looked up to see if I could tell what the weather was doing. Even though the vegetation was thinner than usual, the trees were incredibly high and appeared to have at least one or two layers of jungle vegetation that blocked direct sunlight. I couldn't tell what our weather situation was. Earlier in the day, the weather had been spotty, and in Laos the weather could take a dramatic turn for the worse quickly and without warning.

The weather wasn't the dominant concern in my mind. I wanted to cross the trail and get our ambush set up. If we had a little luck, we could snatch a POW and return to Phu Bai in time to eat supper in our outstanding mess hall. On the north side of the trail were NVA telephone lines. I told Sau I wanted to get across ASAP. Shore moved east and I moved west along the trail to provide security while the team crossed without incident. I moved the team about 100 yards north of the trail as we reconnoitered the area. Sau climbed one of the telephone poles and started a wiretap on the phone lines. Meanwhile Shore, Son and Tuan moved down the mountain and set up our ambush. The wooded area worked to our advantage; it wasn't the thick sort of jungle where you couldn't see 10 feet in front of you. Team members could move quickly, yet had enough cover to avoid being seen from the road. The ambush munitions consisted of two claymore mines facing the trail, with the inner killing arcs crossing in the center of the ambush. ST Idaho had spent hours practicing placement of the claymores at the correct angle and distance from the trail. That practice paid off here. Tuan, Son, and Shore knew exactly how far apart the claymores had to be at the ambush site. Between the arcs of bearings thrown from the detonated mines there was an area big enough for one person to survive. And in the middle of that area, exactly six feet from the trail, was a piece of C-4 plastic explosive that was powerful enough to knock unconscious the one person who survived the claymore killing zone. We knew the C-4 was the right amount because one of our fellow Green Berets, Lynne Black, practiced detonating different quantities of C-4 until he knocked himself out on our firing range at Phu Bai.

Next, Son and Tuan placed claymores at the east and west ends of the ambush zones for team security, and Cau put a claymore north of our team for rear security. It was textbook perfect. With the ambush set up, Shore and I started joking about where we'd spend our bonus and extra R&R. MACV-SOG had promised that all team members who captured a live NVA soldier would get a cash bonus and a five-day R&R anywhere in the world. We had good reason to dream. Sau and Hiep, who spoke French, English, Vietnamese and understood some Laotian, were monitoring the wiretap. As we sat on the north side of the Ho Chi Minh Trail, we observed several more NVA soldiers, including an officer, walking casually without realizing we were contemplating snatching their bodies for a quick trip to Saigon. When Spider returned, I could barely contain my enthusiasm. I told him to scramble the Kingbees and to give me a precise time on target (TOT) at our primary LZ because we'd have one live NVA package. Because I was transmitting in the clear, the NVA POW portion of the message was in code, just in case Charlie was monitoring our frequencies. Then things turned to shit.

"Don't move!" Spider said. "Don't move! Don't breathe! Don't fart! Don't do nothing!" he said in an unusually nervous voice. Before I could ask why, he continued. "I'm at 10,000 feet and I can't see you. You're completely socked in. Right now we couldn't find a mountain down there, let alone a spike team. Cool it. Don't do anything. And above all, don't make contact until this weather breaks." Then I remembered seeing a bank of clouds to the west as we were inserted into the target. Before I could pass on Spider's bad news to the team, we heard tank engines starting and the tanks began to move north of our position farther up the mountain. And it sounded as though a few more were starting their engines as the first tanks moved out. Then we heard the sound of dogs coming from the direction of our LZ. All of a sudden, people on the trail started running. There were no more casual Sunday walkers on the trail. A squad of NVA went past, moving west. Then I thought about Lane. Spider's last warning, "Don't move. Don't do anything," was ringing in my ears.

Within minutes, from the direction of our LZ, we heard the first shots fired by scouts or trackers, who were working with the dogs. We heard a small explosion. Bubba had left a few “toe poppers” behind at the LZ. We knew the NVA were going to be extra peeved with us now. It was also obvious that the damn dogs were heading north and had found our scent. I ordered the ambush disassembled and repacked. Through Hiep, I told Sau to run the wiretap as long as possible. Again, through hours of practice, Sau and several other members of the team knew how to rig the wiretap in such a fashion that they could pull it down with a quick jerk on the wire that led from the Panasonic tape recorder to the phone lines. CIA operatives told us to tap into NVA phones anytime we could because even though we might hear nothing during the wiretap, the spooks could amplify the tape a hundred times and pick up voices from it, thus giving them one more source of information on the enemy. They said the NVA phones, unlike American phones, were open all of the time, even if sitting in the cradle. CIA technicians would get insight and intelligence from listening to any conversations that were picked up by the constantly open lines.

The tanks that were north of us sounded as though they were heading west, so we moved east. Before we left, Sau placed large quantities of ground black pepper in the area where we had set up our ambush, to foul the noses of the dogs. We continued to move east around an enormous mountain as the activity continued to escalate behind us. During that unsettling period of time, we crossed a major trail and a small footpath without incident. At approximately 1800 hours, we encountered a mountain creek that ran south down the hill. It had lots of water in it and steep embankments on each side. We jumped in the creek and moved north, upstream, for 15 minutes without pause. Because of the heavy cloud cover, darkness was beginning to set in. Sau, who had been running missions for three years, agreed that it was best to move as long as we could. Occasionally the team stopped and all eight members walked up the embankments at different spots along the creek, into the jungle, setting false trails for the dogs to follow. Sau again laced one of the false trails with black pepper. By last light the team was exhausted, hungry and wet. To further dampen our spirits, Spider said the weather had gotten worse. Again, we violated recon team protocol, which dictates that an hour before darkness, a team should set up its RON and, if time allows, reconnoiter the area and place claymores outside the RON perimeter. Nothing about this mission was routine, however, and the thought of dogs bearing down on us had me push the team to keep moving up the creek for a short while in the growing darkness.

Finally, we moved up the east embankment to set up a hasty RON. I was the last person up the creek bank. As the team settled in, I found a tree and sat next to it, facing the creek. Since we had an eight-man team, it seemed as though it took us longer to settle into the RON. Here, the vegetation was much thicker. As usual, I had Sau check out the entire perimeter, and handle any team security issues, such as putting out claymores in the direction of all the trucks that we could hear to the south. Dozens of trucks were apparently moving along the trail where we had set up our ambush hours earlier. Sau climbed the biggest tree around to see what was going on. Speaking through Hiep, he told me the trucks were bringing hundreds of NVA troops along the road where we had set up our ambush. They were heading north up the mountain with lanterns, looking for us. The only question was had we moved far enough up the mountain so that the NVA couldn't reach us tonight? Welcome to the deadliest game of hide and go seek I had ever played. We ate our dehydrated rations in shifts. At midnight, the NVA and their dogs were still coming up the mountain. At 0130 hours, Sau said he could see the lanterns approaching our team. Privately, I had been hoping that our first hour on the ground would have put enough distance between us and the NVA. But the NVA had been combating SOG recon teams for several years now. They had studied SOG team habits and reviewed previous encounters with SOG teams while using more aggressive trackers and tactics on LZs.

What the SOG reports failed to mention was that the NVA dogs sounded like the biggest meanest canines to walk the face of God's earth. When they barked, it took them twice the time that it would take a Great Dane. Their bark, combined with the fact that hundreds of NVA soldiers were hunting for us, sparked palpable fear in me. If they found us, there was going to be hell to pay. Additionally, the visibility was zero. The jungle darkness was so black I couldn't see my hand moving in front of my nose, although I could feel the breeze from my hand as it passed my face. With visibility at zero, we had nowhere to run, we had no air assets, and we had no friendly artillery units to call for fire support. Then Mother Nature added one more ingredient: lightning bugs. For several hours the biggest, brightest lightning bugs I had ever seen were fluttering around and inside our RON. When their tails lit up, it seemed to shed unwanted light on all surrounding objects for several feet. They were huge. They seemed bigger than the gargantuan mosquitoes in Massachusetts, which we had combated during field exercises with the 10th Special Forces Group in Ft. Devens. I remember asking myself what we had done to anger the recon gods. We had been swallowed by the jungle, the weather had closed in, someone had unleashed the giant dogs from hell, and now, to add insult to injury, these slow-moving lightning bugs were like an arrow pointed right at us! At one point I remember joking about how all of the lightning bugs were in our RON and none were pestering the NVA. Were they loyal to the NVA out of fear, like the local inhabitants? As far as the dogs were concerned, I had my CAR-15 and it could shut the mouth of any mutt, forever. Lightning bugs, however, were another story. Sometime after 0130 hours, we heard one dog howl after his nose picked up some of the pepper Sau had spread on our trail farther down the mountain.

Several times that night Sau quietly climbed a tree to check on the NVA's progress. Around 0300 hours, the lanterns got low on fuel and most of the NVA finally turned around and went back down the mountain, with the exception of two soldiers. Their lantern was out as they walked up the creek and past us. I thought I heard one soldier speak to the other, but wasn't sure. After they walked past, I gave Hiep, who had a bad cigarette cough, a bottle of cough syrup.

The damp heavy air, the wet ground, and his wet jungle boots had irritated his throat. After a few minutes, the two NVA turned around and came back down the mountain, walking past us in complete darkness. Hiep coughed. The NVA stopped in their tracks. I stopped breathing. Based on what I could tell from listening to them, they were in the creek, just about even with where I was sitting.

For the longest time, there was no further sound or movement. I quietly spread my legs a little farther apart and placed my CAR-15 at an angle facing where I estimated they were standing. On the one hand, I knew that if I opened fire, the muzzle blasts would light them up enough for me to finish them off. On the other hand, the hundreds of NVA who had hunted for us weren't that far away.

Additionally, no one had fired any shots during the night. The NVA and their trackers had maintained complete silence, which was a little surprising. On prior missions in Laos, the trackers had a method of signaling each other with rifle fire. The method was simple, but efficient. If one NVA tracker came across our path in the jungle, he would fire a warning shot or shots. The other trackers would continue to sweep through the jungle, knowing that one of the other tracker teams had picked up our trail and where that team was. Other times, the trackers would have several men moving through the jungle and they would fire several shots in one location, and then one or more shots in another location, in an effort to herd the recon team toward a predetermined location. But that night there had been no warning shots, no herding attempts. Of course, with hundreds of lanterns blazing brightly in the pitch-black jungle, they may have felt no need for firing their weapons.

One of the NVA in the creek started crawling up the embankment toward me. I was still facing the creek. The NVA soldier was good; he only moved when the wind stirred the trees. For a moment, my thoughts drifted to summer camp in New Hampshire years earlier, when we played capture the flag on those clear summer nights. My favorite trick was to use the woods to get as close to the flag as possible. Now, my mind was racing 100 mph, and I realized I was the flag and he was closing in. He was too close for me to tell anyone on my team. The jungle that night seemed deadly quiet, except of course, when the wind stirred. As the NVA soldier crawled closer, I remember thinking that my heart was beating so damned loud that Ho Chi Minh could hear it in Hanoi. I flashed back to my childhood, when we played hide and go seek on West Paul Avenue in Trenton, New Jersey. One of my favorite hiding places was behind the hedges in Mrs. Amico's front yard. I remembered worrying that Teddy Zebrowski or John Wayne Austin, or worse, Barbara Pointon would find me because they could hear my heart beating so loud. I tried to comfort myself by thinking that because I had not been running in recent hours, my heartbeat shouldn't be too loud. Yet my heart sounded like a kettledrum during Beethoven's Ninth. No matter, the NVA soldier kept moving up the embankment. I was very impressed with his stealth. I could barely hear him.

Then it happened. During one windy moment, I heard movement very close to me. It was only a slight sound, but a sound nonetheless. Before the wind stopped, the NVA soldier touched the sole of my size 10 R Army-issue jungle boot. I heard a slight gasp of surprise from him. At that moment, I had a death grip on my CAR-15. I had it on single shot. A CAR-15 on full automatic sounds much different from the bark of an AK-47 on full automatic. If I had to shoot, it would be single shots. For a millisecond I wondered if my left foot was far enough to the left so that when I fired, I wouldn't shoot myself. Time stood still. My pucker factor was minus zero. After a few of the longest seconds in my life, the wind stirred, but there was no movement. He remained still.

After what felt like an eternity, the wind stirred again and I heard the NVA move backward just slightly. He was so cool. I knew he was still facing me. I wondered why I couldn't hear his heart. The jungle around us remained pitch black. The lightning bugs had left the RON. I kept hoping that one lightning bug would have gone down the bank so I could see the NVA soldier's face, just for a second, so I could carry his face in my memory. However, I couldn't see him. I wondered if he could see my CAR-15 pointing at him. At that point, I didn't dare shoot, unless I had to. By now, I felt the very last thing in the world I wanted to do was to fire a round from my CAR-15. I really did not want to alert the trackers' buddies as to where we were. The NVA and their trackers knew this mountain like the back of their hand. We only had the maps provided to us by S-3. As the soldier moved down the embankment, I realized it would have been nice to have more intelligence, make that more accurate intelligence, about this target area before we actually got on the ground.

During his return trip down the embankment, the NVA used the same method—he only moved when the wind blew. When it blew again and the tree branches moved, he moved. If it were a longer breeze, he'd move a little farther. I forget how many times this routine repeated itself before he finally reached the creek and his NVA pal at the bottom of the embankment. The two NVA soldiers moved out, but only when the wind blew. I thought I heard muffled tones between them during one stirring of the leaves and branches. When I finally looked at the luminous dial of my watch, I was amazed to see that it was shortly after 0400 hours. I thought I heard a man slip on a rock down the creek a few minutes later, but as always, that sound occurred simultaneously with a wind movement. As soon as I was certain the NVA were gone, I spread the word to the team that we were going to move out before first light. It was only a question of time before the NVA were all over our RON site. I told Bubba Shore to rig another surprise for the NVA.

Shortly before first light, we moved northeast up the mountain. I wanted the team going in the opposite direction of the road where all of the NVA had driven those trucks the night before, while dropping off hundreds of NVA soldiers, trackers and dogs to search for us. The dog aspect of the previous night heightened the intensity for ST Idaho. The NVA's dogs had never hunted us before. We had to get out of the RON and move as far away from it as possible, as quickly as possible, without running into NVA troops or the Pathet Lao troops which were reported in the area. Speaking through Hiep, I asked Sau to be our tail gunner for the first few hours of team movement because I wanted him to conceal our trail as much as possible. Sau also agreed that during the first few hours, we should push up the mountain as far as we could, as fast as we could move, to put distance between the NVA and us.

As we moved out, I assessed ST Idaho. This was the first mission for Bubba Shore, a young kid out of Florida who I picked for Idaho after I became the One-Zero. I liked Bubba as he learned quickly, he respected the Vietnamese men on the team and he was good with explosives. Henry King was a strong, gangly man from Savannah, Georgia, who was smart and agile like a big cat. Actually, he had more time on the ground than either Shore or me. He had run several successful missions with other teams, but had apparently declined to take a One-Zero slot. The other One-Zeros who ran missions with King spoke highly of him, and although this was our first time on the ground together, his silent confidence was a welcome element for me. A few weeks before this target, King had mentioned that he'd like to run a mission with ST Idaho and offered his services as a strap-hanger—someone with experience in the field who joins the team for just one or two missions. During the week before launching into this target area, King had taken a liking to an experimental 40mm pump weapon. It was one of many experimental weapons that surfaced at C&C during the war.

King asked if he could bring it along as his primary weapon. When the weapon worked, it gave a recon team formidable firepower. It fired the 40mm round we used in the M-79 grenade launcher. It held four or five extra rounds in the magazine tube underneath the barrel. It simply looked like an enlarged shotgun, with grooves on the pump mechanism to assist in chambering the rounds. A person could fire five or six 40mm rounds in a tight pattern in less then 20 seconds. King had the strength to hold the weapon and maximize its potential. He could also hold it over his head, as though he were shooting from behind a boulder, and still fire the rounds into a target. However, the feeding mechanism jammed occasionally. Since King had demonstrated some proficiency with the weapon and because we were going to E-8, I agreed to try it out. He carried a Browning 9mm Hi Power semi-automatic pistol as a backup weapon and more than

100 rounds for the experimental 40mm grenade launcher. The thing I liked most about King was his mental and physical toughness. I knew that if the NVA hit us, King would never stop battling. During the previous day, he had complained about carrying all of the extra rounds for the weapon, especially when the team was moving at a faster pace than a reconnaissance team did on a normal mission. Of course, there was nothing routine about this mission now.

The top priority became survival as I looked at my rebuilt team. This was Son and Cau's first time on the ground in Prairie Fire. Spider had drilled ST Idaho hard when we rebuilt the team and every day that we were in camp, we were either on the range or doing live-fire reaction drills outside FOB 1 or some sort of mission-preparation training. The old football adage came to mind: a team is only as good as its weakest link.

I was thinking about that during the first hour of movement, as we walked into the shrouded, cloudy morning light of Laos, moving almost straight up a steep mountain. Again, I pushed beyond the move-10 minutes, wait-10 minutes type of patrolling that we normally followed in the jungle. Instead, I wanted to get as far away from the RON as possible. No one on ST Idaho argued. At first, we patrolled through the thicker jungle vegetation that was more common in Laos, complete with wait-a-minute vines. But after the first hour or so, the vegetation on the ground thinned out. Instead of limited vision as we advanced up the mountain, we could see 50 to 75 meters to our front. Soon I had Son move at a more lateral angle, instead of almost straight up. The mountain remained steep and the footing was often slippery due to all of the moisture in the area. During one break, I asked Sau if he thought Cau could handle the rear security for the next few hours. I didn't know what we were heading into, but whatever it was, I wanted Sau right there. While speaking through Hiep, Sau said he thought Son was doing a good job of moving and that he wanted to build his confidence. Sau would remain behind Son for the next few hours and I'd be number three in line, with Hiep behind me. Then King, Tuan, Shore and Cau.

By noon, the mountain felt as though it was the largest mountain on earth. Because we were fairly beat, we slowed down our movement and lengthened our breaks. We hadn't trained for moving straight up massive mountains all day while fully loaded for combat. Routinely the Americans carried 80 to 90 pounds of equipment; ammunition for two weapons; hand grenades; claymore mines and batteries for the PRC-25 radio. The Vietnamese traveled with less equipment because they were smaller and weighed much less than the U.S. personnel. Sau only weighed 100 pounds soaking wet. Meanwhile, Spider checked in for a second commo check, admonishing me for not making commo during the night with Batcat, one of the airborne command ships that flew over the Prairie Fire AO twenty-four hours a day. Intelligence reports had warned us that the NVA had strong RDF (radio direction finding) capabilities and so I merely broke squelch or said one or two words in an effort to limit my transmissions. Spider stayed over us long enough to report that the AO was completely socked in. Again, he was at 10,000 feet, unable to see anything beneath him except gray clouds. Before we moved out, King asked me if he could ditch some of the 40mm rounds for his experimental pump weapon. I took an extra ammo bandoleer containing 40mm rounds and I asked Bubba to pick one up, too. The jungle we moved through was thick, but not dense. During one break, Sau climbed up an extremely tall tree, virtually disappearing from our sight. When he came back to earth, he said we should continue moving traversely across the huge mountain and try to get to the top by nightfall. That way, if the NVA hit us, we'd have high ground. King again asked for permission to bury some of his 40mm rounds. I told him to bury some of it and to have Bubba booby-trap it. I signaled Cau to help King bury the ammo away from our break area.

On the ground, the day remained gray and often we were covered with mist or dew. The ground was slippery, as jungle floors under double or triple canopy often are. After Cau gave us the all clear, we moved out, continuing on the general azimuth that Sau had given us a few hours earlier. We had moved only ten minutes when Son signaled the team: Stop. Make no movement. The team remained frozen for several minutes. No one moved, no one said a word, as Sau moved closer to Son. Frankly, I couldn't believe we had moved all day without some sort of contact from the NVA. Sau signaled for the remainder of the team to take a break in place and not to move while he and Son reconnoitered an area off to our left, in the opposite direction we were heading. Sau indicated that Son had heard some noise, but he wasn't sure if the noise was woodcutters or trackers. If the noise came from woodcutters, there was little chance of combat at that moment. The woodcutters would eventually tell the NVA what they had seen or heard, but they were usually unarmed. If the noise was from trackers, I hoped Sau and Son could catch them by surprise and blast them. As Sau and Son moved out, I felt fatigued. I felt bone tired. My rucksack felt like it weighed 200 pounds or more. My bad knee was acting up. A few minutes later, Sau and Son returned. They signaled no sweat, indicating the woodcutters had run away when they spotted them.

Again, we moved out. Everyone appeared tired. King and Hiep had requested that we stop the torturous climb and set up a RON. I met with Hiep and Sau. Sau said we should be near a mountaintop soon. He didn't want to set up a RON on the side of a mountain, on slippery ground, if we could set up a RON on high ground. He reminded us again how critical high ground was to a small recon team when the NVA launched wave attacks—a military tactic I never understood, but grew to both fear and respect. I told King and Hiep that I agreed with them, that it would be easier to stop now, but we had to go on if there was a chance to get to high ground. No sooner did we move out than I slipped on the damn wet terra firma and crashed to the ground. As I tried to get up, my good knee was throbbing from the fall. I again lost my footing on the slippery soil and landed on my right knee, again rolling to the right. My right cheek landed on the wet ground. For an instant, I was so tired, so angry about falling that I felt like quitting the push up the hill. As I lay there for a few seconds, I felt my right elbow complaining about the fall and I didn't know if I had the energy to get up. I wanted to quit moving and sleep. I told myself I couldn't quit. We weren't in contact with the NVA, we were just battling Mother Nature and she was winning at the moment. I slowly got to my feet. For a moment, I longed to be back on my cousin's farm, working the soil, instead of wiping it off of my face. Finally, we moved out. During our next break, Sau reconnoitered the terrain. He came back with a broad smile on his face and pointed straight ahead, indicating a little twist to the left as he signaled the "take a break" hand sign. Sure enough, we had finally reached the peak of that God-forsaken mountain.

It had taken us all day. I had Sau and Son check one side of the mountain to the left of where we approached it while Bubba and Tuan inspected the other. Meanwhile, King and I tried to figure out where we were. The weather was still bleak with gray skies and no sign of sunshine. We took off our rucksacks and studied our maps to see where we were. Based on our insertion, our first line of march from the LZ and then the second line angling away from the NVA, I thought I had our location pinpointed on the map. However, there was an extra mountain between the ones that were shown on the map. When Sau returned, I had him and Hiep look at the map, along with Shore, King and myself. Sure enough, there was an extra mountain in between the mountaintops we observed on the map. After trudging up a steep mountain all day, slipping and sliding and picking off blood-sucking leeches, we found the extra mountain laughable. How could a cartographer miss an entire mountain? What did the CIA pay this clown? The day's tension broke. We would talk about the extra mountain for weeks afterward.

As darkness settled in, Spider flew over for a commo check, with the usual report of being 10,000 feet above us with no break in the weather. I gave him a quick team okay and told him we had a RON on top of a mountain.

"If you've got a good RON, settle back, enjoy the view, but avoid enemy contact, because we can't get the birds in to get you out and we can't use TAC Air to cover you. Don't be a hero." As we settled in for the night, several of the men placed claymore mines along the obvious and easiest paths to our RON atop the rocky mountain. Sau was diligent in checking each team member and setting up a night watch rotation among the Vietnamese, while I told King and Shore to catch some sleep after we took turns digging into our freeze-dried rations, which we referred to as LRPs. My absolute favorite was chicken and rice. In a pinch, I'd eat a chili LRP ration. That night, I was so tired and hungry that I poured some water in the plastic pouch, wrapped it up and let it soak for only a few minutes before digging in with the white plastic spoon supplied with the meal. Finally we could relax, as much as we could in the field. I dug into my ruck and pulled out my wool sweater and thin plastic, waist-length rain jacket. Every time I packed the sweater back in sweltering Phu Bai, I felt silly. We were always trying to find ways to reduce the weight we carried on our backs. But I always placed it in the bottom of my rucksack to help cushion the PRC-25 radio against my lower back. The rucks we wore were called indigenous packs, meaning, I assume, that they were small and designed for the indigenous team members of the recon team. Once I put the PRC-25 in the backpack, it filled up quickly. I'd place extra magazines for the CAR-15 in one of the three outside pouches, extra M-79 rounds in another pouch, and extra hand grenades and smoke grenades in the third pouch. The sweater would be placed in a long, narrow pouch on the inside of the rucksack. I'd jam a few LRPs and a can of fruit in the remaining space.

Shore, King and I rotated guard duty, which essentially meant staying awake without moving from our positions in the haphazard perimeter. Sau oversaw our Vietnamese men. About midnight, the sky cleared. We couldn't believe the dramatic change in the weather. The breeze was chilly, but there wasn't a cloud anywhere. Per our SOP, I made a brief radio contact with Batcat or Moonbeam, codenames for different airborne command ships that flew over the Prairie Fire AO twenty-four hours a day. I told them we would see what the weather offered in the morning before making any further plans. A short while later, Spider flew over us "just to see how my team is doing." I gave him a quick team okay and asked if there were any choppers equipped for night extraction. "Negative," replied Spider. Recon teams seldom heard from Covey at night, but somehow Spider made it over our RON. That extraordinary effort brought a degree of comfort to my aching body. Later that night, I started scanning the PRC-25 FM frequencies, monitoring the airwaves for any radio traffic. A few months before this mission, we had heard about the Russians and Chinese working in "neutral" Laos. I was tired, and switching the frequencies helped to break up the monotony.

As I clicked down each cycle on the FM radio, I heard someone speaking Russian. When I went through Special Forces Training Group in Ft. Bragg, I had a Russian roommate. Often, after he had consumed his first pint or two of vodka, he spoke Russian, usually casting dispersions on the uncouth Yankee imperialists who didn't speak his language. That night in Laos was the first time any recon team from FOB 1 or FOB 3 had audio proof of Russians in Laos. I tried to raise Batcat or Moonbeam, but couldn't. I tried Spider's frequency with no luck. I removed the short antenna from the PRC-25, replacing it with the long antenna that extended the PRC-25's reception and transmission range. I moved to the east side of the mountain and tried to contact Lemon Tree or Leghorn, radio sites manned by MACV-SOG personnel. Again, no luck.

While I was on the radio, Shore came around to my side of the mountain; his eyes wide open with amazement. "You've got to see this to believe it. I think we're in the Twilight Zone," he said. I told him about the Russian radio conversation I had heard and asked him if there was any way we could get the Panasonic tape recorder that we used for wiretaps to record the Russian conversation for the MACV-SOG brass in Saigon. As I monitored the Russian conversation, I walked around to the west side of the mountain. Shore simply pointed west, with his mouth wide open, toward a range of huge Laotian mountains. Only they weren't covered in darkness as our mountaintop. The base of the mountains was lighting up like a massive Christmas tree. It was well after midnight, we had Russians on our radio and the middle of the jungle was lighting up. I frantically dialed each FM frequency I had listed, attempting to raise an American, any American, to let them know about the Russians. Everybody in the world knew the Russians were supplying the North Vietnamese Army, but actually hearing them in Laos added an entirely new dimension to our ugly little war. Off in the distance, I heard a plane. From day one of my involvement in the secret war, the U.S. dominated the air over the Prairie Fire AO. At first, I assumed it was an U.S. plane. However, as Ivan's plane drew closer, we realized we were catching a rare glimpse of a unique aspect of this war that only a few, if any, U.S. intelligence or State Department staff knew about.

As the plane came within range, the lights to our west grew brighter, giving Laos the appearance of Broadway. Weird! The Russians were flying a resupply mission to the lighted side of the mountain. From our RON, the area appeared to be bigger than several football fields put together. I told Bubba to try and raise someone on the URC-10 emergency ultra-high frequency radio. This compact radio had an emergency beeper on it. When activated, the beeper was on a frequency that was allegedly monitored by all U.S. aircraft flying over the AO, whether Navy, Air Force or Marine Corps. By now, everyone was awake, looking at the Laotian mountain base. For several minutes ST Idaho simply stood there in silent amazement, gazing at the incredibly brilliant lights made all the brighter by the inky darkness of the jungle night.

By the time I raised someone on the radio, Ivan's plane had turned around and headed north. When I issued our first verbal report, the radio operator was incredulous.

"You saw what? Where? The pilot was speaking what language?" A short while later, Moonbeam was on the scene, at least on our radio frequency. I requested that we go to an alternate FM frequency. Moonbeam communicators acknowledged that they had our primary, secondary, alternate and emergency frequencies. Again, the male voice was cool and calm, but had a certain edge of incredulity to it. Now that the Russian plane had left our AO, I was very concerned about NVA RDF capabilities and told them that had they been within range, we could have bagged a Russian plane! To complicate matters, Spider flew over in the morning, asking for further details on our sighting and the issue of the extra mountain came into play. Spider wanted to pinpoint Ivan's DZ (drop zone). Although the weather was closing in, Spider tried to locate the DZ and us. But the extra mountain and a possible missing mountain range made it nearly impossible to pinpoint Ivan's DZ. It was too cloudy to flash him with a signal mirror. By 0700 we were socked in again and Spider had to get above the clouds.

We hadn't heard the dogs in over 24 hours, so I sent Sau and Son out to find the tank trail while Shore and Tuan went out to find some water. Sau knew how to operate the URC-10. I gave him King's URC-10 and I kept Hiep nearby me in case Sau radioed. Shore had his own URC-10. Because King was carrying a pump-action 40mm grenade launcher, I kept him on the hill with me. Additionally, I had a personal problem. During the night, my lower left rear molar had fallen apart and I was in a lot of pain. I asked Son for some of his rice and kept packing the cracked tooth with rice to keep the air off of it. I was afraid to use the morphine Syrette we carried, because they were to be used only in emergencies. Meanwhile, Shore and Tuan observed some woodcutters hacking away on the large trees, cutting out one of their slash-and-burn fields that were so plentiful in the Laotian mountains. They returned to our position by noon without incident. Sau and Son searched for several hours before spotting some trackers. Shortly after seeing them, Sau and Son heard the dogs and returned to the hilltop. We hadn't heard anything from the area of our previous RON. Sau felt it was only a matter of time before the trackers pinpointed us and he strongly suggested moving to another location. Ten minutes later we were heading down the backside of the mountain. After descending about 1,000 feet, we moved west, back toward the direction we had come from. I assumed the NVA had searched thoroughly for us in that area the previous day, thus, there was less chance of a large concentration of NVA in that area.

During our travels we crossed several trails that weren't on the map, but were heavily used. As recon men, we hated trails. We disdained them and seldom used them. The reasoning was simple: The NVA knew the area, knew it well, and we didn't. We didn't know where the night rest spots were on the trail, where trail security was posted or how many NVA were patrolling the area while we were on the ground. The general rule of thumb for our teams was to avoid trails, stay in the jungle, and stay alert and unpredictable. There were many stories of recon teams who lost men during contact with the NVA on a trail. Thus, when we crossed a trail, we placed two men out as flank security, one to the left of the trail and one to the right, in an attempt to give us early warning of NVA activity. Once security was in place, the point man would cross it. Then we'd each follow him, trying to walk in his footprints. Security was quickly established on the other side of the road, while the remainder of the team moved across the trail. The tail gunner's job was to cover our tracks as well as possible. The jungle boots worn by our recon teams had a distinctive pattern on the sole and would spark a great deal of NVA activity if discovered on a trail. As we moved down the steep mountain, my knees were aching. King asked for permission to dump a few more rounds of 40mm ammo. I gave him the okay. The experimental 40mm weapon was large, bulky and heavy in the jungle. Several times, King became entangled in jungle vegetation because of it. At last light, we found a series of huge boulders that were reminiscent of the prehistoric Stonehenge monument. There were limited entrances into this rocky area. Several of the stones were huge and high. It would be hard to launch a successful mass assault against us if we were pinpointed.

We set up with claymore mines extended along the two most obvious paths approaching our RON. About midnight, ST Idaho was collectively shocked out of its sleep when we heard barks. The dogs were a good distance away, but just hearing those long barks raised the hair on the back of my neck. The jungle was pitch black again. Before darkness fell, I had given Spider a SITREP and explained why we had moved from the mountaintop. When Moonbeam checked in at midnight, its crewmembers asked if we had any more UFO or Russian sightings. I resisted the temptation to tell them that the only sighting we had was actually an audio "sighting" generated by the largest dogs in the world. And that if they wanted to come down and deal with them,

Gathered on the three-quarter ton Army truck in front of the indig recon billets, fall of 1968. From left: standing is John T. Walton; on the hood is John S. Meyer in white T-shirt; next to him is John Smith. Seated on the dashboard with a broom is Ron Zaiss with Henry King behind the steering wheel and Charles Borg in his ever-present black hat. Standing on running board is Pete Boggs with Rick Howard seated in the rear.

I'd be happy to sit in their air-conditioned plane, sipping champagne and eating strawberries. Fortunately, the dogs moved away from us.

The evening passed without further incident. Before moving out of the RON at first light, Sau backtracked a short distance from our line of approach and laced the trail with pepper. When he returned, he and Shore placed a few toe poppers at two of the entrances to our Laotian Stonehenge. Spider was overhead early and I told him we wanted to be extracted ASAP. Last night, it sounded as though the dogs had picked up our trail coming down the mountain, but were following it in the wrong direction. It was only a matter of time until they were on to us. I wanted out of there and I told Spider about my aching tooth. After getting a fix on our location, Spider gave us an azimuth to follow to an open area big enough for extraction. He returned in about 30 minutes, however, with bad news: because the weather had finally broken, S-3 at Phu Bai ordered him to insert another spike team into the Prairie Fire AO before he extracted us. A short while later, we heard two mines explode at our RON site. It felt good to hurt Charlie with his own tactics.

By 0900 we had located the LZ and secured it. The clear area had several feet of grass on it and the ground was on an angle because it was on the side of a mountain. Again, we heard the dogs. They sounded like they were either in the RON area or near it. I learned that another spike team had declared a Prairie Fire Emergency after making contact with the NVA. They had casualties and needed an immediate extraction. I couldn't argue with the decision to pull that team first because technically, we had not made actual contact with the NVA. We had what was called a tactical emergency, where we were compromised and the chance of successfully continuing the mission appeared to be slim. Meanwhile, the other spike team was inserted and the air assets moved directly to pull out the ST with casualties. I asked Sau and Son to go back up the steep area we had covered in our line of march to the LZ and install more toe poppers to slow down the NVA. Shore went along to set up a claymore mine rigged to a trip wire. Our tactical scenario stunk. We were in a relatively open area, on a hillside, with minimal cover and the NVA had the high ground.

Time seemed to be our worst enemy, although having limited air resources didn't improve our mood. Finally, the other team was extracted without taking further casualties and Spider was overhead, taking ground fire from north of the LZ. He told us the trusty and reliable Marine Corps' UH-1B gunships with the radio call sign Scarface were seconds away. As we heard the choppers approaching us, one of the toe-poppers that Sau and Son had planted exploded. We knew the NVA were going to be hopping mad now. Spider was able to vector the Scarface gunships to our location quickly. There was no time for orientations. We popped a smoke and seconds later the first Scarface chopper roared in. Because the hills were so steep above us, the first run was parallel to us and the door gunners were firing above us, to the north, toward the NVA coming down the steep jungle slope. The jungle north of us erupted with small arms fire. The second Scarface chopper roared in so close I could see the facial expressions of the door gunner as he blasted the area north of our LZ with his M-60 machine gun. Both Scarface aircraft took several hits. When the A-1E Skyraiders made passes, they also took hits from small arms fire that sounded like AK-47s. During the second A-1E gun run, Sau blew a claymore in the face of an NVA scout. Sau then blew a second claymore and returned to the LZ, reporting more NVA troops right behind him.

King climbed a rock and pumped out five or six quick rounds of HE toward the area the NVA were in. Shore and I fired HE rounds from our sawed-off M-79s. Tuan, our M-79 gunner, added to the 40mm barrage. In between M-79 rounds, the other team members fired north into the jungle with their CAR-15s. King quickly reloaded and unleashed one more barrage, while Shore, Tuan and I continued to pump M-79 rounds north. Apparently, the combination of the air assets and our 40mm barrages slowed the NVA troops long enough for the extraction ships to come into the LZ. Spider told me that the 101st Airborne Division was going to extract us. The Marine Corps gunships would make one more gun run and, for the first time for ST

Idaho, slicks from the 101st Airborne Division would follow right behind them and get as close to the LZ as possible. We were used to Kingbees and knew most of the pilots on a first-name basis. The 101st pilots were good too, but because this was our first time with 101st Airborne Division slicks, I told Shore and King that they had to be the first people to approach the ship and that they had to alert the young door gunners to the fact that five of our men were Vietnamese.

The extraction was slick and quick. When the Scarface gunships made their gun run, the NVA opened fire, including with what sounded like machine gun fire from NVA RPDs. As the second gunship went past us, the first 101st Airborne Division slick screamed into the LZ. The landing zone was at too much of an angle for it to land, so it hovered as Shore and King ran to the aircraft with three Vietnamese from ST Idaho. The second slick was there in a heartbeat. I ran out first to tell the door gunner that I had Vietnamese men on my team. Hiep and Sau followed. As we pulled out of the LZ, the slick took several hits. The three of us returned full automatic fire from our CAR-15s. I threw a white phosphorus grenade down as the area north of the LZ lit up with dozens of muzzle flashes from AK-47s and SKSs. The green tracers from the AK-47s appeared as though they were coming up between my legs. I was told later that as our slick pulled out of the LZ, the Scarface gunships laid down a final fusillade of suppressing fire. The lead Marine aircraft, piloted by Lieutenant Colonel Robinson, had the Plexiglass windshield blown out of the aircraft. In addition, his chopper and the second gunship had taken more than a dozen hits.

When we returned to FOB 1, Lieutenant Colonel Robinson asked if everyone was okay. I said yes and thanked him for his crew's bravery. Before I finished my sentence, the veteran aviator told me he hated pulling our team out of Prairie Fire targets because his aircraft always took a beating. I had never observed the Marine officer in such an agitated state. He asked me if there was ever a target I was extracted from where we didn't get shot up. I told the colonel that I'd buy him and his crew all that they could drink for pulling us out. The ass-chewing didn't stop.

When I walked into S-3, the major accused me of panicking and asking for an extraction prematurely. He asked me why I didn't break contact and continue with the mission. I slammed my CAR-15 down on his desk and explained about Lane, how he had disappeared not far away from our target and how I didn't want to disappear in the Prairie Fire AO. I told him about how the NVA were closing in on us, that the number of hits the Spads, gunships and slicks took during the extraction proved that there were a lot of NVA soldiers on our trail. I explained how painful my broken tooth was and how fatigued our team was. And I reminded him that had Mother Nature cooperated, ST Idaho might have had at least one NVA POW for him to interrogate. He didn't care. He told me to go to the dentist and get the tooth either pulled or repaired, as Idaho had a new target to run the next day.

I wanted to hit him, but he was older and there were witnesses, all with a lot more rank than I had. I went over to the team room to make sure that Shore was getting everything the Vietnamese team members needed. Sau wanted a pass to go see his wife in Phu Luong. Hiep also wanted a pass. I told them we had a new target for tomorrow and that we'd only take a six-man team this time. I had to return to S-2 for a debriefing on the Russian aircraft, resupply and radio frequencies they used. I promised to file a more detailed AAR after dinner. Before going to the dentist, I returned to the Green Beret Lounge in FOB 1 to again thank the aircrews. I hadn't set one foot in the door before Lieutenant Colonel Robinson was up and heading in my direction, repeating his earlier message.

"Tilt, every time we pull you out of a target, my birds get shot up. Look at my chopper! They shot out the Plexiglas." I offered to buy him a drink or two, but he kept on going. I was happy to have an ice-cold can of Coke in my hand while I bought the Colonel whatever he was drinking. After a few more minutes of railing at me, I had to say something.

"Colonel, does this mean that the next time we're in trouble and we call for Scarface, you won't respond to the bell?"

"Hell, no," Robinson responded. "I never said that. It just pisses me off when my aircraft gets shot up. Parts are hard to come by and I'd rather be flying."

I went back to my room and picked up a news magazine with a picture on the front page about the biggest, latest anti-war protest stateside. Insane. Whose side were they on? They hadn't seen Charlie like ST Idaho had. They'd never asked Sau, Hiep and the other Vietnamese men on my team what they felt about the war.

What a day. S-3 refused to pull us out when we were ready for extraction, then S-3 questioned my integrity, despite the fact that we were only minutes away from fighting the NVA in close quarters battle had not Scarface, the A-1Es and the 101st Airborne slicks defended us from the sky. And there are people back in the states protesting this war. I shook my head, dropped my rucksack and web gear, picked up a small ammo belt holding several magazines of 5.56mm ammo, and went to S-3 to get a Jeep. The dentist was only a short drive up the road, but I kept my trusty CAR-15 nearby, anyway. I went to the dentist, got my tooth pulled, and drew new rations and PRC-25 batteries.

The next day, ST Idaho got shot out of five LZs.

CHAPTER ELEVEN

THANKSGIVING IN CAMBODIA

As we approached the end of the month, the FOB 1 brass asked me to take ST Idaho south to assist FOB 6 at Ho Ngoc Tao, located north of Saigon. I gladly accepted the offer. The team needed a break and everyone was happy about heading south. Scuttlebutt in camp among the old veterans of SOG was that FOB 6 targets were dangerous, but not as dangerous as FOB 1 targets. But we knew the recon teams had been hammered running Cambodian targets in the Daniel Boone AO. It sounded dangerous enough to me, especially when Pat Watkins warned me about the flat terrain in Daniel Boone targets, which was a startling contrast to the Laotian mountains we had grown accustomed to in the Prairie Fire AO.

Even though it was November, the heat and humidity in Saigon felt thicker and heavier than Phu Bai. When we arrived in the compound, Bubba took the team to the indigenous quarters while I reported to S-3. There was a lot of activity going on. The OIC (Officer in Charge) greeted me and said the CO wanted to talk to me as soon as he could break free. There was some sort of crisis with the State Department and the CIA that involved one of the teams. No more details were offered. I went back to Bubba. He had found some food and lodging for the Vietnamese team members, all of whom wanted passes to Saigon. I asked Bubba to check with the recon company personnel as to SOP for Vietnamese team members going to town without weapons.

I returned to the office of the Commanding Officer for FOB 6, Lieutenant Colonel Ralph R. Drake. I could hear The Beatles' Rubber Soul playing in the distance.

When Drake finally appeared, he took one look at me and the Specialist 4th Class rank on my arm and frowned. "I thought they were sending me an experienced team," he said. "Are you the One-Zero?"

"Yes, sir. My Zero-One and Zero-Two have been running recon for C and C and working with SF for five years. I've had several missions on the ground in the Prairie Fire AO, both as a One-One and as a One-Zero, including the successful insertion of those three-piece Air Force seismic sensors in the middle of the A Shau Valley."

"You know the One-Zero position is an E-8 or E-9 billet?" Drake asked.

"Yes, sir. My time in grade is only a few months, but during that time I've spent a lot of time on the ground and have been shot out of a lot of targets in Laos. My little people are very good. I'd stack them up against any indig troops in Nam, sir. How can we help you?"

Lieutenant Colonel Drake sighed and told me about his "little" problem. "We've got three NVA divisions that are MIA—the first, the third and the seventh divisions, to be specific. The spooks can't find 'em, aerial reconnaissance can't find 'em and, quite frankly, we're worried as hell that they might be lining up another attack on Saigon or one of our A camps. They took a licking from us during Tet, but they're resilient and everyone from General Abrams to the spooks is worried. As I said earlier, welcome to Ho Ngoc Tao."

Drake reviewed the latest intelligence estimates the U.S. had on NVA strength across the Cambodian border; it was 100,000 plus. The terrain was open and as flat as a pancake. The mission for ST

Idaho: locate one of the three NVA divisions that had disappeared. Gather any intelligence or information on those units and, as always, if the opportunity presents itself, capture an enemy soldier or a porter who moves supplies south on the Ho Chi Minh Trail Complex. After apologizing for having to leave, he asked me to make myself available to talk to him later that evening. He asked if we could launch tomorrow. I told him I'd prefer a night at House 10, the MACV-SOG safe house in Saigon, where SF and folks from intelligence agencies stayed. House 10 was a secure hotel with everything from cold drinks to hot women. Drake chuckled as he left the room, shaking his head no.

I went back to the humble hootch where Bubba and I were quartered. He told me that Hiep and Sau had passes and would be back in camp at first light. I told him that we had to be ready to run a mission in the morning. I also told him about the three missing NVA divisions and watched his eyes widen in disbelief.

"Whoa," he said. "Three NVA divisions? Missing? How did that happen? Let's hope they find 'em before we launch."

I told Bubba to get some extra claymores and to make several 5 and 10-second fuses, in case we had to run from the NVA. As I unpacked and geared up for the mission, Bubba found the S-4 sergeant, who gave him extra claymores, det cord, ammo for our CAR-15s, plus sawed-off M-79s and M-26 frag grenades.

As Bubba unpacked the ordnance, he told me of a warning he received from S-4: in the flat terrain, the NVA would literally try to run over a recon team. Several teams had experienced massive frontal attacks by charging NVA troops. I had heard of this happening to recon teams, but from my experience in Laos, the charging NVA were beaten back before they broke into our perimeter. With that warning ringing in my ears, I told Bubba to give every member of our team a claymore mine with a five-second fuse and extra short fuses, in addition to the conventional hand-held detonator that came with the mine.

As we walked to the mess hall for dinner, the oppressive heat seemed unrelenting. Bubba and I thanked the SOG brass for originally stationing us in Phu Bai, more than 400 miles north, where the heat was a little less sweltering. Over dinner we talked about the mission in general terms: Bubba and I would carry our sawed-off M-79s and our CAR-15s, and we'd take Sau, Hiep, Phuoc and Tuan, our reliable M-79 grenadier, who could pop a high-explosive round into a tire at 200 yards. Since this was our first mission into the Daniel Boone Area of Operation, I reiterated that we'd go very light on water and food, and very heavy on ammo, grenades and claymores.

"I'd rather die hungry than run out of ammo," I told Bubba.

"Three divisions?" he asked, and shook his head.

After dinner, Bubba and I went to the CO's office. I told the staff where I would be when Lieutenant Colonel Drake wanted to brief me. Sometime after 2200, someone from the TOC (tactical operations center) told me the CO wanted to talk to me.

When I reported to Drake, he had a series of photos and maps, plus secret and top secret reports sitting on top of a desk. "Can you go tomorrow?" he asked. I told him we were prepping for a mission with a six-man team and gave him a brief rundown on each member of ST Idaho. I also explained that we'd be very light on food and water, heavy on ammo, grenades and claymores.

We started going through the materials spread across the desk. He methodically reviewed each written report and handed it to me when finished. Some of the reports appeared to be very specific in details, as though someone on the ground, near the missing divisions, had written them. Others were more generalized. Then Drake showed me the photographs. They were high resolution, clear shots taken from high altitude. The pictures brought to mind the photographs printed in The New York Times during the Cuban missile crisis and how they had provided the damning evidence of Russia's intentions 90 miles south of the United States. But Lieutenant Colonel Drake had photographs taken from a much higher altitude than the Cuban photos. Curious, I asked where the shots had come from. He mumbled something about the latest in high altitude photoreconnaissance and moved on.

The CO pulled out a map of the Daniel Boone Area of Operation.

He reviewed the status of several Special Forces A camps recently hit by the NVA and camps anticipating enemy contact from NVA troops staging in Cambodia. Drake then pointed to a spot on the map, suggesting it as a landing zone. Based on everything we had looked at, it looked like a good choice to me. By now it was around midnight. Before I left, Lieutenant Colonel Drake reminded me about the significant differences in the rules of engagement in Cambodia as opposed to the ones we operated under in the Prairie Fire AO. First, recon teams were limited to going only 20 klicks, or kilometers, into Cambodia from the border. In Laos, the western limit was much deeper. Second, we were prohibited from using fixed-wing aircraft. That rule stopped me dead in my tracks: no fast movers and no A-1E Skyraiders? I wouldn't have been standing there if that rule had applied to us while we were in Laos. Third, helicopters and recon teams couldn't use white phosphorus weapons. To every Special Forces troop and aircrew member, the rules of engagement forced on us by the State Department were ludicrous and criminal.

He reminded me that we were going to be inserted on Thanksgiving Day. I told him that we were planning to dine on state-of-the-art chicken and rice LRP rations at the launch site before going into the target. When Drake said he would try to get hot Thanksgiving Day meals out to the team and aircrews before we launched, I thought he was kidding.

Shortly after first light on Thanksgiving Day, Sau and Hiep arrived at the compound. Happy from a good night in Saigon with family members, they quickly prepared for the mission. I explained to Hiep what the area of operation looked like, what the intelligence reports had estimated and what we were hunting for. When Hiep interpreted the mission to Sau, the veteran SOG warrior's face turned sour. Speaking through Hiep, he reminded me of the thin vegetation in the target area and said that some of the indigenous troops had warned him about the NVA getting stronger and using more brute force against FOB 6 recon teams.

Finally, we arrived at the launch site in Bu Dop. At the northern end of the runway was an Air Force compound. We settled into a tent on the east side of the runway and south of the Air Force compound. It looked like a quiet, peaceful launch site. Unbeknownst to me, a short distance away from the tents was a Green Beret A Camp that had recently encountered heavy attacks from NVA soldiers who struck the camp at night, then retreated to the sanctuary of Cambodia.

As we discussed the rules of engagement for our new AO, a chopper landed with a Thanksgiving feast, complete with hot turkey, cranberry rolls, gravy and mashed potatoes. Bubba and I were duly impressed; Drake was a man of his word. The fact that we were getting ready to launch into a new target area didn't diminish our appetites. The entire team enjoyed the Thanksgiving Day food. The gallows humor of the day was that if this was our last meal before getting waxed, at least it was a feast. As we finished overindulging, U.S. Air Force UH-1F model Hueys arrived to slip us into Cambodia. The pilots and crewmembers were from the Air Force's 20th Special Operations Squadron. They called themselves the Green Hornets. The Special Forces people at the launch site had told us they were very good and that the UH-1Fs they flew had more power and flew faster than Army versions of the Huey.

During the briefing, the rules of engagement were repeated again. I mentioned how the lack of fixed-wing assets made me uncomfortable. The Green Hornet squadron leader quickly spoke up, saying that once they inserted our team, they'd fly far enough away so that no one would hear them, yet they'd be able to return to the AO in five to ten minutes if we called for an emergency extraction. He said that the Green Hornet gunships had unique weapons systems, including miniguns in the door gunner position, rocket pods and M-60 machine guns. The pilot also said that after our insertion, the lead ship and the backup aircraft would pull dummy insertions in the area to confuse the enemy.

The Green Hornet pilots further impressed us with their knowledge of their aircraft. They said the Hueys they were flying were the most powerful at the time and that with the flat terrain, they would fly strictly nap of the earth. One officer warned us "snake-eaters" not to let our feet hang too low or they'd hit the treetops going into the target.

He wasn't kidding. As we flew into the target area at full speed, we were close to the trees, but what worried me more was the vegetation. Instead of the dense jungle foliage of Laos, it reminded me of the thinly wooded central New Jersey countryside I had hunted with my cousins.

The door gunner gave me the thumbs up sign. We would be on the LZ in a matter of seconds. As soon as I alerted the team, the Huey was flaring for a quick landing. Bubba exited on the left side with Phuoc and Tuan; I went out the right side with Hiep and Sau. The Huey was up and gone, the insertion slick and quick. The ground under the knee-high grass was wet and sloppy, but as we moved into the wooded area, the soil became firmer. Once in the tree line, we set up our first perimeter. We could hear the Air Force choppers executing false insertions away from us. As we looked up, there was no double canopy. No thick jungle overhead. We could see sunlight. And we could see straight ahead, through the trees, more than 100 yards. This was so different from Laos. I called the Green Hornets and gave them a team okay signal, letting them know the insertion was successful.

Instead of waiting at the LZ for the customary 10 minutes, I moved the team out, heading west, toward the area Lieutenant Colonel Drake and I had targeted the night before. With the vegetation so much thinner, we had to increase the amount of space between team members when we moved. The area was quiet, with little or no bird noise, which was always a bad sign when you were on the ground.

After 10 minutes of cautious movement due west, we took our first break. I did a quick commo check with the Air Force command ship. Again, the Air Force pilots were on the money. They were airborne and they could make clear commo with me. And per the briefing, I couldn't hear their helicopters.

Because the vegetation was so thin, I had Hiep remind everyone that they had to have a 5-second fuse in their claymores. I had Phuoc, our point man, and Bubba put 5-second fuses in two additional claymores and 10-second fuses in a few more. The openness of the

John S. Meyer returning from training at FOB 6 Ho Ngoc Tao in November 1968 with ST Idaho South Vietnamese team members, from left: Cau, Son, Nguyen Van Sau, Nguyen Cong Hiep and Minh. ST Idaho was detached to FOB 6 briefly in November 1968 because the recon teams had taken a beating in the Daniel Boone (Cambodia) Area of Operations. (Photo courtesy of John S. Meyer)

wooded area made me cautious. We hadn't been on the ground too long when Sau, my counterpart, spotted smoke and we moved toward it. Sau, who was number two in our line of march between Phuoc and myself, silently mouthed, "No VC," and we continued forward. As always, Sau's reading of the NVA was correct. He and Phuoc moved deeper into what appeared to be a base camp, as Bubba and I set up a perimeter with the remainder of the team.

Sau and Phuoc reported back in a few minutes. They said we were on the periphery of a huge NVA base camp. The smoke was originating from a fading fire. They said there appeared to be other fire sites that still had warm ashes. Now the adrenaline really started pumping. I had never walked into an NVA base camp before. The fact that there were no NVA troops there at that moment seemed almost unreal. I started taking pictures, but Sau was nervous. His eyes were getting bigger. His speech was getting quicker. Hiep was getting nervous just talking to Sau. Sau was quick, smart, agile, and fearless, but he could smell the NVA and he knew how they worked. He had been fighting them for three years, compared to my five months running SOG targets. From my previous experiences with Sau, I knew that his eyes were an accurate gauge of enemy presence in the immediate area. His eyes were growing bigger by the second.

I wanted to see if we could find a weapons or food cache and suggested going farther west. Not waiting for Hiep's interpretation, Sau looked at me and said, "Call helicopters now! Beaucoup VC come now!" I must have had an incredulous look on my face, because I couldn't hear anything, and I certainly didn't see any NVA troops and I really wanted to grab something to take back to FOB 6 for Lieutenant Colonel Drake. Hell, he had given us Thanksgiving dinner before we shipped out, the Green Hornets had given us a perfect insertion and now we were in a base camp of some sort. But in identical situations in Laos, I had doubted Sau and barely survived to tell about it.

When Sau turned to Hiep, he was more agitated. Before Hiep said a word, I turned to Bubba, who was tail gunner in our formation, and to Phuoc and directed them to turn around. I signaled that we were going back to our LZ. If Sau was overreacting, we'd talk about it later.

"Sau say this is big enemy camp. We're beaucoup lucky no VC here. He found hundreds of fresh footprints going there," he pointed south.

"Di (Go)!" Sau hissed. "Di di mau (Go quickly)!" We were in Cambodia, alone, with no fixed-wing aircraft. Sau's eyes were as big as saucers.

I told Bubba to give me a claymore mine with a five-second fuse. I gave Bubba and Phuoc the "move quick" signal. As we moved back to the LZ, I stayed at the rear of the formation with Sau hastily covering our tracks. We had only gone a short distance when Sau hissed, "Beaucoup VC! Beaucoup VC!"

I could see pith helmets in the distance coming from the south. I radioed the Green Hornets' C&C helicopter and told them to return with their gunships and to pick us up at the primary LZ, ASAP! C&C said they'd have assets on site in 10 minutes or less. That fact, if true, was incredible to me. We never had that sort of response time in Laos. Now, even 10 minutes seemed like a long time. Tuan and I fired our M-79s as two high bursts, which slowed the NVA down for a few seconds. Sau opened fire, shooting single shots and moving backwards, no longer bothering to cover our tracks. I yelled to Bubba to move out at double time. The race for life was on.

Sau hissed to Hiep and pointed north. Damn! There were pith helmets and NVA uniforms coming at us from the north, too, and at a dead run. The elements from the south were apparently from the division that had left the base camp, and the NVA from the north were apparently moving into it. The good news: the NVA were no longer MIA. The bad news: green AK-47 tracer rounds were cracking over our heads. The morning quiet turned into a noisy crescendo as weapons on both sides blasted away.

Sau and I placed a claymore behind a tree, pulled the fuse lighter and ran. The NVA were now running and shooting wildly. We sprinted to catch up to the team as the claymore exploded. The

NVA kept on charging. Sau quickly placed his claymore in front of a tree and ran while Tuan and I provided covering fire. We sprinted toward our team as the second claymore detonated. We felt the blast on our backs as we ran. As Phuoc and Bubba pushed towards the LZ, Hiep, Tuan, Sau and I fired and fell back, using the immediate action drills the entire team had practiced for hours on end. Tuan's M-79 rounds were deadly effective. Those, combined with my M-79 rounds and the CAR-15 fire from Hiep and Sau, temporarily stalled the hard-charging NVA troops.

We reached the LZ quickly in comparison to how cautiously we had exited it. As the team set up a hasty perimeter, Hiep placed another claymore in the path of the NVA that were charging us from the south. To the north, Bubba rigged a claymore with a contact detonator on a tripwire. As the tide of pith helmets flowed toward us, Bubba and I opened fire with our M-79s, and Sau and Hiep opened up on full-auto with their CAR-15s. More NVA emerged from the smoke of the M-79 high explosive rounds and tripped Bubba's claymore. That's when the first Green Hornet gunship arrived. I popped a smoke canister and directed a gun run to the west of our perimeter. Within seconds the gunship roared in front of our perimeter, shredding the NVA ranks, slowing them down for a few seconds. The Green Hornet's firepower was incredible.

Finally, the Green Hornet slick that inserted us into the target area arrived on the LZ, as close to our position as possible, with his left door facing us, and the nose pointing north, or northwest. Fortunately, the Air Force made it to us in less than 10 minutes. The relentless NVA kept coming after us. As Tuan and I each unleashed one more M-79 high explosive round at the NVA, Bubba led the team toward the Air Force Huey. We always had an American lead the team's approach to an American helicopter, to avoid any confusion in regard to the South Vietnamese team members on ST Idaho. I fired the last claymore as a wave of NVA troops got in front of it. That last claymore blast gave me a few, precious seconds to make it to the Huey.

I signaled "all clear" as I approached the Green Hornet Huey and jumped into it. As the chopper started to lift out of the LZ, several

NVA burst from the woods, surprised to see our slick and a second chopper that was providing covering fire. They were gunned down instantly. As the Air Force chopper I was riding in started to lift off the ground, an NVA soldier running at full speed burst from the thinly wooded area onto our LZ, just a little to the left of the door gunner. As the NVA soldier dug his boots into the muddy soil to stop his forward momentum, they kicked up clumps of mud. He tried to bring the muzzle of his AK-47, which was pointing skyward, to bear on our chopper.

I remember watching the clumps of mud from his boots slowly kicking upward toward the rotors as the door gunner and I hit him in the chest with a burst of gunfire. It felt as though I could count the spent shell casings flying from the door gunner's M-60. When the rounds struck the NVA soldier, his forward movement stopped suddenly, so suddenly that he reminded me of a cartoon character who is running at full speed and whose head and feet moved forward while his chest and stomach are slammed backwards from the impact of the bullets. The NVA never hit the ground as the rounds drove him backwards into the woods. He disappeared from our sight as the Huey quickly gained air speed and altitude. We could see dozens of NVA soldiers firing at us. For a second it seemed as though all of their green tracers were heading right at our slick. At the last moment, I threw a white phosphorous grenade down toward the NVA as a final, lethal blast from us. It was something I had done on my previous targets in Laos. For a brief, fleeting moment, I thought about the rules of engagement, which prohibited the use of "Willie Peter" in Cambodia, but dismissed it quickly, as we were deep in Cambodia. I didn't give it another thought.

In seconds, the Green Hornets were screaming back toward the launch site at top speed, whisking us away from certain death, flying nap-of-the-earth. I checked my men for casualties. There were none. As the six men of ST Idaho sat in silence, I looked over and saw the Air Force gunner pumping his fist in the air, talking excitedly into his microphone, still enjoying his adrenaline high. ST Idaho was quiet. Real quiet. We had been moments away from a very violent death and we had killed an untold number of NVA soldiers—soldiers who continued to earn our undying respect. I took no pleasure in killing the enemy. It was simply us or them.

When we landed at Bu Dop, it was approximately 1400 hours. I went straight to the SF personnel to send a SITREP to Drake. I told him that the message was simple: you were right in your estimate of where the NVA are located.

Meanwhile, Bubba tracked down cold sodas and cigarettes for the men on our team. A short while later, the Green Hornets invited Bubba and myself to join them for a Thanksgiving dinner at the Air Force mess hall. We told them that we should be the ones buying them dinner. The narrow escape from Cambodia was sobering. As Bubba and I walked north toward the Air Force area, he asked me what would have happened if the Air Force had been delayed a few more minutes. I told him not to think about that, but to be grateful for Uncle Sam's Air Force and for those five-second fuses on the claymore mines. The gods of recon had smiled on ST Idaho one more time.

In the Air Force mess facility, nobody seemed to mind that Bubba and I were the dirtiest folks stuffing our faces with Thanksgiving chow. We were starved. I found myself savoring the flavor of the turkey, suddenly appreciating turkey more than I had in recent years, or hours, for that matter. The mashed potatoes didn't come close to my mother's, but just being alive to enjoy the meal added extra flavor to them. Afterwards, Bubba and I rolled out of the mess hall and headed back to the SF area of tents and dust. One of the SF launch site people said we had to get back to FOB 6 ASAP for a debriefing. I reported directly to Lieutenant Colonel Drake.

"Give me a thumbnail description of what happened, so I can send that to Saigon, then we can eat our Thanksgiving dinner and do the detailed report afterward," Drake said. "That makes two Thanksgiving dinners and one mission. Not bad for a day's work."

"Make that three dinners," I laughed. Bubba and I ate the third dinner, after making sure that Hiep, Sau, Tuan and Phuoc had turkey and the trimmings, too. Again, we gave thanks to God for the Green Hornets.

On Friday, after a morning of training and weapon maintenance, I gave everyone an overnight pass to Saigon, reminding them that they had to return to base at first light for another mission. Bubba made another supply run. We went over to S-3 for a quick preview of the next day's mission: a POW snatch from Cambodia. Nothing was better than a living person who worked in or drove through Cambodia for picking up useful intelligence. S-3 said there were several roads in an area farther northwest from our Thanksgiving Day target and they would make good targets for Saturday. After the briefing, Bubba returned to S-4 to pick up a few land mines to knock out an NVA truck and a couple of Light Anti-Tank Weapons (LAWs).

At first light, ST Idaho was transported back to the Bu Dop for an early morning briefing. The Green Hornets had recently flown over the target area and knew of several LZs that would place us less than a kilometer away from a road. Intelligence reports indicated plenty of troop movement in the target area, but no specifics. Because the Green Hornets performed so well on Thanksgiving Day, we trusted their judgment on the LZ selection. And again, they promised to pull several fake insertions after they dropped us off.

For the second insertion in a row, I was impressed with the speed and alacrity of the Green Hornets. In no time flat, we were on the ground. Again, the choppers pulled several fake insertions away from our target area. I gave a team okay and we moved out toward a road the Green Hornets had spotted. This time, although the vegetation wasn't as thick as Laos, there was a second canopy, making it a bit denser than what we moved through on our prior mission. We didn't need to have such a large interval between team members. We moved for 10 minutes and took the traditional 10 minute break to listen to our surroundings. Because we had good cover and another excellent insertion, I pushed the team to move longer than 10 minutes. Nobody complained. We had a perfect insertion; we were in "Indian Country" and on the move.

It wasn't too long before we heard the first trucks moving from north to south. We advanced toward the road with extreme caution. The intervals of the trucks heading south were irregular. The first few we heard were single trucks. Then there was a group of several trucks. Phuoc went up to inspect the road. He told us the road was wide and that the vegetation next to it was thick. I took out my 35mm camera and moved to the roadside with Bubba and Phuoc. The vegetation was so thick that I could poke my head through it, place the camera up to my eye and take several shots of trucks moving toward us without being observed by the truck drivers or the NVA. For the next hour or so, we moved along the roadside, finding the best spot to set up an ambush. At one point, I came to a swatch of vegetation that was so thin I could pass through it without effort to get onto the road. There was no roadside pull-off area. As I walked north, I came across a road sign that had the number 33 on it. I wondered if this were Route 33 in Cambodia and if it headed toward the shore like the Route 33 in Trenton did.

Bubba picked the best ambush point and prepared to place one of the land mines in the road. After several false starts, Bubba got out into the road and started digging frantically, while the rest of the team remained behind the vegetation. We could hear another truck coming, so Bubba quickly covered up his hole and returned to the team. As he was moving through the brush, I couldn't believe my ears. The truck I heard sounded like a 1946 or 1947 Chevrolet truck. My dad had a 1949 Chevrolet milk truck when I was a kid and I would have known that Chevy truck sound anywhere in the world. Hearing it in Cambodia was one more oddity of the war.

When Bubba said he was ready to plant the mine, we put together a traditional recon ambush, with two claymore mines in the center. The arcs of fire were set at an angle so that everyone would be killed except for the person in the very center of the ambush. At dead center was a piece of C-4 plastic explosive, which was cut to size and had enough force to knock a man out. Then, to the northern and southern flanks, the team placed claymores and we placed one behind us for rear security. Once the ambush was in place, several more trucks passed down the road. These trucks carried NVA troops, but everyone in the trucks seemed unaware of our presence. This was a startling contrast to Thanksgiving Day. I told Bubba to plant the land mine so we could set it off from our ambush site. He looked at me with a huge smile on his face and asked where I wanted to spend the bonus we would get for capturing a POW. SOG had a policy that stated any recon team that captured a live POW would receive a five-day R&R to anywhere in the world and a cash bonus of $100.

As Bubba planted the land mine, I called the Green Hornets' C&C helicopter to notify them that we'd need a lift real quick. I gave them the code term to advise them that we were going to attempt a POW snatch. I was excited as I waited for a response. This was recon at its best. We'd had a perfect insertion. We were deep in enemy territory and the NVA didn't know we were in his backyard. It was a classic scenario for an ambush. John Wayne would have been proud. For a brief moment, I dreamed of an R&R in Hawaii or Hong Kong, somewhere exotic. But the recon gods had other ideas.

The Green Hornet C&C acknowledged my radio transmission but said, "Abort mission. Return to insert LZ ASAP." I looked at the handset as though it was a pit viper that had just bitten me.

"Repeat last transmission," I said, sounding incredulous.

"Abort the mission. Return to LZ ASAP for immediate exfil." I questioned his sanity. I told him we'd have a live POW in a matter of minutes. I was shocked. I asked him to repeat one more time and he said, "Per the direct order of General Abrams, you are ordered to abort the mission and return to the LZ ASAP." SF men knew the old tank commander hated Special Forces troops, but this was taking military rancor too far.

When I told the team to pull in the ambush, they looked at me as though I had eaten a bad batch of peyote buds mixed with Cambodian red marijuana. I told Bubba to replace the handheld detonator with a pressure detonator. I wasn't pulling that mine out of the road for anyone. Reluctantly, the team returned to the LZ. When we were about 100 meters from the LZ, Bubba wanted to fire one LAW at a tree in the distance for practice. I told him that when he was done, to booby-trap the LAW tube with one more deadly surprise for the NVA.

The Green Hornets arrived and we had one of the few uneventful extractions ST Idaho enjoyed during my tenure with the team. I asked the door gunner what had happened. The pilot tried to tell me, but there was too much noise in the aircraft. Finally, I put on the door gunner's helmet and spoke to the pilot on the intercom. He told me that Cambodian Prince Norodom Sihanouk had filed a formal complaint with the U.S. government about the use of a white phosphorus grenade in Cambodia on Thanksgiving Day. It was a clear breach of the State Department's agreement to allow SOG teams to operate in Cambodia. When we returned to FOB 6, Lieutenant Colonel Drake pulled me aside to ask about the white phosphorus grenade. I gave him two versions of the story: off the record, I did it and I had no regrets. I reminded the CO that ST Idaho would have suffered severe casualties had the Green Hornets not reacted so quickly to our call for an extraction. The official version, I didn't know anything about the unfortunate and untimely explosion of the grenade in the lovely country of Cambodia and I was sincerely sorry if any vegetation was damaged by it. That version went into my After Action Report and that was the last we heard of the incident.

Since it was Saturday, I gave everyone passes for Saigon, but told them to be ready for another target Sunday morning and that I wanted everyone to be mission ready. I also said I wanted to take eight men, to give us more firepower in the field and to give the younger men on the team experience on the ground.

Recon didn't rest on Sundays, so we geared up for another Daniel Boone target. This time, our insertion was delayed several hours because another FOB 6 recon team was in heavy enemy contact and the Green Hornets were working the NVA over, but good. After a rough Saturday night in Saigon, all of us took naps at the Bu Dop launch site. This time, the mission was a general reconnoiter of a target northwest of the launch site in Cambodia. If we were able to get a POW, that would become our top priority. We also carried equipment to execute a wiretap if we found any NVA telephone lines. Because the white phosphorus incident was still a political hot potato, the brass strongly suggested that we not blow up any trucks or create any major incidents.

A rare photograph of FOB 1 recon team members inside an H-34 Kingbee, of the South Vietnamese Air Force's Special Operation Squadron, 219. This photo was taken Nov. 29, as this group of recon men volunteered for an Eldest Son Operation in Laos. From left, Lynne M. Black Jr., Rick Howard, John E. Peters, the Kingbee door gunner and John McGovern. Please note the feet of the Kingbee pilot on the right and his co-pilot on the left. This mission was scrapped while the team was enroute to the target due to bad weather. The following day, another group volunteered for the mission and everyone died after anti-aircraft gunfire hit the Kingbee enroute to the target. (Courtesy of John E. Peters)

Later in the afternoon, the Green Hornets arrived. After a quick briefing, we agreed to a two-helicopter insertion with dummy insertions, only this time the dummy insertions would occur before we jumped off of the slick. Again, the insertion was flawless. We were in the wood line and on our way for a general area reconnaissance. This time, we played it by the book, moving 10 minutes, then waiting 10 minutes. As we moved, I swore that I'd never run an eight-man team again. It was too cumbersome. In this target, the vegetation still made me a tad on edge, as it had a second canopy in some areas, but still gave us long lines of sight, something we weren't used to. The younger team members I took with us, Chau, Son and Cau, moved well in the bush. Son was working so well that Sau worked him on point for a while, to give him experience.

As darkness approached, we looked for a good spot to RON. With the flat terrain, finding a good RON became really dicey. Ordinarily we'd look for high ground, dense vegetation, or an area far from any trail. Finally, we found one and Sau set up a perimeter, set up the watch rotation and oversaw the placement of extra claymore mines. In one area where the vegetation was thin, Bubba placed a couple of toe poppers in the ground. I couldn't sleep. The flat terrain played on my mind. Also, I couldn't believe how good the Green Hornets were on insertions. This was the third time they had inserted us without any trackers or dogs getting on our trail. In Laos, it was a different story.

Before first light, the entire team was awake, alert, retrieving the claymore mines and preparing to move out of the RON. After a night on the jungle floor, I wanted an R&R anywhere with firm beds, clean sheets and cold drinks. Because I insisted on carrying the PRC-25, there was little room in my backpack except for essentials. At night, when I slept on the ground, I did so without an air mattress or hammock. The sole item of comfort was an Army-issue pullover sweater that buttoned up to the neck. Whenever I put it on at night, I always worried about Charlie hitting us as I was pulling the sweater over my head. It was one of the few creature comforts I allowed myself or had room for in my rucksack.

Shortly after first light, the Green Hornets' C&C aircraft flew into the edge of our AO for a routine commo check. I gave him a quick team okay and prepared to move the team out of the RON. However, the C&C crew told me to wrap up the mission. There was another problem that he couldn't discuss on an open frequency—we knew the NVA monitored SOG FM radio transmissions and had radio direction finding equipment. The C&C pilot told us to find an LZ and to let him know when we'd be ready for extraction. After a brief discussion with Hiep and Sau, Son and Sau left the team for a few minutes to locate an open area that they had observed the night before when we were approaching our RON. They returned a few minutes later. I called the Green Hornets and told them we'd be ready for extraction in 10 minutes. Since the AO had been so quiet, I gave them a vector from our insertion LZ and told them to look for yellow smoke. A few minutes later, the Green Hornets roared into the new LZ, picked us up and returned us to base.

The reason we were yanked from the field this time stemmed from a tragedy in the Prairie Fire Area of Operation on 30 November. An H-34 Kingbee was shot out of the sky during an Eldest Son operation. Seven Green Berets from FOB 1 and FOB 4 were killed when an anti-aircraft round struck the Sikorsky chopper and ignited the ammunition on the aircraft, killing everyone onboard. Eldest Son missions were quick hit deals. SOG teams would take captured NVA ammunition and mortar rounds that ordnance specialists had rigged to explode and place them along the Ho Chi Minh Trail in Laos. This was one of the psychological operations used against the NVA. The ordnance was placed along the trails with the hope that the NVA moving south would pick it up. Subsequently, when the NVA troops used the ammo it would explode, killing or wounding the enemy soldiers. Recon teams often carried a few clips of Soap Chips ammo or an Eldest Son mortar shell on a mission, leaving the bad ammo where an NVA soldier would find it. Some of the recon men jokingly referred to these missions as "medal missions." That joke ended on 30 November.

One of the men killed in that ill-fated Kingbee was Staff Sergeant Arthur E. Bader, Jr. I liked Bader. On my last night at FOB 1 before shipping out to FOB 6, I played in a poker game where he won a lot of money. The longer we played, the more money Bader won. The more Bader won, the more morose he became. At one point I asked him what was wrong; he was winning and he was ahead several hundred dollars, but kept complaining that he'd never spend the money. His response was that he had had a premonition that he was going to die and that men about to die often win a lot of money, money they would never spend. We all tried to josh him out of his dark mood, but failed.

Bader was a unique Special Forces Green Beret. He had earned and lost three separate fortunes in between three terms in the service. He was in his 30s, but still enjoyed SF, spoke fluent German and a few other languages and merely wanted to accomplish any mission assigned to him. On the long flight back to Phu Bai, I kept hearing him talk to us at the poker table that last night. Now he was gone.

* * *

More than two decades later, a recovery detail brought Bader's remains home to Atlantic City.

Chapter Twelve

COLD AS HELL

In December 1968 ST Idaho was loaded onto Kingbees and flown to the Quang Tri launch site, which was north of FOB 1 and north of Hue. I hated Quang Tri. All it had were smelly old army tents. They always seemed dirty, sandy and dusty from all of the helicopter activity in the area. The site itself was located near an ammo dump for the Marine Corps, possibly its 3rd Force Reconnaissance Company. While personal comforts sucked, when we launched into DMZ targets or Prairie Fire targets from there, the helicopter ride to the target was shorter and that meant the air assets could remain on site much longer than when we launched out of FOB 1. There was a definite tactical edge to launching from Quang Tri.

When we planned to launch from Quang Tri the daily routine consisted of leaving FOB 1 early on Kingbees, then the team would go to the stinking tents and wait for a pre-mission briefing. The time frame between landing at Quang Tri, getting a pre-mission briefing and actually launching into a target depended on a number of elements lining up: having good or acceptable weather, the availability of tactical air and helicopter gunship support and how many other teams were on the ground at that time. If one of those elements failed to come into alignment, the spike team spent the

There weren't many awards and decorations formations at FOB 1, but here's one in the late summer of 1968, held in front of the indig recon team rooms. Among those in the formation are, from the far left in the back row, Sgt. Maj. Harvey Harris. In the front, next row from the left is Stephen Bayliss, with John S. Meyer behind him. At the front of the third row on the left, Lynne M. Black Jr. In the back row between lines four and five is Charles Borg. Standing in the front row of line five is Richard Childress, then a team member of ST Virginia. The second man behind him is Rick Estes—with a moustache. The second man in line six is John E. Peters—with sunglasses. In the back of that row is Robert J. Parks. (Photo courtesy of Ron Zaiss)

remainder of the day getting dirty in Quang Tri, returning to the comfort and security of FOB 1 at the end of the day. Occasionally, an additional delay would occur at a place called the Rock Pile, a god-forsaken Marine firebase where helicopters could land prior to launching into a target.

The DMZ had become a hot target area at the end of '68 as MACV-SOG headquarters received several reports of increased troop movement from North to South Vietnam. The brass wanted to know if the NVA was gearing up for another Tet Offensive. Veteran spike team members had heard rumors that there were Russian advisors with some of the key NVA units that operated north of the DMZ and sometimes into the DMZ. There were also unconfirmed reports of Chinese soldiers fighting side by side with the NVA in the DMZ. Politically, everyone knew the Russians and other Communist bloc nations were supporting the NVA and the communist North Vietnamese government. As far back as 1963, special operations and intelligence agents had photographs of Russian shipping in Haiphong Harbor, outside Hanoi, but the Chinese card was an unknown element at the time. America's military had already experienced the horror of fighting attacking hordes of Chinese 18 years earlier during the Korean War.

By December 1968, we also knew we had a new president back in the United States. Richard M. Nixon had soundly defeated his opponents and one of his platforms included a pledge to scale back American involvement in South Vietnam. How such a political promise would pan out in this war remained to be seen, but if there were Chinese out there, we wanted to capture one and bring him back for the world to see. So on a cloudy day in mid December, ST Idaho flew to Quang Tri to conduct an area reconnaissance of a DMZ target that was further west along what we commonly called the DMZ River.

Despite the living conditions, as a One-Zero I enjoyed launching out of Quang Tri because the launch site men always worked hard to give us as thorough a pre-mission briefing as possible, which included a detailed map with markings showing the latest NVA anti-aircraft weapons within any target area and surrounding areas. SF Major Bill Shelton always went the extra yard for teams preparing to launch. Additionally, my old pal and former recon man Rick Howard was assigned there and always helped make us comfortable, or at least he dug up cold sodas and beers, and passed on any intelligence reports he heard about the AO. During this December morning, the weather was too cruddy to launch a mission, so most of ST Idaho curled up on the dirty cots and slept. During the early afternoon, we were told that Covey said the weather was breaking up over the target area. Because of the bad weather I didn't have a chance to fly a Visual Reconnaissance over the AO prior to the mission. I didn't like skipping a VR. If flown properly, it gave a One-Zero an excellent chance to get a feel for the target area, look for key landmarks, and plan better escape and evasion routes and rallying points. During the early afternoon, we had our briefing that included several new marks on the AO map reflecting more NVA 37mm positions creeping farther south into the DMZ area. Due to those reports, the Kingbee pilots said they would insert us with a direct nap-of-the-earth approach, instead of the more familiar downward spiral, which was the Kingbee trademark on insertions.

We finally boarded the Kingbees and took off from Quang Tri. We had only been in the air a few minutes when it became obvious that we weren't heading toward the AO, but to the Rock Pile instead. After we landed, the Kingbee pilots told us we had a delay because one of the gunships had to top off its fuel tanks. Up the hill from us was an outdoor latrine. Hiep said he wanted to use it before going into the AO. As he started to walk toward the latrine I saw a few young Marines starting to get nervous. They had never seen an armed South Vietnamese man, wearing sunglasses and carrying M-26 frag grenades. Sometime during 1967, when Hiep was at FOB 3 in Khe Sanh waiting to launch into a target, a Marine had attacked Hiep after he had ordered Hiep to pick up some trash lying on the ground and Hiep refused. In plain English, Hiep told the Marine that picking up trash was not his job and that perhaps the Marine should pick it up. The 200-plus-pound Marine hit the 105-pound

Hiep several times before anyone could intervene. Hiep could have shot him, but he didn't. Back at the Rock Pile, I told Hiep to wait a second while I went to talk to the young Marines and avoid any further trouble. As I approached the Marines, one of them locked and loaded his M-16. When the bolt slammed forward, I moved quickly toward them. I explained that I was an American with more rank than any of them and that Hiep, and all of the Vietnamese with me, were on a classified mission. I warned them not to point their weapons toward any of the Vietnamese because they were better shots and were men of purpose. After muttering amongst themselves for a moment, they allowed Hiep to use the latrine. A short while later, we boarded the Kingbees for the DMZ target.

The weather was gloomy and cold by South Vietnam standards. As we flew toward the target, the clouds broke long enough for the Kingbees to fly ST Idaho to the LZ. I was the One-Zero, Lynne Black was the One-One and an old friend, Rick Estes, was our One-Two. Rick and I had gone through Training Group together and wanted to get at least one target under our belts as team members. Black, Hiep and I were inserted on the first Kingbee. We moved to a thin, wooded area as the second Kingbee roared in and deposited the second half of the team, including Estes and the designated point man for that mission, Son, and Tuan, our M-79 man. Before the mission, Sau, our Vietnamese team leader, requested time off to be with his ailing wife. He had worked hard training Son to run point, and we agreed that this target was going to be Son's debut in that crucial slot. After the second Kingbee lifted off of the LZ, we remained silent for a few minutes to see if there was any enemy activity. Instead of the veteran Covey riders such as Spider Parks, Pat Watkins or Don Wolken, we had a young lieutenant on one of his first assignments. He radioed me twice, asking for a team okay. Ordinarily, we waited at least 10 minutes before giving Covey a team okay. Since we were in the DMZ, I assumed we had a few more minutes.

As I looked around, however, Son was at the end of the ragged formation and he was sitting on the ground, grimacing in pain as he unlaced his boot, instead of moving up to me and Hiep. Estes signaled that Son was hurt. Because I was getting frustrated with the young, gung-ho lieutenant Covey rider, and because the DMZ was reportedly so hot, Black and I were primarily focused on the immediate area around our LZ. As Estes was moving towards us instead of Son, I looked skyward; the little hole in the clouds the choppers had flown through to deliver us to the LZ was quickly closing in over us. I radioed the Covey rider that we had trouble and that we might need an extraction ASAP. Had Spider, Watkins or Wolken been in the Cessna O-2, they would have asked for more details and ordered the choppers to return to our LZ. All of them had been on the ground across the fence and they had all been One-Zeros, thus they didn't question the team leader on the ground.

Unfortunately, the young lieutenant's first response had been different. "Negative, your request. Continue mission." Estes told me that Son had severely sprained his ankle. After Estes had exited the chopper, the H-34 had suddenly lurched up several feet off the ground, just as Son had jumped. Son landed on a rock and severely twisted his ankle.

"He's hurt Tilt, and I don't know if he can move, let alone run point." None of us were medics, yet it was plain to see that Son's ankle was hurtin' for certain. I told the "brave" young lieutenant, who had never run a practice mission in-country or run a mission across the fence, that I had a tactical emergency and wanted an extraction ASAP. His second response was no better than his first. My language became more heated. Finally he agreed to send the Kingbees back "if they can find your LZ."

I wanted to hit the SOB desk jockey from the FOB. A light rain started falling. Instead of Kingbees rolling into the LZ, we had clouds rolling in. Off in the distance we could hear the Cessna O-2 searching for us, but he was too high in the air to see anything. I was angry. I wanted to place the butt of my CAR-15 between the beady little eyes of that ferret of a lieutenant. I imagined how he proudly reported back to base that he had inserted a team and when the team asked for a tactical withdrawal, he denied it. At the same time, I thought about how much time I had been on the radio talking to that lieutenant. I asked Black if the NVA had RDF in this area. He shrugged his shoulders and gave me that "I sure as hell hope not" look. The young lieutenant radioed me several more times, saying that neither he nor the Covey pilot could find our LZ. The weather had sealed our fate: we were stuck in the LZ with a point man who couldn't walk.

"We're screwed," I said, as we surveyed the desolate-looking DMZ target. We agreed that we had to get to high ground, secure it and set up an RON ASAP. There had been so much Marine and Army artillery activity, that there were few tall trees standing. There were fewer trees with leaves. The land was so lifeless, we couldn't tell if artillery and air strikes had caused the massive devastation or, if the highly touted Agent Orange defoliant had done the job. There was one more option as well: the USS New Jersey was off the coast and had conducted several fire missions in that area. Whatever the cause, the DMZ was an ugly god-forsaken place reminiscent of Pork Chop Hill and other dreaded battlegrounds from the Korean War. It was bleak and gray and the rain kept falling. I asked Hiep to run point with Black behind him and get us up to the small ridgeline I had observed when we flew into the LZ and asked Tuan and Estes to assist Son. The terrain was so open we could see for long distances. And in a few minutes, Hiep and Black had moved far ahead of me, while I had moved far ahead of Estes, Son and Tuan. As we moved up the hill, I wondered again if the NVA's RDF had picked up any of my radio transmissions. The thought of the NVA triangulating our position due to my excessive commo with the FNG lieutenant exasperated me no end.

When the team reached the top of the hill, we began setting up a RON. Estes and I ended up next to each other. "Sorry I got you into this mess, man," I said.

"Well, I've been trying to get outta the comm center for months," he said. "I'd rather be on the ground than back there in the comm center, although a nice cup of hot coffee and some cake would hit the spot right about now."

Our smiles quickly faded as the rain picked up in intensity. Instead of placing claymores or doing any further security checks, I told Estes I wanted to put on my sweater. And then it hit me: ever since the Echo Four target in October, I carried nothing except bare essentials. Instead of carrying two or three cans of fruit, I carried only one. I cut back the number of canteens in order to carry more magazines for my CAR-15, rounds for my M-79 and frag grenades. The last grenade, the last bullets fired during the extraction from the Echo Four target were deeply ingrained into my psyche. But at this particular moment, I regretted the lack of rain gear.

I carried no sleeping gear, no poncho liner, and no hammock. The sole piece of rain gear I had was a thin, plastic, hooded rain jacket cut off at the waist. Because it was so short, the rain would run down my back and flow straight to my bare lower back, when I sat down. The bright yellow, hooded rain jacket I wore as a patrol boy at Jefferson School would have felt great. Instead, the only head gear I had was the green cravat that I wore on missions, as it broke up the light color of my hair. For the rest of me all I had was an Army-issue sweater that buttoned up to the neck and my black contact gloves, which were cloth on top with leather on the undersides.

Instead of worrying about security, I took off my rucksack and pulled the sweater out. I asked Estes to hold my web gear while I removed my jungle fatigue jacket and slipped on the sweater. For a few moments, it felt warm and comfortable. But, by the time I had gotten my gear back on, the sweater was damp. In minutes I was completely miserable and there was no relief in sight. The weather conditions were so bad even the brave desk jockey lieutenant couldn't fly. At dusk, the DMZ looked more gray and bleak than ever. I stayed on my feet for a long time, trying to avoid sitting on the sloppy, leech-infested jungle floor. It was only a matter of time before the rain hit my backside and a leech would chomp into my wet hide. I was only postponing the inevitable.

Things got worse. It had been dark a few hours when the rain began to slack off. It didn't stop, but it wasn't pouring anymore. Through the light rain we heard the unmistakable sound of metal striking metal from the valley to the west of our position. Then there was another sound from the canyon. My pucker factor was minus zero. Then there was another sound. Hiep moved close to me and said, "Tuan say beaucoup VC down there. Beaucoup." Was the NVA staging to hit us?

Fortunately, the NVA continued south. The enemy troop movement was unusually noisy and there were a lot of troops moving past us. If they hit us, the odds were steeply stacked against us. Because we had been inserted so late, there was little time to discuss E&E (escape and evasion) routes. Fear dominated my mind while I cursed all of the things that had gone wrong on this miserable mission, beginning with getting a rookie Covey rider. I wondered if they even knew we were in their midst. I also worried that we hadn't placed enough claymores on the west perimeter. I checked the black electrical tape wrapped around the end of my CAR-15 barrel to make sure it was secure, tight and preventing any water or mud from entering the barrel. I found myself shivering, mentally and physically and my teeth started to chatter. I thought of the old line from a Bugs Bunny cartoon, "What a revolt'n development this is!" By midnight, the NVA had passed, but the rain had picked up, and temperatures felt as though they were hovering in the 40s. When Moonbeam, the night airborne command aircraft radioed for a commo check, I simply broke squelch on the PRC-25. I wondered if those Air Force troops were eating steak or veal tonight in their nice dry, heated aircraft. Were they washing down their exotic dinners with an expensive Cabernet Sauvignon or Dom Perignon?

I sat there in the dark with Estes, both of us trying to keep our teeth from chattering. "Look," I said, "I know you're from California, but we're going to need each other's body heat to survive out here. I've never been so cold in my entire life. So don't pull any funny stuff." Estes wanted to know how someone from the smog-congested Garden State could cast aspersions on an elite warrior from the Golden State. After a few more mutual insults, we agreed to take turns staying awake for guard duty, while the other man slept. I mentally checked my body to see if I could find one dry spot, anywhere. There were none.

By now the first leeches had struck. SF medics stressed that when a leech attached itself, troops had to resist the temptation to yank it off. Once a leech grabbed hold, with its teeth deep into the skin, it poured anticoagulants into the blood making it flow easier. If the leech was snapped off, leaving its head or teeth in the wound, the bite usually would become infected. Whenever I felt one on my body, my first reaction was complete revulsion to the point of vomiting. I struggled to resist the natural urge to rip it off my body and forced myself to dig into one of my jungle fatigue pants pockets and pull out my insect repellant. The spray caused the leech to loosen its grip and it usually fell off. Then I had a chance to feel it to see how much blood it had sucked from my body before I sliced it into pieces with my Ka-Bar knife. After I dealt with the first leech my mind would play tricks on me throughout the night. I would imagine that I had several chomping into my flesh. After a series of false alarms, I would become less apprehensive only to have the real deal go for blood. I dreamed of the sensation, the revulsion, of them crawling on my body. Dreams aside, by December 1968, I had a series of circular scars in various stages of healing around my waist, just above the belt line, from my encounters with the bloodsuckers.

During the night, the rain continued with varying degrees of intensity. We heard the clanging of metal against metal again, as more NVA troops noisily moved south. It was difficult to believe they didn't know we were there. When it was my turn for guard duty, I remember that I sat there in the rain and mud, feeling the water running down my backside. After pulling off my gloves—I always wore black contact gloves to protect my hands from jungle brush—my hands were shriveled, as though I had been in a swimming pool too long. In my mind, I tried to measure how deep my butt had sunk into the wet, cold mud. I tried once more, unsuccessfully to find a dry spot.

Fearing an NVA attack, the entire team was awake before dawn. There was no movement through the canyons, which made me more apprehensive. After an hour of darkness, our intense alert ended, but the rain didn't. The weather had us completely socked in, precluding us from calling in any air or artillery strikes. Realizing that Mother Nature had sealed our fate, we returned to alternating guard duty among ourselves. The weather was so bad there were no Covey commo checks. At some point during the rain, I checked out Tuan, Hiep and Son. They had an extra poncho and a poncho liner rigged to keep them dry from the rain. Son's ankle looked worse. There was no chance of him being able to walk on it for any distance. At various times during the day, Black and Tuan or Estes and Tuan would leave the RON to do short reconnoiters. By dusk Black and Tuan had a good feel for the terrain. We were surrounded on all sides by canyons. The NVA troops had moved through the ones east and west of us during the previous night. When the airborne command aircraft made radio contact with us, I merely broke squelch on the PRC-25. Since I could hear them, I assumed they had picked up my brief signal. There was nothing they could do for us, anyway. We remained socked in by the weather and when the NVA moved, we didn't have an exact location on our RON where I felt comfortable calling in artillery. So, we sat there and suffered for a total of five days.

The weather finally broke a little bit on the fifth day, the low clouds beginning to lift. The rookie Covey rider flew over our position after making several attempts to get a response from me on the PRC-25. The O-2 Cessna was so close I couldn't understand why he didn't hear me. I changed batteries. I told him I wanted an extraction ASAP: Son was still hurt, the NVA had moved around us every night, and we all were tired of being wet and cold to the core. The brave lieutenant ordered us to continue with the mission. He said many feared that something had happened to us because of the commo drought in the last three days. I slammed down the handset. Within a minute or two, the O-2 flew close to the southern perimeter of our RON. As the aircraft passed, I fired two or three single shots into the air away from the O-2. All of a sudden the radio came to life.

From left, Sgt. John S. Meyer, Sgt. Rick Estes and Sp. 4 Lynne M. Black Jr., standing on the walkway outside of the Recon Company area at CCN, Da Nang, a few months after they ran the DMZ target in late December 1968. (Photo courtesy of John S. Meyer)

"We're taking enemy fire! We're taking enemy fire!" He asked me if I had heard the enemy shots.

"Affirmative," I replied. Now his voice had a new nervousness about it.

"We took enemy fire, we're moving out of here," the lieutenant said. I reminded him again that I wanted an extraction ASAP. "Affirmative," came his quick reply. He said he would call in fast movers and Marine gunships to suppress the enemy fire before bringing in the Kingbees. I told him to get the Kingbees in first and fast as the cloud cover was closing in again and that I was out of food, out of clean water and completely out of patience. If the NVA hit us, we'd worry about it when they surfaced directly against us. And, I reminded the lieutenant, for the last four days, the NVA apparently didn't know we were on the ground. Now with his aircraft buzzing our position, any NVA within a mile was alerted and would go searching for SOG teams.

Ten minutes later, we heard the Kingbees. Black and Tuan ran back to the northwestern slope and went down hill. As the Kingbee made its final approach to our LZ, they returned for the extraction. I put the entire team on the Kingbee and we exited the LZ with only a few NVA rounds being fired at us. Compared to other extractions, this was a cakewalk. Black explained that he and Tuan went back to set booby traps on and around one trail, including rigging an old M-72 Light Anti-Tank Weapon tube which had been left behind by another American unit at some time.

When we returned to FOB 1, Black, Estes and I joked about how never before had we been so cold and so wet for so long. Before we left for Vietnam none of us had ever imagined such a painful experience could occur in Southeast Asia. We all agreed that we never would have been able to fight in the Korean War where the temperatures were 30 and 43 degrees below zero during combat. Then the topic turned to the brave lieutenant.

"I'm going to kill the little fucker," said Black.

"Even in a secret war, there are rules and regulations against hurting officers," I reminded him.

"At least I want to knock him out," Black quickly responded.

"Don't kill him," Estes chimed in, "it'll interfere with you running missions with Tilt." He paused for a second. "If you hit him, make sure there are no witnesses. Then it'll come down to his word versus yours and even though everyone would know you did it, no one in camp would support him because we all respect you." Then Estes asked me if the brave lieutenant had asked me if he could run a mission with ST Idaho. I told him, yes, that was correct and that I had politely declined his request to join the team. Estes said he thought I didn't have to worry about the lieutenant ever requesting to run a mission with our team again. Later, during the initial debriefing, I told the senior NCO in S-3 that I never wanted that lieutenant flying as the Covey rider over my team again. I suggested that the S-3 shop should reconsider assigning him to less sensitive position until he had spent some time on the ground in the Prairie Fire AO.

CHAPTER THIRTEEN

CAPTAINS COURAGEOUS

Christmas Day 1968 was just another day for Spike Team Idaho. Early that morning ST Idaho was loaded onto Kingbees and flown to the Quang Tri launch site. The early morning rush came to a halt at Quang Tri, as there was some sort of complication with our support elements. We finally went in for the briefing. That day's target was one of the MA targets west of the DMZ in Laos, along the river that ran through the DMZ. In the briefing room there was a large map and on it were all of the DMZ targets, and all of the MA targets in Laos. Maps of the target area that we carried to the field were just small sections of the larger maps, the theory being that if captured, the small map was useless to the enemy.

On the target map, there were a series of MA targets, MA-10 through MA-16 or 18. The smaller numbers, MA-10 and MA-11, were the first target areas directly west of the South Vietnamese border. Our MA target was a larger number and thus, farther into Laos, near an area where NVA fuel lines were reported to be under construction. The NVA needed fuel to move its trucks and men down the Ho Chi Minh Trail Complex and it was more efficient to have a pipeline, instead of individual trucks, moving the gasoline south.

As we looked at the map, we noticed a disturbing trend: there

Despite the rain, Robert J. "Spider" Parks is running to a Jeep to get to Phu Bai Airport, which was south of FOB 1. Parks is running because an FOB 1 recon team is in trouble in Laos. Parks was a Covey rider for several months, where he would sit in the co-pilot seat while an Air Force pilot would fly the O-2. At FOB 1 the Covey Rider was selected because he had experience on the ground in the C&C area of operations and could better relate to the SF teams or Hatchet Force elements in the target area. Note the Covey equipment Parks is carrying, including a parachute. (Photo courtesy of Stephen Bayliss)

were more anti-aircraft weapons cropping up throughout the AO. The launch site staff was vigilant in warning the helicopter pilots and Covey about any new 37mm or 12.7mm sites in the AO. More than once, the Kingbee pilots would point out a location where they had come under fire from NVA gunners. Because of the increase in anti-aircraft batteries along the DMZ and MA targets, the Kingbee pilots said they would fly straight to the LZ along the nap-of-the-earth. There would be no auto-rotation, downward spiral insertions into the LZ today.

"We don't want another Bader," said one of the briefing officers. The briefing officers also warned us about reports of NVA sappers being in the area. Spike teams from Kontum had made contact with NVA sappers at least once in the last year.

Finally, it was time to saddle up. The lead Kingbee pilot, Captain Tuong, said he would carry the entire spike team on his H-34, as the weather conditions and height of the mountains allowed the old chopper enough lift to carry us. At the briefing we were told that Covey had found an LZ in a remote valley with no enemy activity. The hope was that the LZ's remoteness meant less chance for the NVA to have watchers on the LZ or enemy trackers in the surrounding area. We would soon find out. As we boarded the chopper, I felt good about my team: Lynne Black had joined Bubba Shore and me. Both were fearless, but not reckless, smart and smart-mouthed. Phuoc was our point man, Hiep our interpreter, and Tuan was our M-79 man. I had been on ST Idaho seven months and I was the senior American on the team. I still viewed myself as a green kid in-country and yet the wear and tear of running targets made me feel that I was much older than 22. I still wondered if I'd see my 23rd birthday, now 25 days away.

In our favor was the fact that we had one of the best-damned Kingbee pilots in the 219th Vietnamese Air Force, Captain Tuong. His nerves of steel and amazing flying skills made him one of the most respected Kingbee pilots in the C&C project. I was optimistic about the chances to have a good mission, especially if Covey had found a remote LZ. As we headed west, flying parallel with the

DMZ river, Captain Tuong followed the briefing officer's suggested route of approach. Shortly before we crossed the border into Laos, the door gunner test fired his ancient .30 caliber air-cooled machine gun. It misfired several times before a round finally exploded from the barrel. Those old machine guns misfired as often as they fired. I always wondered why they didn't replace them with a 7.62mm M-60 or a .50 caliber machine gun.

Tuong started to dip the H-34 down, losing altitude before easing into a graceful right turn, which brought us into a canyon, between two mountains. The Kingbee felt strong as it climbed the steepening grade. I was sitting in the doorway, facing east. As we continued the climb up the canyon, I saw a small native shack carved into the side of the mountain with one or two people inside of it. They appeared to be indigenous to the area. No NVA uniforms. No obvious radios or antennae. They appeared to be just as surprised to see us, as we were to see them. Seconds later, Captain Tuong flared the Kingbee onto the LZ, a small knoll covered with elephant grass. I resisted the first urge to jump out of the Kingbee when I thought we had reached the ground and delayed a few moments. When I felt the right wheel touch the ground and could see the dark soil, I jumped out.

ST Idaho was on the ground. The insertion, other than scaring a few locals, was as quick as the slam-bam inserts Bubba and I had enjoyed a month ago in Cambodia. The damned elephant grass was thicker and taller than it had appeared from the air. It was at least 10 feet tall. Instead of quickly moving off of the LZ, we paused right there. I asked Black if he thought the locals would help the NVA. He asked me if I was nuts. The locals had no choice. The real question was could we get off the LZ and far enough away from it to lose any NVA trackers or sappers. Another thing that bothered me about the LZ was the fact that the grassy knoll we were on was much farther from the top of the mountain than I had imagined during the briefing. We had to get to high ground before dark; our team safety was endangered. After a few minutes we started to move east off of the LZ towards the thick, triple canopy jungle. I hated elephant grass. Moving through it took a lot of energy and the blades of grass always irritated my eyes. When moving in it, our team made a lot of noise, noise that hindered our efforts to move with stealth, which was critical to our survival in the jungle.

I radioed Spider and asked him if he could keep the assets on stand-by beyond the normal 10-minute period of time. I told him there was no choice because we had flown past a small, inhabited hootch that was built into the side of the mountain. Spider was surprised by that news. He and the Covey pilot hadn't seen it earlier. I explained that no one could see it from the air due to the heavy jungle canopy growing over it. While I finished the commo check with Spider, Black continued to move the team east, following Phuoc. Tuan and I brought up the rear. It seemed to take forever to move through the elephant grass. I began to get a sinking feeling in my stomach. This elephant grass reminded me of Echo Four two months earlier and it was really slowing us down. Now, as I looked skyward, the gray day seemed to be taking on a stormy appearance. I had packed an extra sweater in the rucksack, but no extra raingear. Spider radioed to ask if he could release the assets. I clicked the handset signaling affirmative, release them.

Although we were still in the elephant grass, we were moving closer to the triple-canopy jungle that appeared to be taller than the Empire State Building. Then Phuoc opened fire on full automatic. There were one or two possible enemy shots fired. From my location at the rear of the formation, I might as well have been on Broadway because I couldn't see Phuoc, Black, Hiep or Bubba. I quickly radioed Spider and told him we had light contact with the enemy and requested an extraction.

"Tilt, I released the assets," Spider said. I knew he was joking.

"Thank God the young, desk jockey lieutenant wasn't flying Covey today," I said to myself. There was no more gunfire as the remainder of the team moved back towards me. As I waited, I felt a leech inside my pant leg. It was too near to my private parts for comfort. To hell with the NVA, the clouds, rain and cold! If that leech bit me...! I shook my right leg violently and reached down into my pants. It had to be an NVA leech; it was still moving up my inner thigh. I flicked it down into the bottom of my pant leg, pulled my fatigues out of my boot and shook that communist out. I then stomped him into the ground for several, long moments.

"This damned elephant grass," cursed Black. "They could have heard us coming from Hanoi!" With Hiep interpreting, Phuoc said he had heard someone in the jungle, as he was about to emerge from the elephant grass on an eastern azimuth. He opened fire on them and they returned fire with one or two shots. Phuoc said the weapons weren't AK-47s. As we spoke in muffled tones, we heard movement to the southeast of our position. They were far enough away that we couldn't see them, yet they were down hill from us and close enough that I threw one frag grenade in their direction. There was no response. The elephant grass seemed taller and more vexing than ever; every time we moved, we made too much noise. As we all peered to the southeast, wondering what was going on out there, we heard movement to our northeast. Again, it wasn't a lot of movement, but someone was trying to flank us. Shore loosened his throwing arm and indicated he wanted to throw an M-26 toward the northeast. He quietly removed the pin and let the spoon fly, counted to two and threw the frag toward the noise. By holding it an extra two seconds and throwing it in an exaggerated arc, the M-26 exploded in the air, increasing the shrapnel's lethality, hopefully right over the enemy's head. We were all sweating. We heard no aircraft sounds, but now we heard movement to the southeast.

Spider called me on the radio. There was a certain edge to his voice when he said it was imperative that we not move to the northeast.

"I repeat, negative on moving team to northeast!" He demanded that I confirm receiving that message.

"Affirmative. Do not move team to northeast!" I was surprised by the urgency in his voice. I passed the word to Black. Northeast seemed to be the path of least resistance and the last chance to get on with the mission. Spider's terse message and the sounds to the northeast negated this. He said he had an intelligence report that backed up his order to us that we not go to the northeast. We slipped into survival mode. I was curious as to what sort of intel report could make him so certain. I stopped pondering the hypothetical and returned to our tactical situation on the ground.

Due to the elephant grass, both in terms of the noise we were making and how it muffled other sounds, we couldn't tell exactly how many NVA were moving or even if they were NVA. Were they the sappers we had heard about during the briefing? If they were, they'd have to move through the same stinking elephant grass we were stuck in. Some earlier intelligence reports said the sappers wore only a loincloth, an ammo vest and carried a new version of the AK-47 with the folding metal stock, which some folks called an AK-50. They had to carry a knife, but where? The sounds to the northeast ended my theoretical sapper questions. Black threw a hand grenade toward the noise to our southeast.

Black said, "I smell smoke. Either our hand grenades or the NVA have started fires."

"Things are really heating up on the LZ, literally," I radioed Spider. I told him we were surrounded and had fires on two sides of our perimeter. Due to the location of the knoll in the canyon, with mountains rising on the east and west of it, using fixed-wing air support was ruled out immediately. Working helicopter gun runs would also be difficult due to the terrain and where the enemy was located. Within minutes, we could all smell the smoke. The popping noises grew in number and volume. Black went to the western edge of our perimeter looking for a way out. If we tried to escape down that route, the elephant grass-covered terrain would leave us in a deep hole. There were no trees nearby to climb for improved visual reconnoitering.

Now, there was no noise discipline. Black was pushing the elephant grass down. I tried going north, but the elephant grass remained thick and high. The NVA moved to our north. We were surrounded on three sides. Since we were on the highest ground, we attempted to form a perimeter in the elephant grass by knocking it down—which was no easy task. Bubba and I whacked away at

Capt. Nguyen Van Tuong at the controls of his H-34 Kingbee flying north from FOB 1 to the Quang Tri launch site. (Photo courtesy of John S. Meyer)

the thick stalks of the elephant grass with machete-type hand tools; Black jumped into it, using his body weight and the weight of his gear to flatten it. Black and I figured that if we were able to get enough elephant grass knocked down, we would be able to see any NVA emerging from it into our perimeter. Spider radioed to say the Kingbees were about two minutes out from the LZ. Then he asked me how the firefight was going because he could hear all of the popping noise in the background and assumed it was enemy gunfire. I told him that if the Kingbees didn't get there ASAP ST Idaho would be engaged in fighting fires as well as firefights.

The wind was blowing up the canyon from the south. That fire was gaining strength as more smoke wafted up the hill and through our perimeter. The pops from the burning elephant grass were so loud that some of them sounded like single shot gunfire.

"Kingbee come soon?" Hiep asked. I told him Captain Tuong was approximately one minute away.

"They're starting more fires," Bubba said. By now, the noise from the fire forced us to raise our voices when talking to each other. The smoke was getting thicker. I began to sweat. We threw a few more hand grenades down the hill to force the NVA to keep their heads down. The noise from both fires was so loud we would not have been able to hear the NVA had they launched an attack. At this point, the most likely avenue of attack would be the knoll ridgeline from the east to our LZ. Bubba said he had a claymore mine strung out there. Black reported that the fire was sweeping through the elephant grass on our western flank, on the steep slope below our LZ, which led down to the canyon.

The southern fire's intensity grew by the second and continued to move up the slope toward us and around to the east. There was a fire or fires to the north and northeast, but they weren't heading toward ST Idaho with the speed of the southern flames. Black and Shore took out several one-pound bars of C-4 plastic explosive, cut them in half and primed them with blasting caps. With the fire advancing so quickly up the southern side of the hill, they got as close as possible, placed the C-4 at the fire's edge and set it off.

The theory was that the C-4 would temporarily blow the flames back down the mountain. By now the smoke was so thick, I had my green cravat over my face with the top pulled over my nose. Burning embers from the south kicked up and flew over our small, jagged perimeter, dumping ashes, soot and small, burning sparks on the elephant grass and us. Only Hiep and Tuan wore hats. Several of us soaked our hair.

The heat from the fires became so intense that Black and Shore got heat blisters the second time they attempted to stop the flames' charge toward us. All of us were flicking ashes or small sparks off of our clothing and any exposed skin or hair. Black told me that the NVA weren't far behind the flames. Tuan had first reported seeing images a short distance behind the flames to the south and southeast. Black had observed the same images, unsure as to whether the images were real or some phenomenon produced by the flames and the rising heat waves. Then Bubba reported seeing the same thing, noting that it was odd that the NVA soldiers were not holding their AK-47s in a firing position, but rather in a relaxed, almost casual way. Black and Phuoc placed a few more claymores on the slope heading south and southeast.

When Spider said the Kingbee was 30 seconds out, I signaled Tuan, Black, Phuoc and Shore to blow their claymores. Finally we could hear the Kingbee. Because we had the most enemy activity to our south and southeast, I told Spider to bring Captain Tuong's Kingbee in from the north, which made for a radically, steep descent into the mountainous canyon area. The smoke was stifling, choking us while sending up a huge plume of black and gray smoke. Black pointed out that the fires had burnt so long in the southeast, that the NVA might use that burnt area as a line of attack against us. Black, Shore, Tuan and I fired a volley of M-79 high explosive rounds toward the south and southeast. I turned my attention to the Kingbee, and Black and Bubba set off two more C-4 charges in an effort to keep the flames at bay. The explosions slowed the flames and any NVA movement behind them. Black, Bubba and Tuan fired a few more M-79 rounds to the south, arching them as though they were small mortars.

Captain Tuong knew exactly where we were, as he brought the

H-34 down the canyon toward us. The smoke was thick, however, and made it difficult for him to see our LZ. It felt as though we were trapped in some sort of Twilight Zone episode, with the smoke and fire rushing up the mountain, enemy soldiers firing at us, and salvation within sight, but out of reach. When the old Sikorsky was about 75 feet from our LZ and flaring toward us, it appeared to me that the rotor blades were moving in slow motion. For a brief moment, I thought the Kingbee was going to pull out of the landing pattern due to the smoke that covered the LZ. My heart stopped. If he left, we would die.

Seconds became hours. My vision was clearer than ever and I was acutely aware of the smoke, fire, popping sounds and enemy gunfire. I stood on the western edge of the perimeter, waving a colored panel skyward trying to catch the pilot's eye. The H-34 continued its slow motion descent. All I saw was the bottom of the chopper, with the front struts sticking out to the right and left coming down like a giant praying mantis. The rotor wash from the Kingbee began to hit us. Finally, the chopper's nose turned slightly to the left and I could see Captain Tuong. Seeing his face, seeing him sitting there so calmly in the pilot's seat, made my confidence surge. We would survive.

There was an additional benefit from the rotor wash: it pushed the smoke and fire back from the top of the knoll. Normally during an extraction, the powerful rotor wash was a disruptive force as it kicked up dirt, leaves, small branches and stones while the noise eliminated most verbal communication and the swirling blasts of air hurt the eyes. But, on Christmas Day 1968, the powerful rotor wash became a unique saving grace for ST Idaho. It pushed the fire and smoke back as the entire team jumped into the Kingbee. The rotor wash was so strong it pushed the flames farther down hill, forcing the NVA to back up or to be burnt by their own fires. As the last man aboard the chopper, I signaled to the door gunner to exit the area. I sat in the door as Tuong lifted the Kingbee straight up for several feet before heading south. As we pulled away from the knoll, fire swept up the hill and engulfed the area where we had

John S. Meyer in Kingbee co-pilot seat, with Capt. Nguyen Van Tuong, the pilot at Quang Tri Launch Site, Dec. 1968. (Photo courtesy of John S. Meyer)

been standing moments earlier.

Captain Tuong roared down the canyon we had chugged along only a short while ago. I radioed Spider and gave him a team okay. Once again, ST Idaho entered that magical, post-mission moment. The adrenaline was still flowing; we had survived another target. Every breath of air was sweeter. There was no thought of Christmas, mom or holiday presents. Our gift was to be alive. I looked at Black and Bubba. They had burnt eyebrows, burnt arm hair and all sorts of soot and black ashes smeared on their sweaty faces. I started to shiver as the Kingbee headed southeast to Quang Tri. The shivers were triggered by several elements: the cold air hitting my sweaty, fear-laced body, the chopper gaining altitude where the temperature was much colder than that of the LZ and realizing once again just how close ST Idaho had come to getting wiped out. As the One-Zero, the team leader of this small, valiant band of recon brothers, I had extra shivers.

Captain Tuong flew us back to Quang Tri first because he was getting low on aviation fuel. We returned to Phu Bai in near darkness. As he had in the past, Captain Tuong allowed me to ride in the co-pilot seat with him during that last leg of the flight. I asked Captain Tuong if he was getting tired of pulling ST Idaho out of hot spots.

"No sweat," he said. "Beaucoup smoke, but no sweat. Kingbee go home now. We fly you tomorrow?" I told him I could use a day off. He said Kingbees would fly tomorrow, for sure. Kingbees never rest. When we landed at FOB 1, he wished me a Merry Christmas, but declined my offer for a Christmas drink at the club. His family was waiting for him in Da Nang, where the 219th South Vietnamese Air Force was based.

Black and Shore gathered up food and drinks for the team while I went into S-3 for the initial de-briefing. Later, I took a shower in the cold water at Phu Bai. By that time, I was used to cold showers and it felt good. After-mission showers were special. Not only did I wash away the physical sweat and dirt from being on the ground, but for a few moments, I always appreciated the fact that I had survived another day on the ground in the Prairie Fire AO. While walking back to my room I heard Silent Night playing from a tinny-sounding AM radio, complete with static and interference. The old German Christmas carol stopped me in my tracks. It was Christmas.

Christmas was my favorite holiday, more so than my birthday, because Granddad Meyer, Grandmom Stryker and Uncle Rob Meyer would always join us for Christmas dinner and opening presents. Two years earlier, on Christmas, there had been snow in Trenton, when I had leave from basic training at Ft. Dix. I thought of the snow, my mother's mashed potatoes and gravy, and the warm house in the cold winter. It all seemed so far away. But standing there listening to Silent Night in the safety and darkness of FOB 1, it felt like Christmas. I relished the moment because only a few hours earlier I had feared the worst. I also felt very tired and very old. I returned to the room I shared with Spider and Don Wolken.

The nightmare began that night. All of a sudden I was back on the LZ. I could feel the heat of the fires, I could smell the smoke and I was coughing. Once more I was standing on the western edge of the LZ, flapping my orange and pink panel trying to get the attention of the Kingbee pilot descending toward us. The flashback was an instant replay of the day's earlier trauma with one major exception: at the point where the Kingbee appeared to abort the descent I could see a young lieutenant in the pilot's seat instead of Captain Tuong. It was the lieutenant who had failed to pull out the second half of a spike team in an A Shau Valley target earlier in the year after a veteran Kingbee pilot had pulled out the first half. The veteran Kingbee pilot, Captain Thinh, returned for the remainder of the men after the young lieutenant had panicked. Thinh got them out during one of the more courageous and gutsy extractions in C&C history.

In my dream, I knew the young lieutenant because the veteran Kingbee pilots were patiently working with him. Quietly the word had spread among the One-Zeros in camp, if he's flying and you're under enemy fire, just bend over and kiss your ass good-bye. He didn't have the flying acumen and courage of Kingbee captains

Thinh and Tuong, or lieutenants Trung and Trong, who had all earned the respect of Special Forces men at FOB 1. In my dream, when I saw the young lieutenant's face my panic changed to sheer, unadulterated fear. I yelled into the PRC-25 to Spider, "Where's Captain Tuong! Where's Captain Tuong, God dammit!" As I yelled into the FM radio, I saw panic roll across the young Kingbee pilot's round, oriental face and the lieutenant gave me a mournful look as he pulled out of the landing approach, leaving us on the ground. I felt the flames, the heat, and the smoke closing in. My throat tightened, my eyes were watering.

I sat straight up in bed. I was soaked with sweat, my throat felt raw and my eyes ached from the imagined smoke. The terror was so real I hadn't noticed a rat scurrying off my bed until I heard it hit the floor.

Two days later, Bubba and I sat talking to his buddy, ST Virginia team member, Doug "the Frenchman" Le Tourneau. The Frenchman and his team had been extracted earlier after making contact with the enemy on the fifth day of their mission.

He asked Bubba if he was on the ground Christmas Day. The Frenchman said that by the time the third day of their mission arrived, there was no enemy activity to report and he had forgotten that it was Christmas. Bored, he began exploring the various FM frequencies on his PRC-25. After a few clicks on the dial he came across a clear Vietnamese channel, where the conversation sounded urgent. Unable to understand what the Vietnamese were saying, or who they were, the Frenchman asked ST Virginia interpreter Hoahn to listen to the conversation. In a few moments, a frown creased Hoahn's brow. He told the Frenchman that he was listening to NVA soldiers and it sounded like they were setting up an ambush for American troops. He was having a difficult time understanding exactly what the North Vietnamese soldiers were saying because their dialect was different and he was unfamiliar with their slang.

Then Hoahn stared in horror at the PRC-25. He told the Frenchman that the North Vietnamese were attempting to set up an ambush for ST Idaho. The Frenchman told ST Virginia's One-Zero,

Mike Childress, what Hoahn had heard on the radio and requested permission to go to an emergency frequency as soon as possible to alert ST Idaho. Permission granted. As Hoahn listened to the PRC-25, Le Tourneau turned on his emergency radio and quickly raised Covey. At the time, he didn't realize Spider was already in the area of operation. As he started to explain what Hoahn had heard on the radio, the interpreter grabbed his arm and told him to tell ST Idaho that the NVA had an ambush waiting to the northeast of their position. The Frenchman immediately passed the word to Spider. After a few more minutes of monitoring the NVA radio transmissions, the FM frequency suddenly went dead. Covey was focused on getting us extracted and didn't return to the ST Virginia frequency. Now I knew where Spider had gotten his information and why he wouldn't let us move northeast.

The Frenchman continued his story. On the fifth day of ST Virginia's mission, the team moved to another location on the trail and he positioned himself behind a large log where he could view the trail and still be able to signal his team members. Around 1400 hours, a scout for an NVA company came down the trail and stopped at the log where the Frenchman was hiding. For some reason, the AK-47 toting scout stepped backwards toward the log and lifted one leg over it, as if he was about to slide across it. Before the NVA soldier's foot touched the ground, the Frenchman stood up right alongside the startled NVA troop. There was a brief moment when the NVA looked into the Frenchman's eyes, saw Le Tourneau's CAR-15 rising toward him and realized that he had made a tragic mistake. The Frenchman, on his second mission with ST Virginia, was so unnerved that he opened fire on full automatic, emptying the entire magazine into the NVA soldier, killing him instantly. The NVA company chased ST Virginia for more than an hour, with Le Tourneau calling in air strikes, until finally getting extracted on ropes by a Kingbee.

For the Frenchman, however, the adventure didn't end there. As the helicopter lifted him off the ground, his CAR-15 became tangled in the rope above him and then he was flipped upside down. That fucking D-ring! The NVA were still hot on their trail, so he lobbed hand grenades at the enemy and managed to fire off a couple of rounds from his M-79 as he was pulled from the jungle.

Bubba and I filled in the missing pieces for Le Tourneau about what happened on Christmas Day and how lucky we were. We didn't want to think about what would've happened if the Frenchman hadn't intercepted that transmission. Bubba and I both knew he had saved our lives.

* * *

What I didn't know was that Christmas 1968 would haunt me sporadically for more than 25 years. After a while, I was able to stop sitting upright, sweating with fear when the nightmares hit. It's been almost 10 years since I last had that dream, but every Christmas, nightmares or not, I always take a moment to think of Captain Tuong's courage. No sweat. Kingbees never rest.

Chapter Fourteen

HAPPY NEW YEAR

The day after Christmas, the S-3 brass asked ST Idaho to run another MA target in Laos. I respectfully declined, citing fatigue and general weariness. I didn't tell the brass that I had a funny feeling about the target. I felt apprehensive about it for some reason. The S-3 shrugged and asked a team led by Rodney Headman to run the target. Shortly before he launched into the target, he asked me what the real reason was behind me declining the target. I explained that I simply felt that something very bad was going to happen to ST Idaho if we ran that target and that I was bone weary from running so many targets in the past three months. On the morning of 31 December, Headman's team was extracted from the target without incident, while ST Asp from FOB 4 in Da Nang was inserted into another MA target without incident.

While Headman's team was on the ground, I worried about my premonition turning into a bad mission for the southerner and his troops. Every day I checked with my friends in the commo center for the latest SITREP on his team. When the team landed on the helicopter pad at FOB 1, I was there to greet Headman and I told him I was glad he and his team returned without any pain or suffering. I

This is one of the few photographs of four ST Idaho One-Zeroes together with some of their South Vietnamese team members. From left, kneeling, Nguyen Van Sau—the Vietnamese team leader and counterpart to the One-Zero, Tuan—the M-79 grenadier, Cau and Nguyen Cong Hiep—interpreter. And yes, Hiep always wore those sunglasses, even in the jungle in the dark of night.
Standing from left, Lynne M. "Blackjack" Black Jr., Don Wolken, Phouc—fearless point man for ST Idaho for many months, John S. "Tilt" Meyer and Robert J. "Spider" Parks. (Photo courtesy of Doug LeTourneau)

asked him how it went.

"What was your worry about that target again? It was a dry hole. We moved around for four days, took some pictures, but couldn't find any fuel line. When we were extracted, there was some small arms fire, but that's all," Headman responded with a slight smirk. I was relieved and surprised. Perhaps it showed on my face because Headman held his head to the side and said, "Really, what was your worry, again?" Headman was a fine One-Zero, a tough card player and he sincerely cared about his indigenous team members.

Because it was New Year's Eve, FOB 1 Camp Commander Major William Shelton had ordered extra base security, including having all reconnaissance teams and Hatchet Force personnel on alert in case the local VC or NVA had attack plans up their communist sleeves. Months earlier, a VC had placed a marker on the roof of the lounge, which VC or NVA mortarmen could use as target guide-on. It was also revealed that in the last day or two, one of the Hatchet Force NCOs had found a camp worker carefully counting his steps as he walked away from the clubhouse. That was a common practice for mortarmen or artillerymen to improve their accuracy against a proposed target. As we prepared to ring in the New Year, the jukebox blared, the drinks flowed, the men played the slot machines, and the poker stakes were high. But there was an edge to the evening's festivities. Shelton ordered it closed early, in case of enemy activity.

Before the club closed, the conversation around our poker table turned to the FOB 4 team that was on the ground in the MA target. Headman told us how happy he was to have been extracted in time to spend New Year's Eve at FOB 1, instead of across the fence. A few comments were made about how the team in the target area planned to celebrate New Year's Eve. Someone mentioned that the Americans had taken a bottle of Jim Beam to the field for the occasion. Headman and I gave each other a skeptical look. Personally, I wondered how they could carry a glass bottle and not break it. Another recon man said the two SF troops were unhappy about having to run a target on New Year's Eve. However, the S-3 brass cut them no slack and sent them out anyway. I knew one of the troops from Training Group and considered him a good recon man. The other I knew only slightly, but there was no reason to believe that either man would be so foolish on the ground.

Around 2200, Spider told us that he and the Covey pilot were going to fly into the team's AO at midnight to wish the men a "Happy New Year." While Spider's O-2 was over the target area, the mortarmen at FOB 1 lit up the sky with flares of various colors and other rudimentary explosive devices, welcoming in the New Year. When he returned to base, Spider told me it sounded as though the Americans had had too much Jim Beam. He gave the team holiday greetings and a reminder that they were in Laos. The only activity we had at FOB 1 was from a poorly trained VC mortar crew who lobbed some mortar rounds at us, but they landed in the ARVN compound to the south instead.

On 1 January 1969, Spider left FOB 1 early for a commo check with RT Asp. He talked to the team's radio operator and returned to Phu Bai. Later in the morning, however, the One-Two requested a tactical extraction from the AO because there had been a lot of enemy activity around them. While Spider was talking to the SF troop, he heard a burst of AK-47 fire and screams. Then silence. For a long time he was unable to raise anyone on the radio. He knew something was terribly wrong. He finally got an indigenous team member on the radio who said that the Americans were dead, but the indig had survived the attack.

Back at FOB 1, around 1200 hours, someone from the commo shack came into the club and said a Vietnamese team member from RT Asp was on the radio, talking to Spider. That was very bad news. Several of the recon team members in FOB 1 headed toward the commo shack. Before we got there, Tony Herrell, a veteran recon man, came around the corner with more bad news.

"They were hit by sappers. It doesn't look good," he said. As we tried to walk through S-3 to the commo shack, the S-3 major told the team members to stay outside so the SF commo troops could do their job. The major was universally despised by every recon team member in camp because he showed no sympathy toward any team member and acted as though he didn't care whether a team lived or died in a target area. The fact that he still had a thick German accent didn't help matters either. It never occurred to me that perhaps his gruffness was a buffer between having to send teams into targets where the probability of casualties was extremely high and keeping his own sanity.

As always, when a team was in trouble, several team members pulled out their PRC-25s, attached a long antennae, and monitored any radio traffic they could pick up. From FOB 1, SF troops usually would be able to hear the Covey rider talking to the team on the ground. The transmissions from the team on the ground, however, were too far away to be picked up in Phu Bai. The only news this first day of the New Year was bad. We could hear the Covey rider patiently talking to the Vietnamese team members on the ground. They were obviously shaken. At first, we assumed the Vietnamese team members were wounded. But as time passed, it was apparent that the three Vietnamese were alive and had suffered no combat wounds. In addition, there were no NVA casualties.

It appeared the Americans had been slow to react. In a matter of seconds, the sappers killed the three SF troops and chose to leave the South Vietnamese team members alive. The news about the sappers was a triple dose of bad news: First, we had three dead Green Berets. Second, reports One-Zeros had received for months about NVA sappers being a lethal force were now confirmed. Third, by killing only the Americans, the NVA pulled off a major psychological coup. By leaving the Vietnamese team members alive, their survival would plant seeds of doubt and dissension between SF troops and our little people.

That tactic worked momentarily at Phu Bai. Some of the U.S. personnel in camp who didn't work daily with the little people were openly questioning the loyalty of the Vietnamese team members. I went over to the ST Idaho hootch and told Hiep and Sau to have the team be alert for any untoward comments from U.S. personnel in camp. I also asked them to learn as much as they could about the Vietnamese team members on RT Asp as quickly as possible.

During early 1969 FOB 1 was closed. ST Idaho was transferred to CCN at Da Nang, where on occasions the team pulled guard duty atop Marble Mountain. As the team hunkers down for another cold night on the mountain team members enjoy a light moment. From left: Hung, Douglas L. LeTourneau, Cau, Son, Chau, Lynne Maurice Black Jr. and John S. Meyer. (Photo courtesy of Rick Howard)

I headed back to the comm center. This time, the major was gone and no one stopped me. The radio room usually took on an eerie silence after a team had been pulled out of a target. That afternoon was no different. The only sounds in the comm center were radio tones, hums and static while the men waited for the helicopters to return to base. And whenever a team was hit as badly as RT Asp had been, the comm center took on an additional somberness. On the first day of 1969, it was tomb-like. Three Americans dead, no apparent intelligence other than the fact that all of C&C now knew that the NVA sappers were as good as they had been touted in earlier briefings. For Herrell and me, it was hard to swallow because we had lost a friend. Forever. For several minutes we just sat there, deep in our own thoughts. It had been about 10 minutes since the pilots had called in to report that all of the RT Asp team members had been recovered and were returning to Quang Tri.

Oddly, none of the aircraft extracting RT Asp received any significant ground fire from the NVA. To me, that was a definite indicator that the NVA wanted to send a psychological message along with the carnage the sappers had wrought on RT Asp. On 30 November, we lost seven SF troops and an entire Kingbee crew. Thirty-two days later, we lost three Americans. And since this was a secret war, Walter Cronkite could tell viewers that he no longer believed in the war, but he couldn't tell the American public about another day in SOG. I stood up and started to walk out of the comm center. A war-weary voice broke the long silence in the comm center with a short, clear transmission: "Happy New Year."

His words caught me off guard. I thought of those three words in the context of the many close calls ST Idaho had survived since the day I joined it, the same day Sergeant First Class Glen Oliver Lane and an entire ST Idaho team had disappeared in the Prairie Fire AO. I thought of how every member of ST Idaho would probably have been killed in action had it not been for the heroics of Kingbee pilots, Marine and Army helicopter gunship crews and Uncle Sam's Air Force. On 1 January 1969, the NVA had upped the ante and the thought of going across the fence sent a sobering chill down my spine. I walked over to the club and had my first drink since August. Within days, ST Idaho boarded Kingbees to launch into an MA target in another attempt to find the NVA gasoline pipeline.

And while we headed north to Quang Tri, the 101st Airborne Division choppers carried the six men south. When the choppers landed on the helicopter pad, Colonel Jack Warren had ordered every man in FOB 4 out to the site. He was held in high regard by SF troops because he genuinely cared about his men. It had been said that because of his dedication to the SF mission and the men of SF, that he would never advance beyond the rank of colonel. He had remained in SF too long, a career decision the traditional Army hierarchy despised and punished. Asp was from FOB 4, which Warren commanded. At the time, FOB 4 was transitioning into becoming Command and Control North (CCN) as part of a major consolidation of resources within SOG. FOB 1 would join FOB 4 in Da Nang. Where once there had been six FOBs, there would now be three bases, CCN in Da Nang, Command and Control Central (CCC) in Kontum, and Command and Control South (CCS) at Ban Me Thuot.

After the three corpses were unloaded from the helicopter, Warren gave a terse, teary-eyed speech to his captive audience. Warren warned everyone that if they were careless in the field, death was the result of that carelessness. Then he bent down, opened a body bag and picked up a portion of a body of one of the dead Americans. Now he was crying and screaming at his men to never be careless in the field. Warren was never the same after that. Neither was C&C.

During January, ST Idaho was moved to CCN at Da Nang and ST Idaho became RT Idaho. Da Nang was two or three times the size of FOB 1. Gone forever was the camaraderie of FOB 1. Additionally, team member Bubba Shore requested to be transferred to headquarters. Bubba and I had run many targets together during his brief tenure on the team. It was a request I respected and granted instantly. Now it was simply Black and myself. Black recruited Do Ti Quang from ST Alabama, a man born in North Vietnam, who moved south with his family to escape communism. We didn't bring any additional Americans on the team because our Vietnamese team members were so strong and we felt they were better in the jungle than most Americans in camp.

The daily grind of running missions across the fence was wearing on me physically and mentally. As '69 dawned, I began a mental examination of life in SOG. Being in an elite unit within America's finest special operations was where I wanted to be. The adrenaline-enhanced high of deadly firefights against a relentless enemy under extremely lopsided odds was intoxicating. I had never experienced such exhilaration or sheer terror. Yet there was a little voice in the back of my head which spoke of survival, surviving not only a vigorous enemy campaign directed against SOG teams, but merely surviving the odds of going home in one piece.

My mind also began the mental debate between rising to the new challenges inherent in a secret war and returning to a safer assignment. My one-year tour of duty was scheduled to end at the end of April. Under the general rules of SOG, after running targets across the fence for six months, I could request a cushy assignment. I had already spent seven months with the team. I was alive, however, thanks to Hiep, Sau, Phuoc, Tuan, and the other men of ST Idaho. I couldn't just walk away.

CHAPTER FIFTEEN

WALKING AMONG SOG LEGENDS

At five-foot-four, 120 pounds, Louis J. "Jake Three-Zero" DeSeta wasn't exactly what you'd call the All-American John Wayne type. Still, after spending most of 1967 with A Company 4th Battalion of the 173rd Airborne Brigade, where he survived the horrific battle of Hill 875 at Dak To, the Delaware native son volunteered for Special Forces duty in January 1968.

DeSeta went to Nha Trang to process into the 5th Special Forces Group where a sergeant told him he had bad news for the young paratrooper. "You're going to C&C in Da Nang."

"What's C&C?" DeSeta asked.

"You'll find out soon enough," was the sergeant's response.

In late February, 1968, after receiving his C&C briefing at FOB 4 in Da Nang, signing documents promising not to talk about the top secret operation for 20 years, DeSeta flew to FOB 2 Kontum. While airborne, DeSeta wondered what he had volunteered for. He had fought NVA troops for a year with artillery support and backup units, but the thought of fighting the NVA in Laos and Cambodia without that sort of support sent a chill down his spine.

Wearing new, polished jungle boots, new fatigues and carrying

Louis J. DeSeta standing in ST Nevada Team Room, FOB 2, 1968. (Courtesy of Louis J. DeSeta)

a carbine and a duffle bag, DeSeta walked into camp where he ran into another surprise: FOB 2 had a road, Highway 14, running right through the middle of it. DeSeta thought FOB 2 had to be the most insecure camp in Vietnam.

As he walked toward S-1, ST Nevada's One-Zero Spec 4 Howard Taylor noticed DeSeta's 173rd combat patch on his right shoulder, welcomed him to FOB 2, and asked if he'd be interested in running recon. DeSeta shrugged his shoulders and said "Why not." Since DeSeta was a sergeant and Taylor was one rank lower, he told Taylor that he would not have any trouble taking orders from him. A little later in the day, Taylor introduced him to Special Forces staff sergeant and Trenton, N.J. native, Fred Zabitosky.

Later, the three went to Zabitosky's team room to talk about general recon tactics. The two veteran recon men shared insights and lessons learned about running recon in the Prairie Fire and Daniel Boone areas of operation. Then, they retired to the club for a few beers. Never once did Zabitosky mention he had been nominated for the Medal of Honor.

Over the next few days, Taylor and Zabitosky spent time with DeSeta before ST Nevada was scheduled to run a mission.

At that pre-mission briefing, a sergeant told Taylor and DeSeta they were going to run an Eldest Son mission. They would carry 7.62 mm rounds for NVA AK-47s that would be left in enemy territory. The ammunition was rigged by U.S. specialists to explode in an AK-47 when fired by an enemy soldier. Mortar rounds were also rigged to explode in enemy mortar tubes. Missions where this doctored ammo was inserted were called Eldest Son or Soap Chips.

The briefing sergeant casually told Taylor and DeSeta that one of the ways to get Eldest Son ammo into enemy hands was to take an AK-47 away from an NVA soldier, put in the bad ammo and leave the weapon in enemy territory.

DeSeta was dumbfounded by that remark. As he left the briefing room he turned to Taylor and asked him if anyone in that briefing had ever tried to take an AK-47 from a live NVA soldier. Taylor just laughed.

Although he'd only been at FOB 2 for about a week, DeSeta realized that nearly every guy he'd run into was crazier than the one before. He began to question his own sanity for volunteering for C&C duty.

The Eldest Son mission into Cambodia ended on the third day, when ST Nevada made contact with NVA troops and was extracted under heavy enemy fire. The helicopters took several hits from enemy gunfire, but no one on ST Nevada was wounded.

That night, DeSeta went to watch a movie inside FOB 2. He carried his CAR-15 to the outdoor theater area. Before the movie started, a captain approached DeSeta and asked for his CAR-15 because no weapons were allowed in the movie area. DeSeta asked the captain why he wanted his CAR-15; the officer answered that there were NVA infiltrators in camp. DeSeta told the captain to point out the NVA to him and he'd "take care of them." But, he wasn't going to surrender his CAR-15 to anyone.

When he sat down, a young-looking Special Forces soldier told DeSeta he liked his answer to the officer, shook his hand and introduced himself as David "Babysan" Davidson, a veteran recon man in C&C. They struck up a friendship that night.

After running an in-country mission, Taylor and DeSeta were briefed to run a mission in a target designated as: Charlie 50, a tri-border target that was in Laos, Cambodia and South Vietnam. They were told it was a tough target. When Taylor and DeSeta exited the S-3 briefing, an SF soldier with no rank or name on his fatigues approached Taylor and asked what target ST Nevada was given. The SF soldier, who Taylor later identified as Jerry "Mad Dog" Shriver, told DeSeta that no American had come out alive from Charlie 50 in the last six months.

DeSeta stood there for a second. If there hasn't been an American to come out of that target alive in six months why in the hell are we going in? This place really is crazy. And, that guy Mad Dog has the correct moniker!

But being a good infantryman, DeSeta went into Charlie 50

with ST Nevada for three days without questioning his orders. The team successfully inserted an Air Force sensor along a major trail that reported enemy activity to planes. It also deposited Eldest Son ammunition. On day three in the mission, ST Nevada made heavy contact with NVA regulars and Pathet Lao troops. Before getting extracted from the target, DeSeta dropped the rest of the doctored ammo among dead enemy soldiers, hoping their live comrades would pick it up and use it.

Again RT Nevada was extracted while under heavy enemy fire. And, again it was extracted without taking any team casualties

At that time, DeSeta received a letter from a 173rd paratrooper friend asking him if he should transfer from "The Herd" to SF. DeSeta wrote him a quick note telling him to stay with the 173rd because it was a safer assignment and that the missions and some of the men in C&C were crazy. He also told his friend that transferring was the biggest mistake of his life. He didn't expect to survive his time in C&C.

The following day, DeSeta was introduced to a new member of the team, an Irishman from Brooklyn, N.Y., Spec 5, John J. Kedenburg. The tall handsome soldier would have made a perfect poster boy for Special Forces. During the following days as Kedenburg trained intensely with ST Nevada, DeSeta marveled at an M-1 carbine bayonet that he carried strapped to his web gear.

When ST Nevada was slated for a new mission, DeSeta and Kedenburg went over to S-4 to pick up a bayonet. When they walked inside, Zabitosky was joking around with the supply sergeant, SFC Bob Howard. He introduced DeSeta to Howard.

DeSeta explained that he was looking for an M-1 carbine bayonet similar to the one Kedenburg carried. Howard disappeared into the bowels of S-4 for a few minutes before returning to the counter and handed DeSeta a box. "Will this do?"

DeSeta opened the box and a knife slid out. It was an official SOG knife—No. 2704. Howard, a tall, friendly soldier didn't know DeSeta from the man in the moon, but he knew that he was running recon. DeSeta was impressed. He had never seen

From left, Louis J. DeSeta, two indigenous team members of ST Nevada, and Sp. 5 John Kedenburg, who was killed in action, June 13, 1968. He received the Medal of Honor posthumously. This is a photo that Kedenburg shot with his new camera using the time-delay switch. (Courtesy of Louis J. DeSeta)

anything like it. From that date forward SOG knife No. 2704 was never dull, DeSeta always kept it razor sharp and strapped it to his web gear for all future missions.

A few days later, ST Nevada, with Taylor as One-Zero, and Kedenburg and DeSeta, were inserted into a target and remained on the ground for a few days before being extracted on ropes without any casualties.

After that mission, Kedenburg and DeSeta drove downtown to buy a shoulder holster for DeSeta's Browning 9 mm pistol. Before they left, Kedenburg looked at DeSeta and told him that the way he wore his beret didn't look right. He handed DeSeta his beret and told him that he would shape his for him. So, they swapped berets and headed downtown.

On the way back to FOB 2, they were discussing the next target that S-3 had assigned to ST Nevada and DeSeta complained to Kedenburg that the Army couldn't do anything worse to him because as a short-timer, with about four months left to his tour of duty, he was running missions in C&C across the fence with no artillery support and he didn't think he'd live to see the end of his tour of duty. Kedenburg gave him that all-American smile and told him he worried too much.

After Taylor, Kedenburg and DeSeta discussed the upcoming mission for ST Nevada, Taylor told DeSeta to go to S-4 for a resupply of grenades for the team. While walking to S-4, Sgt. Maj. Rupert G. Stratton saw DeSeta and told him to "pack his shit" because he was going to FOB 3 at Khe Sanh. DeSeta's jaw dropped in surprise. As he mentally processed those words, Stratton again told him to pack and that a chopper would take him to Da Nang for processing, prior to shipping him to FOB 3.

DeSeta turned around, went back to his team room and apologized to Taylor for not getting the grenades, but Sgt. Maj. Stratton had just made his life worse. In January, when he was home on leave before reporting for duty to Kontum, DeSeta had watched live TV coverage of Marines fighting during the siege of Khe Sanh. He also had viewed the Special Forces A Camp at Lang Vei a short distance west of Khe Sanh get overrun by NVA tanks. That portion of South Vietnam was the hottest combat spot in Southeast Asia and the Army was sending DeSeta there.

Just when he thought the Army could do nothing worse to him, it sent him to Khe Sanh!

Forty-eight hours later, DeSeta reported to FOB 3. When the Kingbee approached the LZ, the door gunner told DeSeta to grab his gear and jump out before the chopper set down as the Khe Sanh base was under NVA artillery attack. DeSeta jumped out of the chopper and ran to the nearest bunker, as he heard the familiar sound of incoming artillery rounds. For a few seconds, his mind flashed back to the horror and ruthless pounding he experienced while on Hill 875 with the 173rd Airborne the previous November.

DeSeta finally made it to S-1, where he was greeted by Staff Sgt. Pat Watkins, the One-Zero of ST Lion. Within a few weeks, DeSeta was on the ground in Laos, in target Oscar 8, the deadliest Laotian target in the FOB 3 area of operations. During the team's first night in Oscar 8, an enemy soldier approached an indig ST Lion team member and told him to pull guard duty without realizing who he was talking to.

DeSeta survived that mission and ran several more with ST Lion, before FOB 3 was shut down in July. Watkins, the best one-zero he had during his time in C&C, headed south to FOB 1 and DeSeta returned to FOB 2, where he learned that Kedenburg was killed in action June 13, 1968. SF medic Joe Parnar was in the chase ship that was picking up the second half of ST Nevada on ropes. Parnar said Kedenburg had unhooked his D-ring on the rope to make room for an indigenous team member. Before Kedenburg could get hooked in, the chopper pulled out because it was receiving heavy enemy gunfire, leaving the Irishman alone on the ground confronting a wave of NVA. The following day an FOB 2 Brightlight team was inserted to recover Kedenburg's body. Every member on that team was wounded, with one indig KIA. And to Parnar fell the gruesome task of preparing Kedenburg's body for its final flight home.

DeSeta finished his C&C tour of duty with the Hatchet Force which ran a few operations in Laos and the tri-border area, including one with ST Nevada a few days before he left Vietnam on Aug. 18, 1968.

During his six months in C&C he rubbed shoulders with three SF soldiers who earned the Medal of Honor at FOB 2 in 1968: Fred Zabitosky, Bob Howard and John Kedenburg. Kedenburg's was awarded posthumously. Howard was nominated two more times for the Medal of Honor and left Southeast Asia as the most highly decorated soldier of the Vietnam War. Jerry "Mad Dog" Shriver and David "Babysan" Davidson were later killed in action running C&C missions across the fence.

Among DeSeta's most prized possessions are Kedenburg's beret and SOG knife No. 2704.

MARINE AIR

(LEFT)
U.S.M.C. Scarface pilot 1st Lt. Mark Byrd, whose call sign was "Scarface 47", is standing in front of (Marine Light Helicopter Squadron 367) sign at the squadron's headquarters on the Phu Bai airfield in 1969. Byrd flew many Prairie Fire missions including the Dec 2, 1969 emergency extraction of RT Mississippi led by CCN One-Zero Nick Manning. During that mission the Eagle Claw lead aircraft was shot down. On Prairie Fire missions Scarface's call sign was "Eagle Claw".
For several years HML-367, known as VMO-3 prior to the summer of 1967, provided at least two UH-1E Huey gun ships daily to lead the helicopter assets on SOG's Prairie Fire missions in the FOB 1, 3 and 4 areas of operations and later for CCN missions.
Other Marine squadrons participated in SOG missions. In the 1967-68 time frame VMO-6, call sign Klondike, based in Chu Lai, provided a semi-permanent detachment of four UH-1E gunships at Khe Sanh to support SOG's operations and their aircraft led the SOG helicopter package during the ill-fated raid of Target Oscar-8 in June, 1967. In December 1969 HML-367 was converted to the AH-1G Cobra and transferred to Marble Mountain Air Field and HML-167, call sign "Comprise" was thereafter assigned most of the Prairie Fire missions flown by U.S. Marine aviators.
As of January 2011, according to Bryd, no complete history of Marine aviation unit operations and sacrifices in SOG or SOG-type missions in the Vietnam conflict has been published.

(Photo courtesy of Mark Byrd)

CHAPTER SIXTEEN

STUFF WE CARRIED
STUFF WE DIDN'T CARRY

Since Across The Fence was published in 2003, and because most of our missions with the Military Assistance Command Vietnam Studies and Observations Group (MACV-SOG) were classified top secret, I've received many inquiries about the equipment that I and fellow Special Forces soldiers carried when we ran reconnaissance missions into Laos, Cambodia and N. Vietnam and about the state-of-the-art weaponry, communications and surveillance equipment that we tested at the time—some of which we used in the field.

First, I turned to Lynne M. "Blackjack" Black Jr., to see what he carried as a conventional infantryman in South Vietnam with the 173rd Airborne Brigade during 1965 and 1966.

"When we went out on patrol the enemy could hear us coming a mile away," Black said. "The canteens were metal, with a metal chain that attached the black plastic cap to the body of the canteen. The metal canteen sat inside of a metal cup. As we walked that chain would bang on the canteen and the canteen sometimes rattled inside the metal cup. A squad of guys sounded like a Chinese drum line. Our weapon sling swivels would bang on the weapons providing even more noise. Dog tags would rattle as we walked."

This photo shows some of the equipment worn by ST Idaho members in the spring of 1969. Here, during an inspection by Lt. Gen. Richard Stilwell, the I Corps commander in S. Vietnam at that time, inspects the gear of Son, the ST Idaho point man for the special mission the team was preparing to run in Laos. Son, was dressed in NVA garb and equipment. Note his NVA vest across his chest, the AK-47 on his right hip and AK-47 magazines in his pouch. On far left, is John S. Meyer. On Meyer, note his Frank & Warren Survival Axe Type II, the radio wire connecting the handset in his jacket to the PRC-25 in his rucksack, his black contact gloves and sawed-off M-79 under his left arm.

The paratroopers also wore metal helmets with the paratrooper chinstrap, with plastic helmet liners. Many paratroopers smoked and used Zippo lighters, which had a distinct, metallic clicking sound when opened and closed. They also wore jewelry such as silver or gold colored watches and rings, carried entrenching tools and L-shaped flashlights that attached to the upper web gear and often got caught in the brush. At night, if available, they would drink beer or soda from old tin cans that had to be opened with a can opener, as there were no pull tabs on drinks at that time.

The infantrymen also carried: sleeping bags, gas masks, bayonets, personal knives, and rubber ponchos that were rolled and folded onto the back of the pistol belt. It provided a cushioned seat for sitting, but also a hiding place for small snakes, leeches, spiders and other jungle insects and creatures. Some paratroopers carried the claymore mine, with a hand generator, a PRC-25 radio, compass, maps and protractor. The basic ammo load for the M-16 or M-14 was 200 rounds plus hand grenades. Some wore heavy armored vests that absorbed water and were hot as hell, often quickly dehydrating the young soldiers.

The early paratroopers also wore their jump boots that Black called "fungus factories." Jungle boots, with canvas sides and a metal plate in the sole, were standard issue when I arrived in S. Vietnam in April 1968. The early paratroopers also wore military issued underwear that caused rashes and infections and socks that caused a foot fungus, a fungus some are still fighting today. It wasn't until a visit from the Secretary of State, who caught the fungus, that a cream was developed to fight it.

Nearly everyone smoked in those days. Five cigarettes were packed in neat little packs with each C-Ration meal. The smell of American cigarettes in Southeast Asia was unmistakable.

Louis J. DeSeta also served with the 173rd in 1967 before he volunteered for SOG duty. "We were noisy as hell in the 173rd," he said. "We used to carry those metal ammo boxes that always banged against the metal canteens. Even taking a drink of water with the metal canteen made a metallic noise that could be heard off in the distance. A lot of us carried a poncho, but often didn't use it in the field because they were so noisy when you unfolded them. And, once it started to rain, the rain hitting them gave off a different noise that the enemy could hear.

"SOG was just the total, complete opposite. We carried nothing that made any noise. Everything was taped down or tied down."

DeSeta and Black agreed that the men who served in the early phases of the war had to learn what not to do and to pass along their lessons learned to the FNG's.

Stuff We Didn't Carry

To avoid rashes, infections and fungus, Black and I didn't wear underwear or socks. All SOG recon men didn't wear helmets, helmet liners or armored vests of any sort. Most of us didn't carry entrenching tools, bayonets, sleeping bags, hammocks, ponchos, ponchos liners or air mattresses because they added weight to our total load. I weighed my gear on a small scale once at Phu Bai and it weighed approximately 90 pounds. No one carried an M-16, an M-14 or a 9 mm weapon as his primary weapon.

For all missions we never carried any form of identification: no dog tags, no military ID cards, no letters from home—nothing with any personal information on it. Our uniforms were sterile: no rank, no unit designator, no jump wings, no CIB or South Vietnamese jump wings were displayed. Our green beret remained at FOB 1. We went to extreme measures to insure that our anonymity remained in tact to provide deniability to the U.S. government in the event we were killed or captured. We cut out the section of a target map to carry to the field, thus only showing the grid in the target area, with no further information about the map or the cartographers who produced them. Additionally, we never smoked or cooked in the field.

Stuff We Carried

The most important piece of equipment we carried was the CAR-15. The sling for it would vary: sometimes I used a cravat or a canvas strap taped tightly to both ends of the weapon for soundless movements. That was the preferred weapon of choice by everyone on ST Idaho. The only exception was an AK-47 for Son when he was our point man wearing an NVA uniform, and an M-79 carried by our grenadier. In November 1968, Henry King carried the experimental pump M-79 weapon on one mission. It held up to five rounds of 40 mm high explosive ammunition. His secondary weapon was the Model 1911 Colt .45. On occasions, Black would carry the M-60 machine gun.

Every American on ST Idaho carried a sawed-off M-79 for additional firepower. We thought of it as our hand-held artillery. During patrol, the Americans would load a special M-79 round with fleshettes or double-ought (00) buckshot for close contact. The sawed-off M-79 would be secured either with a canvas or rope lanyard or a D-ring that was covered with black electrical tape to prevent any metallic banging. During the fall of 1968, I had a one-of-a-kind sawed-off M-79 holster, which I lost in when I was unconscious after a rope extraction in Laos.

I would carry at least thirty-four 20-round magazines for the CAR-15—we only placed 18 rounds in each magazine, which gave me 612 rounds for that weapon, and at least 12 rounds for the M-79. The CAR-15 magazines were placed in ammo pouches or cloth canteen pouches, with the bottoms facing up to prevent debris from getting into the magazine and all of the rounds pointing away from the body. We taped black electrical tape to the bottom of each magazine to make it easier to grab them out of the pouch during firefights. I also carried 10 to 12 fragmentation grenades, a few of the older M-26, the newer M-33 "baseball" grenades and one or two V-22 minigrenades.

For headgear, I only wore a green cravat, a triangular bandage, on missions. It was light, didn't get caught on jungle branches, or knocked off my head by prop wash and it broke up the color of my blond hair. As a practical matter, it kept the sweat out of my eyes—hats didn't do that. I often wore camouflage "paint" on my face.

I wore the traditional Army jungle fatigues because they dried quicker while on the ground than the camouflage fatigues available

Among the weapons carried by SOG recon teams included, from the top:

First row: a CAR-15, with 20-round magazine and weapon sling.

Second row: a traditional 40 mm M-79 grenade launcher.

Third row: from left, an M-79 ammo pouch that holds three rounds, a 40 mm tear gas round and a high-explosive round (gold-colored tip) for the M-79, a sawed-off M-79 with rappelling D-ring in the trigger guard.

Bottom row: from left: a claymore mine with connector wire and detonator; a Browning Hi Power 9 mm semiautomatic pistol and a mini-grenade.

Photo courtesy of Alan R. Wise Collection

at the time. I had the Phu Bai tailor sew an extra zipped pocket on the upper right and left arm (see cover of book) where I carried pens, notebooks, pen flares, one plastic spoon and my signal mirror. The tailor also sewed zipped pockets between the front top and bottom buttoned pockets, where I'd place maps, morphine syrettes, an extra notebook with any mission specific notes and the URC-10 emergency radio.

On my right wrist I wore a black, self-winding, luminescent Seiko watch, which was so bright at night that I wore it face down on the bottom of my wrist, under my glove. Thus, even in the pitch-black jungle, I knew when to make communication checks with the airborne command aircraft, usually at midnight, or at 2 a.m. In the jungle I always wore black contact gloves for protection against jungle plants, thorns and insects. I cut the thumb, index finger and middle finger off of the right glove down to the first joint, for improved grip. I always wore an extra cravat around my neck.

On my left harness strap, I taped my K-Bar knife, with handle facing down, hand grenades, small smoke canisters and a sterile bandage. On my right harness strap was a strobe light, held in a cloth pouch, hand grenades, a rappelling D-ring, and a smoke grenade. My preferred web gear was the WW II BAR (Browning Automatic Rifle) ammo belt and shoulder straps because five CAR-15 magazines fit snugly into each individual pouch. One pouch would be used for M-79 rounds. A plastic water canteen in a cloth canteen holder would be fit onto the belt, as well as one white phosphorous grenade and my survival ax.

The amount of water available in the AO would determine how many plastic canteens of water I'd carry to the field. One canteen would have a small bottle of water purification pills taped to it. I used those pills for all water outside of camp. The water in our AO's was often tainted with the defoliant Agent Orange—we hoped the purification tablets would counteract it. On the right side of my harness I always carried the Frank & Warren Survival Ax Type II, MIL-S-8642C. I preferred it to the machete because the backside had a nasty sharp hook that cut through jungle vines on the return swing. I carried my folding compass around my neck, held by green parachute cord.

I used a cravat as a belt, because it was silent. In my right pocket was the Swiss Army knife, secured by a green parachute cord to a belt loop on my pants. Because I always wore the bulky gas mask bag on my left side, which held the black M-17 gas mask, I rarely put anything in my upper left pocket. (If the charcoal air filters on the M-17 got wet they had to be replaced.) In my lower left pant pocket I carried a small and large colored panels to mark our position for Covey and tactical air strikes. In my lower right pocket were extra pen flares, a dehydrated Long-Range Reconnaissance Patrol ration (LRRP, pronounced LURP), bug repellant to squirt on leeches and an extra cravat and sterile bandage. I always carried the Swiss rope. The 12-foot section of green-colored rope was used for a Swiss seat for extractions by helicopter. We would hook a D-ring through the seat's rope and onto 150-foot-long pieces of rope that hung from the chopper.

On all missions, I carried the PRC-25, our primary radio contact with the outside world. It took up the most space in my indig rucksack. Most times I had the short, flexible antenna screwed into it, which was folded under my right arm and tucked into my jungle fatigue jacket because the NVA always searched for the radio operator, knowing he was the primary link to U.S. air power. I carried the long antenna, folded in sections, in my rucksack.

Other items included: one can of C-Ration fresh fruit, either peaches or apricots, extra hand grenades, the remainder of my CAR-15 magazines, extra M-79 rounds—including one tear-gas round, an Army long-sleeved sweater, a thin, hooded waist-length plastic rain jacket and toilet paper. Both the sweater and rain jacket would be folded under the PRC-25 to buffer where it hit my back. I also carried an extra PRC-25 battery, an extra URC-10 battery, extra smoke grenades, an extra canteen of water if needed, and extra LRRPs.

On a few occasions, especially when we ran targets in Cambodia, which was flatter and more wide open, I'd carry a claymore mine and a few pre-cut fuses: five-second, 10-second and longer-duration fuses, used to break contact with enemy troops chasing us. On several occasions I carried .22-caliber High Standard semi-automatic pistol with a silencer for ambushes or to kill enemy tracker dogs. I also carried cough syrup for Hiep or anyone who coughed at night, cans of black pepper and powdered mace for enemy tracker dogs and a compact toothbrush.

There are some redundancies, such as bullets, bandages and smoke grenades carried in various locations on my body because each could be crucial to surviving a firefight and successfully directing helicopter gun ships, F-4 Phantom jets that delivered ordnance on target faster than the speed of sound and the old deadly propeller-driven A-1E Skyraiders.

The emphasis was packing firepower for survival. I preferred to go hungry as to running out of ammo. Items for creature comfort were discarded in favor of carrying an extra grenade or a high-explosive M-79 round. Why?

In the Prairie Fire AO there were several times when we were in contact with NVA troops for two or three hours before making radio contact with Covey or any U.S. aircraft. Then, depending on weather and the status of other teams in the field, there would be further delays in getting air assets on scene, especially when the team was surrounded and there were no routes for escape and evasion. On most missions, I preferred six-man teams due to helicopter extraction considerations: height, altitude, weight and weather conditions dictated how many men could board an extraction chopper. The type of helicopter used for the extraction could vary from the old H-34, to Hueys, or on rare occasions, the Air Force's HH-3 Jolly Green Giant, the larger, more powerful chopper during that war. Which one picked up the team, usually under heavy enemy gunfire, made a difference in how many men it could carry in extreme weather conditions.

There were at least two missions when ST Idaho was extracted from the target, I was down to my last CAR-15 magazine, M-26 grenade and M-79 round. The NVA was relentless and fearless.

Other equipment SOG teams carried included, from the upper left:

First row: Pentax single-lens reflex camera; signal mirror; Air Force pen light; strobe light and smoke canisters.

Second row: a mini-grenade, a hand-held, single-shot pen flare launcher and flares and an URC-10 ultra-high frequency emergency radio.

Bottom row: one-pound of C-4 plastic explosive and a box of blasting caps.

Photo courtesy of Alan R. Wise Collection

We had an intimate knowledge of all the weapons we carried to the field. Not only did we know how they worked but we could dismantle them and clean them at night—that was mandatory training, not optional. We fired thousands of rounds through our CAR-15s and M-79s during live-fire reaction drills and firing at static targets. Before we carried any new weapon or device to the field on a mission we practiced using them for hours in order to gain familiarity with them and to see how they functioned under repetitive conditions. With ST Idaho, if the team wasn't on a mission we were training on the range or doing local training patrols, which included both silent and live-fire reaction drills.

For wiretaps, Sau was the quickest team member to climb an NVA telephone pole or tree to install a wiretap. He trained several other men on the team, including Phouc, Hung, Quang and Son. They had to climb the pole, install the wiretap and cover the wire leading from the telephone wire down to our cassette tape recorder with mud or wood putty, to hide it from passing enemy troops.

For Bright Light missions, we carried extra rounds, hand grenades, claymore mines, bandages and medical supplies, and at least one machine gun. We carried one canteen of water, no food.

On a few missions we carried antitank and antivehicular mines. Before going to the field, Black or Shore would spend hours cross training our Vietnamese team members to insure installing the devices as quickly as possible without detection by enemy troops while the remainder of the team provided security for them. On those missions we'd usually carry at least one M-72 Light Antitank Weapon (LAW), but only after the entire team had drilled on them for several days.

For POW snatches, ST Idaho spent hours practicing setting up the jungle ambush. This entailed each team member quickly placing a claymore mine in the kill zone and for flank security, in addition to installing the pre-cut block of plastic explosive that would knock out an enemy soldier. The claymore mine, officially designated the M-18A1 fragmentation, antipersonnel mine, weighed 3.5 pounds and contained 1.5 pounds of plastic explosive which propelled 700 steel balls in a deadly, killing arc that was dangerous out to 250 meters.

During the course of 1968 there were experimental weapons that S-4 shared with recon men for our assessment of their performance capabilities, such as the Gyrojet rocket pistol that fired a 13 mm round similar in gauge but longer than the standard .45 caliber round. There were many variations of silenced weapons such as the M-1 carbine, the old WW II Sten submachine gun, the 9 mm Karl Gustav Swedish K submachine gun, the XM-21 sniper rifle, various night-vision devices and the experimental pump M-79 weapon. The Air Force and the CIA often came to us with experimental explosive devices, communications equipment and various trail sensors. Later, in the early 70s, the Air Force used recon team experiences combating the NVA at night to design complicated enemy-targeting devices, some of which lead to technology used in the wars in Iraq and Afghanistan following the terrorists attacks on the Twin Towers in New York City on Sept. 11, 2001.

Sometimes team members were issued devices that were unknown to me. For example, in 2005 Doug LeTourneau told me about a team perimeter security device that he carried with him on all missions. It was a small box that held a small strand of nylon filament he placed around the team's perimeter. He would place the listening device near his ear. If a person or an animal walked through the team's perimeter, it would sound a barely audible alert signal. For a short period of time, Black used a seismic alert system made up of four probes, each emitting its own signal. He had a receiver in his breast pocket with an ear jack that allowed him to hear the warning signals from each probe. Unfortunately, if it was used in heavy grassed areas any wind moving the grass would set off the probes, falsely indicating the team was surrounded. Once we discovered this flaw in the system it was abandoned. Not all technology worked out.

Lastly, LeTourneau also reminded me that he took "no-shit" pills before a mission, which prevented bowel movements. I didn't use them. Enough said on that topic.

Editor's note: *To see instructions on tying a Swiss seat, go to:* http://www.youtube.com/watch?v=ssmYruwGTzM

POSTSCRIPT—JANUARY 2011

Roy Bahr retired in Florida.

Bill Barclay works part time at Ft. Bragg, N.C. training future Green Berets.

Mike Byard retired in Lawrenceville, N.J. in 2008.

Lynne M. Black Jr., retired in 2010 from The Boeing Company where he'd been an IT manager for 30 years.

Charles Borg is a successful Nebraska farmer.

Thomas Cunningham Jr., recently retired as an administrative hearing judge.

Ralph R. Drake retired and lives in Alabama.

Louis "Jake Three Finger" DeSeta teaches welding in Delaware.

Rick Estes is a successful, semi-retired realtor.

Tony Herrell retired in 2010 as a successful businessman/restaurateur.

Nguyen Cong Hiep, ST Idaho Interpreter, owns a pet shop in Houston, Texas.

Rick Howard trains federal agents in marksmanship.

John Hutchens retired in Ohio.

Douglas "The Frenchman" LeTourneau, like his father, is a private contractor living in Tennessee. In 2010 he emerged as an award-winning showman of livestock.

John MacIntyre died in Garrison, NY, in 2000.

John McGovern, restired from the Army and lives in Iowa.

Frank McCloskey continues to fly hospital-based emergency

Special Operations Association Reunion
September, 2003
Las Vegas, Nevada

Nine Kingbee pilots and crew members received numerous standing ovations and heart felt rounds of applause during a special salute honoring their service to SOG during the secret war from 1964 to 1972. A few of them continued to fly special missions until the fall of Saigon on April 30, 1975. The special acknowledgement was given during the formal banquet at the 27th annual reunion of the Special Operations Association in September 2003 in Las Vegas.
Among the Kingbee pilots were: from left Tran Quang Trong, Thu X. Huynh, Nguyen Phuc Thieu. From the right is Thinh Dinh, who spent 13-1/2 years in a communist reeducation camp after the fall of Saigon on April 30, 1975, and Nguyen Quy An. Please note that An has prosthetics in lieu of hands because the communists cut off his hands to insure that he'd never fly Kingbees again.
Standing at the podium is then-SOA President Jim Hetrick. To the far left is Nguyen Cong Hiep, the event's official interpreter, former ST Idaho interpreter.

helicopters in Maryland.

John S. Meyer is an associate director for homeless veterans programs at a 32-year-old, non-profit agency in north San Diego County, Interfaith Community Services.

Robert J. "Spider" Parks, retired as a sergeant major, retired from the Department of Veterans Affairs. He retired to Alabama.

Joe Parnar lives in Gardner, MA.

John E. Peters retired to Tennessee.

Do Ti Quang, died in early 2010, served with Black on Oct. 5, 1968, joined RT Idaho '69.

Bill Shelton retired as a lieutenant colonel, lives in Las Vegas.

John Shore lives in Georgia.

Clyde J. Sincere Jr., recipient of a DSC, retired in Utah.

George "The Troll" Sternberg, retired in Tennessee.

John T. Walton was a successful businessman and philanthropist before dying in an experimental airplane crash in Wyoming on June 27, 2005.

Patrick Watkins retired as a sergeant major before retiring from the Department of Veterans Affairs. He lives in Utah.

Don Wolken retired after 30 years in the Army. He lives in Missouri.

Ron Zaiss works for Frontier Airlines, lives in Colorado.

Kingbee pilot **Nguyen Van Tuong** lives in Santa Ana, CA. He spent eight years in a reeducation camp after the fall of Saigon before escaping and coming to the U.S.

Kingbee pilot **Maj. Nguyen Quy An**, works for the IRS in San Jose, Ca.

This photograph was also taken at the Special Operations Association reunion in September 2003 in Las Vegas. It's one of the few photos with Tom Cunningham and John T. Walton standing side by side. Walton was the medic on ST Louisiana who saved Cunningham's life in August 1968 (see Chap. 4.) From left are men who served at FOB 1 in Phu Bai: Col. Roy Bahr, the commanding officer for FOB 1 and 3, Cunningham, Walton, John E. Peters, John S. Meyer, George "The Troll" Sternberg and Tony Herrell. (Photo courtesy of Bill Hoopes)

Kingbee pilot **Maj. Thu X. Huynh**, is a successful businessman in Carlsbad, CA.

Kingbee pilot **Col. Thinh Dinh**, spent 13 1/2 years in a communist reeducation camp after the fall of Saigon. He recently retired from a factory job in Fargo, N.D.

Muskets gunship pilot **Dan "The Executioner" Cook** was a career military officer, had a career in private industry, retired in Monument, CO.

Muskets gunship pilot and Anchorage, Alaska native **Mike "The Judge" Arline** died in a 1997 fixed-wing aircraft crash in Alaska.

Muskets gunship pilot **Jerry W. Herman** retired and lives in Ohio.

Scarface pilot **George Miller** recently retired after more than 35 years of service flying emergency air ambulances.

Scarface pilot **Mark Byrd** is a sculptor/historian. He lives and works in Dallas, Tex.

Scarface pilot **Lt. Col. Robinson** died in a helicopter crash in Thailand, 1970.

GLOSSARY

AA – Antiaircraft.

AAA – Antiaircraft artillery.

ABCCC – Airborne Command and Control Center. Code names Hillsborough, Moon Beam, Alleycat, Batcat. They were Air Force aircraft that were airborne 24/7 over Southeast Asia.

After Action Report (AAR) – After a recon team or hatchet force returned from a mission, team members were interviewed by intelligence officers while the team leaders would write a detailed report on the mission, which included such minutiae as vegetation coloration, height of triple-canopy jungle and soil composition.

A-1E Skyraider – Code names, Sandy, Spads, or Hobos. A Douglas-manufactured propeller-driven, single-reciprocal engine, land or carrier-based aircraft capable of carrying heavy bomb loads with long loiter time over a targets. Loved by SOG teams, dreaded by enemy troops.

Arc Light – Code name for a B-52 strikes. Arc Lights were devastating because no one could hear the B-52s flying overhead. Only when the ordnance began exploding on enemy targets did people know they were under attack.

Article 15 – Under the Military Code of Uniform Justice, a soldier could be fined and have his rank reduced for Article 51 infractions.

Area of Operation – Four primary target areas for SOG teams: Laos first codenamed Shining Brass, then Prairie Fire; Cambodia—Daniel Boone, North Vietnam—Nickle Steel, and the DMZ.

ARVN – Army of the Republic of (South) Vietnam.

Army Signal Agency/National Security Agency (ASA/NSA) – U.S. intelligence organizations that intercepted enemy radio transmissions, broadcasts with highly specialized trained linguists, some of whom worked at SOG radio relay sites and with SF A Teams. ASA had a camp at Phu Bai on the west side of Highway 1, near the Hue/Phu Bai Airport.

AK-47 – 7.62 mm assault rifle used by NVA forces.

Authentication – A procedure used to confirm an individual's identity while talking with rescue forces on a survival radio.

Beeper – A radio transmitter that also emits a distinctive, high-pitch, wavering audible tone used as a homing device when tracked by a radio compass. All U.S. and Vietnamese team leaders on Spike Teams carried the URC-10, emergency radio that had the beeper transmitter.

Billets – Common term for military housing.

Bingo – Word used when Covey passes over recon team in AO to help pinpoint location of team in the jungle.

Bomb Damage Assessment (BDA) – Reconnaissance of targets after B-52 strikes hit them.

Blackbirds – Black-painted U.S. Air Force C-130 and C-123 aircraft used to transport SOG teams and for other transport and resupply missions.

Bright Light – SOG code name for heavily-armed Spike Teams inserted behind enemy lines to rescue downed pilots, recon team members escaping and evading the enemy or to locate and retrieve U.S. personnel killed in action, or proof of their death.

Browning Hi-Power – A 9 mm pistol carried by some SOG members due to large magazine capacity.

BRU – Many Montagnard tribesmen were recruited for SOG recon teams and hatchet forces.

CAR-15 – The Colt submachine gun, the preferred weapon of choice among SOG Spike Team and Hatchet Force men which had a shorter barrel than the M-16 and a collapsible stock.

CBU – Cluster bomb unit. Air Force ordnance dropped on enemy targets. The ordnance would have canisters packed with hundreds of small, explosive packets that would detonate when they hit enemy troops or the ground, shooting out hundreds of fleshettes or darts. Not all rounds would explode. Those remaining on the ground would explode if enemy or friendly troops stepped on them. When dropped on enemy targets they sounded similar to a mini-arc light.

Charlie – Nickname commonly used by US personnel for the Viet Cong, the so-called local communists who fought in South Vietnam. The word was also used interchangeably referring to NVA troops, although the NVA troops were uniformed and generally better trained than VC troops. After the VC was devastated during the Tet Offensive of 1968, the VC/NVA propaganda arms portrayed the VC as indigenous troops, when in reality the NVA commanded or dominated most VC units. The only people who believed the VC propagandists were the media.

Chief SOG – Official title of SOG commander.

CIB – Combat Infantryman Badge. Awarded to infantrymen after they engaged enemy forces in combat. The CIB was established during WW II to honor Army infantrymen.

Claymore Mine – A deadly, plastic anti-personnel mine that contained 700 steel ball bearings that were fired by 1.5 pounds of plastic explosive that could wreak havoc up to 250 meters. It could be detonated by firing cord or time fuse that sent out a swath of ball bearings that could cut down small trees.

Commanding Officer (CO) – The ranking officer in charge at a military base or operation.

Command and Control Detachment (C&C) – The field headquarters in Da Nang for SOG missions into Laos, DMZ and North Vietnam.

Command and Control Central (CCC) – SOG base in Kontum, South Vietnam. Also called FOB 2.

Command and Control North (CCN) – SOG base north of Marble Mountain in Da Nang. Originally called FOB 4, before becoming CCN when FOB 1 teams were reassigned to Da Nang in 1969.

Command and Control South (CCS) – SOG base at Ban Me Thuot, ran mostly Cambodian and in-country targets. CCS combined the manpower of FOB 5 and FOB 6 in 1969.

Covey – Call sign for U.S. Air Force Forward Air Controllers for SOG. They flew in two-engine O-2 Cessna Skymaster, until late 1969 when the OV-10 Bronco entered the AO.

Covey Rider – Experienced, cool-under pressure Special Forces veteran recon men who flew with Covey to better relate with teams on the ground during SOG missions across the fence and to assist in directing air strikes.

Cravat – A large triangular bandage that doubled as a head bandana for many SOG troops because they made no noise in the jungle.

Daniel Boone – Code name for Cambodia AO. In early days of SOG, called Salem House.

Demilitarized Zone (DMZ) – 17th parallel dividing North and South Vietnam.

Det Cord – Abbreviation for detonation cord. An explosive cord use to detonate ordnance or to clear LZs of small trees.

Distinguished Service Cross (DSC) – Second highest Army valor award, second only to the Medal of Honor.

Drop Zone (DZ) – A landing area for parachutists or supplies dropped from an aircraft rigged to parachutes.

Dry Holes – A target where the SOG team had no contact with the enemy during the mission.

Executive officer (XO) – the second in command at a military base.

5th Special Forces Group (Airborne) – Official headquarters in Nha Trang for Green Berets assigned to Vietnam. SOG personnel were recruited from the 5th.

1st Special Forces Group (Airborne) – Okinawa-based Green Berets assigned to SOG missions and Forward Observations Base for six-months temporary duty before 5th Group volunteers assumed SOG missions.

Flash – A cloth, colored SF group designator sewn on green berets.

Flashy – A nickname for signal mirrors.

FNU – First name unknown.

Fucking new guy (FNG) – An insulting reference to new men in camp.

Forward Operating Base (FOB) – SOG operations bases that reported to CCN, CCC & CCS: Ho Nunc Tao, FOB 6; Ba Me Thuot, FOB 5; Da Nang, FOB 4; Khe Sanh, FOB 3; Kontum, FOB 2 and Phu Bai FOB 1. After Khe Sanh was closed in June 1968, Mai Loc was called FOB 3 for several months, before it was shut down. In the early SOG years FOB 1 was in Kham Duc. In early days of SOG most of the FOBs reported to C&C Detachment in Da Nang. C&C was moved to FOB 4, in '68.

Green Bombers – A nickname for stimulant pills designed to keep people awake.

Green Hornets – Code name for U.S. Air Force's 20th Special Operations Squadron which flew SOG missions into Cambodia without TAC AIR cover from fastmovers and A1-E Skyraiders.

Grease gun – An older 9 mm submachine gun replaced by the CAR-15.

Hatchet Force – Code name for SOG operational platoons and companies.

Hickory – SOG radio relay sight for reconnaissance teams in Laos and North Vietnam. ASA/NSA personnel also ran radio intercepts from site northeast of FOB 3 at Khe Sanh.

Head Shed – A nickname for headquarters staff office.

Ho Chi Minh Trail Complex – A series of supply trails that ran from North Vietnam, into Laos, through the Tri-Border Area and into Cambodia, established by the NVA. The North Vietnamese government established the 559th Transportation Group to move supplies down the trail. The group is so named because that was when the orders were signed officially establishing it after communists had begun moving south a year earlier. Its sole mission was to expand the trail and keep out SOG troops. A series of small trails branched off of the trail into South Vietnam, with the A Shau Valley a major intersection. Many portions of the trail could not be observed from the air because the routes were camouflaged under jungle canopy.

Immediate Action Drill (IA Drill) – Practiced maneuvers for recon teams to break contact with the enemy.

Indig – An abbreviation of the word indigenous, as in indigenous SOG troops, pronounced (in-didge).

Jolly Green Giant – When no other aircraft could rescue recon teams during an extraction, the Sikorsky HH-3E helicopters were called because they were heavily armored and carried more firepower than conventional Army and Marine troop-carrying choppers. Later upgraded to HH-53.

Jump Wings – The U.S. parachutist's badge awarded upon completion of airborne training, which includes making five parachute jumps. Most soldiers had to obtain their jump wings prior to applying for acceptance in the U.S. Special Forces Qualification Training course at Ft. Bragg, N.C.

KIA – Killed in action.

Kingbee – The code name for the South Vietnamese Air Force 219th Special Operations Squadron-flown helicopters that supported SOG missions. South Vietnamese pilots and crews manned the Sikorsky nine-cylinder H-34s helicopters. Most SOG teams preferred extraction by Kingbee because the ship could take more hits from enemy gunfire than the lighter Bell model helicopters.

KKK – Cambodian mercenaries assigned to SOG Hatchet Force platoons and companies. They wore distinctive red scarfs.

LLDB – Luc Luong Dac Biet (South Vietnamese Special Forces).

Landing Zone – A clear area of jungle large enough for a helicopter to land and deposit or pick up SOG troops.

Leghorn – SOG radio relay and NSA/ASA signal intercept site in Laos.

Little People – A term of endearment by SF troops for their indigenous personnel.

LRP or LRRP – Long-Range Reconnaissance Patrol rations, pronounced: LURP. LRRPs were dehydrated, men only had to add water to the plastic bag, wrap it up, place the bag against their stomach while the food absorbs the water and body heat.

M-26 – Older U.S. produced fragmentation grenade.

M-33 – New, "baseball" grenade.

M-60 – 7.62 mm machine gun occasionally carried for additional firepower.

M-72 – Light Anti-Tank Weapon (LAW), 66 mm, disposable, single-shot anti-tank rocket launcher.

M-79 – Many SOG spike teams carried sawed-off N-79 grenade launchers that fired a 40 mm high-explosive round.

MIA – Missing in action.

McGuire Rig – A harness at the end of 150-foot ropes dropped into jungle to pick up SOG personnel from heavily wooded areas that had no clear spots for a helicopter to land for a team extraction.

Military Assistance Command Vietnam – Studies and Observations Group (MACV-SOG) – A joint-service high command for unconventional warfare engaged in classified operations throughout Southeast Asia. The 5th Special Forces Group shipped personnel to SOG through Special Operations Augmentations (SOA) that provided the cover name given to the secret war conducted from 1964 through 1972 where billions of operational dollars were hidden in Navy and CIA budgets.

Montagnards – Hill tribesmen and social outcasts from South Vietnam who were fearless fighters recruited by SF for A Camps and SOG units. SF affectionately called them 'Yards'.

Nakhon Phanom Royal Thai Air Force Base (NKP) – SOG launch site, MLT-3, for operations into Laos and North Vietnam, especially when poor weather prevented teams from launching from South Vietnam into the AO.

NCO – Non-commissioned officer.

NCOIC – Non-commissioner officer in charge.

Nightingale device – A diversionary device that was dropped on an LZ. It was designed to sound like an on-going firefight complete with gunfire and explosions, enabling SOG teams to safely insert into another LZ.

Nungs – Highly respected tribesmen and warriors of Chinese origin employed by several SF grougs and SOG.

OIC – Officer in charge.

One-One – Code name of SF SOG recon team assistant team leader.

One-Two – Code name of SF SOG recon team radio operator, usually the latest member to join team.

One-Zero – Code name of SF SOG recon team leader. Position based on experience, generally. One-Zeroes had final say on teams, including rejecting officers and senior NCOs as potential team members.

OSS (Office of Strategic Services) – During World War II the OSS ran many secret operations in Europe and Southeast Asia. Several OSS operators went on to serve in clandestine operations in Korea during the Korean War. Some would rise to the position of Chief SOG during the Vietnam War. The OSS proceeded the CIA.

Panels – Bright-colored panels of various sizes that teams used as markers for aircraft.

PDQ – Pretty damned quick, as in: get here PDQ or we're dead.

Pen Flares – A small, single-round flare that was fired from a hand-held launcher, used to get the attention of friendly aircraft in the area. Sometimes it would be confused with enemy tracers.

Prairie Fire – Code name for SOG area of operations in Laos.

Earlier code name for Laos was Shining Brass.

Prairie Fire Emergency – An emergency alert for recon team in Laos. It signaled that a team was in contact with enemy forces and could not continue mission; and probably was fighting for its life. Once a One-Zero declared a PFE, all air assets within range were diverted to assist team, including Air Force, Marines Corps and Navy.

Project Delta – SF unit designed to operate in South Vietnam but was occasionally called to assist SOG teams or hatchet forces that were engaged in heavy combat with the enemy.

Project Eldest Son – Enemy mortar rounds or rifle-propelled grenades that SOG had rigged to explode when used by NVA troops. SOG teams inserted Eldest Son ammo in enemy ammo caches, or along enemy trails.

Quang Tri – Launch site for FOB 1 and later CCN teams going to PF AO or DMZ.

Rear Eschelon Mother F — — (REMF) – Personnel who stayed behind in base camps and often hassled troops going to the field; people generally despised by operational troops.

Remain Over Night (RON) – Code name for site where team spends the night in AO.

Radio Direction Finding (RDF) – NVA and Russian personnel had strong radio direction finding equipment where they could triangulate between two listening posts and a team on the ground to ascertain the team's location.

RPD – A quality communist machine gun.

Rocket propelled grenade (RPG) – used by NVA and VC elements.

Round-eye – An expression connoting American troops.

Rucksack – A type of backpack used in SOG, which always seemed uncomfortable and ill-fitting.

S-1 – Personnel staff on base and at FOBs.

S-2 – Intelligence staff on base and at FOBs.

S-3 – Operations staff, men who planned missions.

S-4 – Supply staff.

SAM – Surface-to-air missiles.

Scarface – Radio call sign of Marine gunships assigned to SOG from HMLA 367 Squadron. This squadron is still on active duty at Camp Pendleton, Calif.

Shining Brass – Code name for Laos area of operation until 1967 when changed to Prairie Fire.

Sigma and Omega projects– Early SOG projects for Daniel Boone and Tri-Border AO later absorbed into CCS.

Sihanoukville – Cambodian seaport where communist bloc nations shipped tons of supplies to NVA troops who trained in and launched military operations from Cambodia. By 1970 the NVA had 100,000 combat troops in 'neutral' Cambodia.

Situation Report (SITREP) – Radio reports from teams on the ground explaining their situation during the mission.

Slicks – A nickname for UH-1 series of troop, transport helicopters designed by Bell that replaced the Sikorsky H-34 in Regular Army units. Also called Hueys, in lieu of UH-1.

SKS – Early rifle used by NVA and Viet Cong forces.

Smoke – SOG teams carried smoke grenades to assist in directing air strikes, with varied colors from violet to white.

Soap Chips – A version of Eldest Son, where AK-47 ammo was tampered to explode when used by enemy troops. Most SOG teams carried it and dropped it in the AO or enemy weapons/ ammo caches.

SOP – Standard Operating Procedure, a common phrase in military meaning there is a standard procedure or way to do something, which is not always a good thing.

Spectre – Heavily armed Air Force C-130 transport aircraft with computerized weapons systems that linked to ground troops by locking in on the team's strobe light.**Special Forces (SF)** – The official military term for Green Berets, men who completed the Special Forces Qualification Course, earning the right to wear the distinctive headgear awarded to America's unconventional soldiers.

Spike Team – Code name for SOG recon team. At FOB 1 in '68, spike team was common phraseology for recon teams. As the war went on, by '69, recon team became the common term and designator among SOG personnel at CCN.

Sterile – All SOG personnel and weapons were unmarked and untraceable, for plausible deniability if captured by enemy troops.

Strap-hanger – The term for someone who is assigned to a recon team at the last minute, to run a mission. Usually, not a member of that team, but used to fill out the number of U.S. personnel on a team. Could be from another team, who runs only one mission with another team.

Strobe Light – A small but bright, blinking light carried by SOG teams. Air Force gun ships in '68 deployed aircraft that could link to the strobe light, and direct ordnance against any enemy targets surrounding the team.

Strings – A term for ropes, hung from helicopters to extract SOG troops from jungle, with no LZs. First strings were 150-ft.

ropes, with sand bags attached to end to carry rope to jungle floor. Team members wore only a rope, Swiss seat, which entwined around legs and waist. Later, a MaGuire rig was attached to rope for extractions. STABO rig was designed as a part of SOG teams web gear for safer extractions.

High Standard HD – A .22 caliber, silenced pistol SOG members carried for assassinations or silent kills on trails.

Sten Gun – The WW II Sten Mk IIS submachine gun replaced by CAR-15.

Swedish K – A 9 mm submachine gun, popular in early SOG years, replaced by CAR-15

Syrette – A small syringe, that had a metallic tube containing morphine, with a needle attached to the end, complete with a plunger to open the flow of the needle, all contained in a clear, plastic tube. Every team carried at least one packet of morphine syrettes to the field.

TAC Air – An abbreviation for tactical air power. When a recon team used TAC Air, it would usually mean fixed-wing aircraft, such as F-4 Phantom jets, or A1-E Skyraiders.

The Peoples Army of North Vietnam (NVA) – The North Vietnamese Army, uniformed personnel from communist-controlled North Vietnam who began moving south in force in 1959 to boost the VC's – a fact little reported in the early years of the war.

TOC – Tactical operations center.

Toe-popper – The M-14 anti-personnel mine that was large enough to blow off a person's toes upon detonation. SOG teams left them in their trail to slow down NVA trackers.

TOT – Time On Target.

URC-10 – Ultra-high frequency emergency radio/emergency beeper all SF carried.

UZI – Israeli-manufactured submachine gun used by some SOG teams. UZI had 9 mm and .45 caliber models.

'Yard – American slang for Montagnard tribesman.

Viet Cong, (VC) – Indigenous South Vietnamese communists. Only operated in South Vietnam.

Visual Reconnaissance (VR) – Over flight of target area to pick LZs before SOG missions across the fence.

WIA – Wounded in action.

Zero-One – Indigenous counterpart on spike team to One-Zero. On ST Idaho Nguyen Van Sau had run SOG missions for several years by '68.

Zero-Two – SOG spike team interpreter. On ST Idaho Nguyen Cong Hiep had run SOG mission for several years by '68.

Zero-Nine – SOG spike team M-79 team member, who also carried a Colt .45 Model 1911A pistol.

INDEX

ABOUT THE AUTHOR

Born 19 January 1946, John Stryker Meyer entered the Army on 1 December 1966. He completed basic training at Ft. Dix, New Jersey, advanced infantry training at Ft. Gordon, Georgia, jump school at Ft. Benning, Georgia, and graduated from the Special Forces Qualification Course in December 1967. After a 12-week training session in Ft. Gordon, on radio teletype, Meyer landed in South Vietnam in April 1968, and arrived at FOB 1 in Phu Bai in May 1968, where he joined Spike Team Idaho. When FOB 1 was closed in January 1969, ST Idaho was helicoptered to FOB 4 in Da Nang, which became designated Command and Control North, CCN. He remained on ST Idaho through the end of his tour of duty in late April. Returned to the U.S. and was assigned to E Company in the 10th Special Forces Group at Ft. Devens, Massachusetts until October 1969, when he rejoined ST Idaho at CCN. That tour of duty ended suddenly in April 1970 after the CCN commander refused Meyer's first request to pull his four-man team from an A Shau Valley target. He returned to the States, completed his college education at Trenton State College, where he was editor of the school newspaper, The Signal, for two years, worked at the Trenton Times for 10 years, eight years at the San Diego Union and 15 years at the North County Times in Oceanside, California. Meyer received his 20-year membership pin from the Special Operations Association in 2002. In February 2011, Meyer was an associate director in the veterans department at Interfaith Community Services, a non-profit organization that maintained 170 beds for homeless veterans. He and his wife Anna have five children and live in Oceanside, Ca.